During the 1900s, the United States engaged in four major conflicts, in Europe, in the Far East with Japan, Korea, and Vietnam. During this time, many members of our parishes served, some were injured and some were killed. We thank you for their efforts, which resulted in peace, freedom, and security for your people around the world; and for all who continue to work for these values.

We thank you, Good Lord.

Also, in the 1900s, your Church struggled with issues of Prayer Book and Hymnal Revision, Racial Relations, Inclusion of Women and Minorities, Social Services, and Liturgical Renewal. We thank you for the learning and growth that took place through these efforts.

We thank you, Good Lord.

Bishop Mikell died on February 20, 1942, and was succeeded by the Reverend John Moore Walker Jr. one month later. The succession of Bishops since Bishop Walker includes John Buchman Walthour; Randolph Royall Claiborne Jr.; Milton LeGrand Wood III, as Suffragan; Bennett Jones Sims; Charles Judson Child, as Suffragan and then Bishop; Frank Kellogg Allan; Robert Tharp, Assisting Bishop. We thank you for the leadership of all these clerics and the imprint they have made on our Diocesan family.

We thank you, Good Lord.

March 31, 2001, our Diocesan Council, through the wisdom of the Holy Spirit, elected the Reverend Dr. John Neil Alexander as our Bishop. We thank you for bringing this great scholar and servant to our Diocese as we continue to enjoy the fruits of his ministry among us.

We thank you, Good Lord.

Soon, we will celebrate the 100th Anniversary of the formation of the Diocese of Atlanta. We thank you for the life of this church community and, as the 100th Anniversary Committee, the privilege of designing the services, activities, and symbols related to this commemoration.

We thank you, Good Lord.

Finally, Almighty God, you sent your son Jesus Christ to reconcile the world to yourself: We praise and bless you for those whom you have sent in the power of the Spirit—past and present—to preach the Gospel especially here in the state of Georgia. We thank you that in all parts of the earth a community of love has been gathered together by their prayers and labors. Help us in the Diocese of Atlanta to continue to call upon your Name and proclaim your saving grace here and throughout the world; for the kingdom and the power and the glory are yours for ever. **Amen.**

The Reverend William P. McLemore

THE
DIOCESE OF ATLANTA
✠
CENTENNIAL CELEBRATION
1907–2007

THE
DIOCESE OF ATLANTA

✝

CENTENNIAL CELEBRATION

1907–2007

By
The Centennial Celebration History Committee

Compiled and Edited
by
James P. Marshall Jr.
with
The Reverend William P. McLemore
Diocesan Archivist

Dust jacket: The dust jacket image is a detail from the William Conrad Turpin Jr. Memorial Window in Christ Church, Macon. Mr. Turpin was the former Chancellor and Chancellor Emeritus of the Diocese. Installed in 1974, the window was designed and produced by Willet Stained Glass Studios, Philadelphia. The Diocese is indebted to Christ Church, Macon, for permission to use it, and to Dale and Susan Myers of Macon for providing the electronic image. The Editors.

Endsheet, title page, and copyright page: Sanctuary decorative detail from the Christ Church, Macon. Photo by Dale and Susan Myers.

Half title page: The nave and chancel of St. Philip's Cathedral, Atlanta.

The Donning Company Publishers
184 Business Park Drive, Suite 206
Virginia Beach, VA 23462

Steve Mull, *General Manager*
Barbara B. Buchanan, *Office Manager*
Richard A. Horwege, *Senior Editor*
Stephanie Danko, *Graphic Designer*
Amy Thomann, *Imaging Artist*
Lori Kennedy, *Project Research Coordinator*
Scott Rule, *Director of Marketing*
Stephanie Linneman, *Marketing Coordinator*

B. L. Walton Jr., *Project Director*

Library of Congress Cataloging-in-Publication Data

The Diocese of Atlanta, 1907–2007 : centennial celebration / by Centennial Celebration History Committee ;
compiled and edited by James P. Marshall Jr. and William P. McLemore.

　　　　　p.　　　　cm.

　　Includes bibliographical references and index.

　　ISBN-13: 978-1-57864-364-6 (hard cover : alk. paper)

　　ISBN-10: 1-57864-364-3 (hard cover : alk. paper)

1. Episcopal Church. Diocese of Atlanta—History. 2. Atlanta (Ga.)—Church history. I. Marshall, James P.,
1945– II. McLemore, William P., 1937–

　　BX5918.A95D56 2006

　　283'.758—dc22　　　　　　　　　　　　　　　　2006017605

Walsworth International Limited
Printed in China

CONTENTS

✠

PREVIOUS BISHOPS OF THE DIOCESE OF ATLANTA

✛

The Right Reverend Cleland Kinloch Nelson, Bishop of Atlanta, 1907–1917.

The Right Reverend Henry Judah Mikell, Bishop of Atlanta, 1917–1942.

The Right Reverend John Moore Walker Jr., Bishop of Atlanta, 1942–1951.

The Right Reverend John Buchman Walthour, Bishop of Atlanta, 1951.

The Right Reverend Randolph Royall Claiborne Jr., Bishop of Atlanta, 1952–1972.

The Right Reverend Milton LeGrand Wood III, Suffragan Bishop of Atlanta, 1967–1974.

The Right Reverend Bennett Jones Sims, Bishop of Atlanta, 1972–1984.

The Right Reverend Charles Judson Child, Suffragan Bishop of Atlanta, 1978–1983; Bishop of Atlanta, 1984–1989.

The Right Reverend Frank Kellogg Allan, Bishop Coadjutor, 1987–1988; Bishop of Atlanta, 1989–1999.

FOREWORD

☩

Grace to you and peace in Jesus Christ our Lord!

The pages of this book celebrate one hundred years of faithful mission and ministry by the parishes and institutions of the Diocese of Atlanta. Since our beginning a century ago, our diocese has experienced phenomenal growth and an exponential increase in gospel-centered service both at home and beyond. Our life together has been richly blessed by God through these one hundred years and our hearts are full of joy as we take stock of the wonderful things that God has done among us, and through us and, at times, in spite of us. To God be the Glory!

As you read these stories and look at these pictures, I hope that you will be able to see yourself in the rich tapestry of the Diocese of Atlanta. In the end, our church is not about programs or places, not about magnificent buildings or even good things accomplished. The church is our people: servants of the Risen Christ who are called together by the Gospel of Jesus and committed to each other out of a common loyalty to serve the church's mission. The New Testament vision of the church is not a collective of individual believers, but a holy assembly whose members take up their lives together as the embodiment of the Gospel. We are not an enclave of the like-minded, but a community of ragtag misfits made one in the waters of Holy Baptism.

This book that you hold in your hands is far more than a chronicle of the past. It is the story of a living and vital diocese "that is straining forward toward the upward call of God in Christ Jesus," as Saint Paul so eloquently put it. It is my sincere hope that these pages will inspire you and perhaps offer you a glimpse of those new things that the living God is always up to in our midst. The most important aspect of our centennial is not celebrating the past, but laying the groundwork for a vigorous and faithful future. Our second century must be stronger than the first or the shame is on us. God is always faithful. I am confident that we will rise to the challenges placed before us in our second century of service.

With gratitude for the faithful servants who have gone before us in these last one hundred years, with delight for each other and our common life in our own time, and with joyful expectation of what God has in store for us, let us rejoice!

Faithfully, in Christ,
The Right Reverend John Neil Alexander, Th.D., D.D.
Ninth Bishop of Atlanta

HIS WORK IS DEDICATED TO THE GLORY OF GOD AND IN PRAYERFUL THANKSGIVING FOR THE BOUNTEOUS GOODNESS WITH WHICH HE BLESSES US EACH DAY AND FOR ALL THE SAINTS who have witnessed before us. We humbly offer up this book as a testament of the loving work and miracles wrought amongst us and our forebears. Through their faith in God, courage and vision, they created and expanded the Diocese of Atlanta as a vehicle for the spread of His word. We also acknowledge the leadership, guidance, and devotion to duty of all the clergy and laity of this diocese. Through the clergy's and laity's ministries, this community of steadfast Episcopalians grew in faith, broadened its acceptance and love of all humankind, increased its number of communicants, and positively impacted the spiritual and human needs of those both in our midst and those far away.

James P. Marshall Jr., Chair of the Centennial Celebration History Committee.

Left to right: James P. Marshall Jr., chair, History Sub-Committee; Anne R. King, chair, Visual Arts Sub-Committee; Arthur Villarreal, chair, Corporate Sponsorship Sub-Committee; Wynn Callaway, secretary and Diocesan liaison; Liz Schellingerhout, co-chair, Communications Sub-Committee; Angela Williamson, chair, Centennial Celebration Steering Committee; The Right Reverend J. Neil Alexander, Bishop of the Diocese of Atlanta; Bruce Neswick, chair, Music Sub-Committee; Ernie Radaker, treasurer; The Reverend William P. McLemore, chaplain and chair, Archives; John Andrews, chair, Funding and Events Sub-Committee; and Chancellor Richard Perry, legal counsel.

Left to right: Deacon Gene Waller Owens and the Reverend Harold Lockett, co-chairs, Outreach Sub-Committee; and Janet Patterson, Annual Council liaison. Not pictured: The Reverend Doris Graf Smith, chair, Education Sub-Committee; Bruce Lafitte, chair, Marketing Sub-Committee; and Joni Woolf, co-chair Communications and Grants Sub-Committee.

ACKNOWLEDGMENTS

☩

SOMEONE ONCE SAID THE ONLY HARD PART TO CREATING AN "ACKNOWLEDGMENTS" PAGE IS THE CHANCE YOU MIGHT LEAVE SOMEONE OFF THE LIST OF THOSE WHO CONTRIBUTED IN special and meaningful ways to the production of the book. This is certainly the case with this work and if I have overlooked anyone, it is purely by accident.

This project has been a deeply moving and rewarding one, both spiritually and intellectually. While having managed many large projects involving many volunteers over the span of my working career, I can truly say that this opportunity posed the greatest challenges. The sheer number of volunteers to be recruited across the Diocese to meet our Bishop's goal of involving as many Episcopalians as possible in every parish in telling its own story was daunting. The logistics of finding the "right" people to tell the stories was a difficult task. I turned to prayer many times during the growth of the book to ask for guidance in making right decisions. I will forever be humbled by the sheer number of "people-hours" and the cooperation of people I'd never met face to face that went into the production of this material. The hours of research, the struggle to capture a "parish personality" in so few words, and the local vetting process were challenging. Finally, the sheer effort of finalizing all the stories and gathering them together to give a real sense of where we've come from together as a faith tradition was staggering.

My first "thank you" goes to my own parish priest, the Reverend Bob Dendtler, who first suggested to our Bishop that I might have an interest in serving on the Centennial Steering Committee. I am also thankful for the trust and freedom which Bishop Alexander gave me and our committee in developing our plan to gather so many wonderful stories. And of course, the support and availability of Angela Williamson, Chair of the Centennial Steering Committee, was a Godsend. She was a great resource as the plan emerged. The entire group of Centennial Celebration Steering Committee members each provided their support in many different ways and I am thankful to each one.

A project of this size, when taken on in addition to a "real" job, invariably impacts one's personal life. I am truly grateful to my beloved wife Nancy and son Matthew who stood by and supported me at every stage of the work—even when I knew that I was neglecting my responsibilities to them. From assistance in managing phone calls, messages, and e-mails to the final frantic proofreading before the manuscript went to Hong Kong for printing, they were both truly "there" for me.

Perhaps the biggest thanks of all goes to the over three hundred volunteer Parish Chroniclers and Parish Photographers whose knowledge of their local parish stories made this publication possible. All have gone above and beyond the call of duty. Their names and credits appear at the end of each story. Thank them when you see them.

Special thanks go Mrs. Carolyn Reynolds Parker for her generous financial contribution; to the Reverend William P. McLemore, Diocesan Archivist, for the chapter introductions and Diocesan Archives photos; multiple parish text composers Dr. Virginia C. Hinton and Robert E. Van Keuren Jr.; to volunteer professional photographers Dale and Susan Myers, Anderson Scott, Bill Monk, and John Whitt; to imaging artists Ruben Burney, Patt Wagner, and Elizabeth Hood; to all the Parish Administrators, secretaries, and volunteers—especially clergy spouses and partners who helped track down the story tellers; to special "expediters" Mrs. Maryel Battin, Mrs. Marianne Joris, Dr. Glenn T. Eskew, and Mrs. Jane C. Symmes who helped locate special resources; to Cathedral of St. Philip and Diocesan staff: Wynn Callaway, Nan Ross, Lara Lowman, Tom Smith, and Cary Patrick—all of whom responded to "panic" requests for materials and information; and special thanks for proofreading assistance to: Sue S. Ashmore, Janice A. Hardy, Mrs. Ramon Lantz, Nancy Marshall, Matthew Marshall, and Anna M. Haslbauer; and for their countless hours spent extensively indexing this work, I will be forever indebted to Janice A. Hardy and Mrs. Ramon Lantz. And finally, our heartfelt thanks goes out to the staff at Donning Company Publishers, without whom, we would not have so artfully crafted a work: Bernie Walton, Richard Horwege, Amy Thomann, and Stephanie Danko. Thanks be to God for all!

James P. Marshall Jr., Editor.

CHAPTER ONE

A DIOCESE IS BORN

GEORGIANS DROVE THE BRITISH OUT IN 1782 AND THREE SMALL ENGLISH PARISHES—ST. PAUL'S (AUGUSTA), CHRIST CHURCH (SAVANNAH), AND CHRIST CHURCH (ST. SIMON'S Island)—struggled to find their new American identity. Until the War of 1812 ended all hope for Britain in the Colonies, stubborn Loyalists complicated their efforts. The few clergy and laity in the new "Episcopal churches" in Georgia realized growth would only come by forming their own diocese. In February 1823, delegates met at St. Paul's, Augusta, and adopted a constitution and four canon laws. Insuring that the new diocese would join with the national church effort, this constitution stated that "this Convention do hereby accede to the Constitution of the Protestant Episcopal Church of the United States of America. . . ."

For eighteen years, the parishes functioned with occasional assistance from the Bishop of South Carolina. On May 5, 1840, the diocese numbered the required six congregations for episcopal leadership and eight clergy and nineteen delegates nominated and elected a College of South Carolina theology professor, the Reverend Stephen Elliott Jr., as their bishop. Congregations represented at the Convention at Grace Church, Gainesville, were: St. Paul's, Augusta; Grace, Clarksville; Trinity, Columbus; Grace, Gainesville; Christ, Macon; Christ, Savannah; St. Michael's, Springfield; and Christ, St. Simon's Island.

Bishop Elliott found a weak and fractured diocese. The only congregation with sufficient member and financial strength was Christ Church, Savannah. Elliott made that port city his home immediately and named himself Rector of newly formed St. John's, Savannah. In spite of travel and communication hardships, Elliott celebrated his tenth anniversary in 1850 with his flock numbering 870 members and twenty-one congregations. Christ Church, Savannah, remained dominant with 160 members and paid the lion's share of the Bishop's salary. A few years later, at the death of the revered rector of Christ Church, Savannah, the Reverend Edward Nuefville, Bishop Elliott assumed that position and remained there until his own death in 1866.

The Civil War wreaked havoc on the Diocese of Georgia. Reconstruction caused great transition among the population. Some parishes benefited and others were decimated of both members and resources. The Forty-fifth Convention at Christ Church, Macon, May 9, 1867, elected the Reverend John Watrus Beckwith of Trinity Church, New Orleans, as the second Bishop of Georgia. His first convention address reveals conditions he faced: "The late political strife which convulsed the Nation and has desolated the South, has subjected the religious Bodies in our country to a fearful test. . . . May God hasten the day when divisions may cease, and all Christians, having only the one Faith and regenerated by the one Baptism, may be gathered into one Fold under the one Shepherd."

Text submitted by the Reverend William P. McLemore.

CHRIST CHURCH, MACON

✛

Georgia Episcopalians held their first Convention of the Diocese of Georgia in February 1823. They initiated a missionary tour of the state led by the Reverend Lot Jones. In February 1825, Jones visited Macon. This central Georgia city had been established by the state legislature in 1823, but almost two years later, the residents had not yet formed any official churches and there were no resident ministers. The Reverend Jones conducted an Episcopal service, and shortly thereafter, on March 5, 1825, a group of Macon residents formed the city's first church, an Episcopal congregation known as Christ Church.

The Reverend Jones became Christ Church's first rector. The parish grew rapidly, and by the end of the year, Sunday school attendance numbered fifty pupils. In the December 1, 1825 edition of the *Savannah Georgian*, the newspaper's editor commented on the progress of the young town of Macon: "I was delighted with the place and its growing prosperity. Last March two years ago, it was a wilderness. It has now thirty-two stores; has cotton stored from sixteen counties, and perhaps nothing characterizes its refinement more conclusively than the fact that it maintains an Episcopal minister."

In December 1826, the Georgia legislature formally incorporated Christ Church and set aside a grant of land on which to build a house of worship. Within a year, the legislature had also granted property for Presbyterian, Methodist, and Baptist congregations to erect buildings in the city.

In January 1833, Christ Church secured the services of the Reverend Seneca G. Bragg as rector. Members of the parish sold the church lot originally allocated and eventually purchased the lot on Walnut Street presently occupied by Christ Church. As the parish solicited funds from its members to erect a dedicated church on the new lot, services were held in various buildings in downtown Macon. In 1834, construction was completed on the new church, designed in the form of a Roman cross with a central dome and Gothic windows. The interior space seated between three and four hundred persons and had a gallery opposite the chancel. All but four of the pews were rented to parishioners; the others were reserved for strangers. By 1835, the church had received donations of a chandelier and a "sweet-toned organ." By tradition, this organ was the first brought to any Macon church, and some of the town's religious leaders considered its use rather controversial.

Right: Christ Church, Macon.

Christ Church grew and flourished in its new facility. By 1850, the Vestry noted a need for additional space and resolved to obtain subscriptions for a new structure. Christ Church dismantled the original building, but salvaged many of its bricks for use in the walls of the new structure. The new Gothic-style church was consecrated on May 2, 1852, by Bishop Stephen Elliott. Completed at a cost of about $15,000, the building was embellished with twelve pinnacles symbolizing Christ's disciples. Each of the four corners of the one-hundred-foot-tall tower was surmounted by a pinnacle, which symbolized one of the four gospels. The interior included ninety-two pews on the main floor, with two side galleries and a rear organ gallery. Bishop Elliott described the new structure as "a very chaste and capacious Church, having nearly double the sitting of the former Church. It reflects great credit on the congregation of Christ Church, Macon, who have built it entirely out of their own resources."

As war ravaged the South in the 1860s, Christ Church persevered under the leadership of the Reverend Henry Kollock Rees, who proved to be a stabilizing force during those troubled times. He stressed missionary work, and is credited with establishing several Episcopal Churches in and around Macon. In addition to developing new parishes in Griffin (1858–59) and Hawkinsville (1864), Rees founded the Macon missions of St. Barnabas in 1869 and St. Paul's in 1868.

Establishment of the mission at St. Paul's would alter Episcopal liturgical practices in Macon. Located in a growing residential section just beyond downtown, St. Paul's featured a Sunday afternoon service with lay reading and "a full musical choral service." This musical service followed the tenets of England's Oxford Movement, which sought, in part, to add the singing of creeds and prayers to the spoken

Anglican service as a means of reviving ritual. The Reverend Rees introduced these same musical elements at Christ Church as well. Members of Christ Church swiftly revolted and expressed concerns that this ritualism was too papist and Catholic in nature. By contrast, the mission at St. Paul's enthusiastically embraced the expanded role of music in worship. Following several months of controversy, Father Rees resigned as Rector of Christ Church to lead the newly established parish at St. Paul's.

Christ Church installed a new rector who promised to follow the strict tenets of the Prayer Book "as, in its glorious simplicity, our Protestant forefathers compiled

Chancel of Christ Church, Macon.

and used it." The communicants of Christ Church redevoted themselves to ministry and outreach. The Ladies Aid Society donated countless hours of physical labor and raised considerable funds to support mission churches, community outreach programs, and improvements to the church property. The interior of the church building was redecorated at least four times between 1882 and 1922, first with delicate stencil patterns and then with polychromatic stenciled borders. New memorial windows were added in place of some of the original geometric stained-glass windows, a new pulpit, lectern, and altar rail were added, the altar was replaced, and the oak reredos was installed and embellished.

In 1880, the Church erected a new Sunday school building, Jones Chapel, in memory of parishioner John Jones. In 1890, the church established the Julia Parkman Jones Benevolent Home to take care of indigent women in the parish and other persons deemed by the Vestry to be in need of protection. In 1926, Christ Church built a new Parish House to accommodate growing Sunday school classes and all of the parish societies.

In 1907 the Diocese of Georgia divided, and the Diocese of Atlanta was created at a meeting in the Macon parish. Christ Church became the mother church of the new diocese. Throughout the twentieth century, as Macon grew and residences of Christ Church's members spread far into the suburbs of the city, the Church remained committed to its urban setting. The Guild of the Helping Hand was established to promote personal assistance by parish families to needy families throughout the city, regardless of their church affiliation. Membership in this guild later extended to include members of other local churches. Although the Julia Jones Benevolent Home closed in 1931, the endowment fund known as the Julia Jones Trust continued to support indigent individuals recommended by the Outreach Committee of the Vestry. Christ Church also supported the efforts of the Appleton Church Home. In 1969, Christ Church's Episcopal Church Women underwrote and administered a church kindergarten for culturally deprived children in the community, which operated for a number of

years. In 1976, Christ Church helped to organize the Meals on Wheels program for Macon. Operated by forty-five volunteers and housed in Jones Chapel, it continues today as one of the church's best known and most successful outreach ministries. Nearly twenty years ago, the church also established a Weekend Lunch Program. Twelve teams from seven churches alternate each weekend to prepare and serve hot lunches in Jones Chapel for citizens in need.

In 2000, Christ Church completed massive renovations to the historic sanctuary and installed a new Fisk tracker organ. Positioning the new organ in the rear gallery allowed the chancel area to be reopened and the altar to be moved, allowing the celebrant to face the congregation. After documenting all of the previous decorative treatments of the sanctuary through historic photographs, written descriptions, and chemical paint analysis, the congregation selected a new palette of sable, green, and red and a collection of wall stencil patterns that relate to the Mother Church, Christ's sacrifice, the New Covenant, and the promise of the Resurrection. The new Fisk tracker organ, Opus 115, rises to the full height of the roof trusses and has 2,006 wood and metal pipes.

Christ Church has entered the twenty-first century as a vibrant and growing community of faith. Outreach remains a hallmark of this church's ministry in the community. Christ Church also supports the Loaves and Fishes Ministry; Habitat for Humanity; Salvation Army's Safe House; Rebuilding Together; and the Macon Volunteer Clinic. Christian education programs for both children and adults have expanded, and there is a strong youth ministry. Music is an important component of worship, and the church offers three choirs for members. Christ Church has chapters of both Daughters of the King and the Order of St. Luke. There are three worship services each Sunday, a Wednesday noon healing service, and a Wonderful Wednesday Evening Prayer Service and dinner program. Rooted in a strong sense of history, Christ Church is committed to its contemporary mission: "Growing by God's Grace into a Family of Faith and Ministry."

Text submitted by Julie Groce. Photos by Dale and Susan Myers.

TRINITY EPISCOPAL CHURCH, COLUMBUS

✠

Trinity's story began in August 1834, in a house located where the parking lot is today. At the invitation of Dr. Edwin de Graffenried and his Presbyterian wife Sarah, an auspicious gathering was held, attended by some leading citizens of the new boomtown Columbus. The first page of the Vestry minutes records that the group resolved to organize an Episcopal congregation in Columbus with all deliberate speed. A chairman, secretary, and treasurer were appointed, and within weeks, committees were hard at work looking for a building lot and lobbying the legislature for a charter.

Another committee wrote the Reverend Seneca Bragg, rector of Christ Church, Macon, asking for pastoral assistance. Responding enthusiastically, he reached Columbus in early September. The Presbyterian minister's invitation to meet there was accepted and the minutes record on September 6, 1834, the Lord's Day, at "half past 10 o'clock a.m., the first public meeting was held in Columbus for the worship of God according to . . . the Protestant Episcopal Church."

Born in a borrowed building with a borrowed rector, and despite the resolve of its leaders, the odds for success weren't in Trinity's favor. The Episcopal denomination in Georgia—with only four other churches—still suffered from its association with the Church of England and the British Crown. It relied on visits from the Bishop of South Carolina or missionary bishops from General Convention.

Rectors were hard to come by. The new congregation found that it could be formally chartered, elect vestry and wardens, adopt bylaws, send delegates to convention, purchase property, draw plans, and nearly complete a church as quickly as they could locate a rector. For over two years, lay leaders led periodic services with sacraments performed by occasional visiting priests.

Trinity's early leaders were committed to establish a new church, one hundred miles from the nearest congregation and clerical leadership. They built a beautiful classical church and bell tower—with no funds to pay for the building, no minister to preach or administer the sacraments, and not even a bell for the tower! Much ridiculed, according to contemporary accounts, they gave their best for God in order to worship in their tradition.

Prayers were answered as the new building neared completion, when the Reverend William D. Cairns answered the call, arriving in Columbus in early 1837. Almost simultaneously, a nine-hundred-pound bell, an unexpected gift to Trinity arrived from Trinity, Wall Street Vestryman Robert Hyslop, and was hung in time to peal during Cairns' first service.

All forty-six pews were immediately rented for one year at public auction for $3,369. With a new fourteen-stop organ, a salaried choirmaster, two stoves, five-piece communion service, three German silver collection plates, fine carpets, marble baptismal font, a hired sexton, and property insurance, Trinity's leaders must have marveled at God's bounty so quickly provided. Chief among Trinity's early leaders were

Trinity Episcopal Church, Columbus, in 1998.

Virginians Dr. de Graffenried, Thomas Nelson, and Robert Carter; Richard P. Spencer of tidewater Maryland; and Georgians Dr. John A. Urquhart and attorney John Schley, both formerly of St. Paul's, Augusta; William P. Yonge of Savannah's Christ Church; and Gustavus de Launay of Milledgeville. Other early leaders included Columbus newspaper editor John Forsyth Jr. and the brothers Charles, John, and George Peabody.

The spring of 1838 was a high point for Trinity and the Georgia Church, when Missionary Bishop Jackson Kemper, joined by Trinity's Reverend Cairns and Macon's Reverend Bragg consecrated the new church, "setting it apart to the service of God, separated forever from all common and unholy uses." Later that year—just as Columbus's first boom reached its height—the American economy bottomed and Trinity's Vestry was beset by creditors.

Banks failed and bankruptcy swept the town with creditors so desperate that even a religious institution was fair game. The Reverend Cairns and a handful of members held fast, in the face of foreclosure and a series of lawsuits. Cairns took a teaching job and reduced his salary; Treasurer John Schley gave free legal services; and some of the most faithful paid out of their pockets—when least able—to save Trinity.

Bishop Elliott helped raise funds to cover Trinity's crippling debts. The ladies of Christ Church, Savannah; St. Paul's, Augusta; and Christ Church, Macon, contributed several thousand dollars. On his 1846 Columbus visit, Elliott reported the parish had grown in ten years from the feeblest diocesan missionary station to strength second only to Savannah. The 125 communicants—98 whites and 27 blacks (both slave and free)—worshiped at Trinity and the plantation mission St. John's in the Wilderness, across the river in Alabama.

Prior to the Civil War, Trinity grew into an established, respected religious institution. Parishioners, both black and white, witnessed the splitting of their nation and the national Church. For four years they dutifully gave their offering in Confederate money, prayed publicly for President Davis and the Confederacy, and helped bury sons of Trinity killed in battle. The 1865 Easter morning service, led by the Reverend Charles Quintard, preceded by only a few hours the Battle of Columbus.

After Reconstruction, came a period of renewed prosperity and church growth. A capital campaign resulted in a successful public fundraising concert in February 1871 as the opening of the new Springer Opera House. Much planning and fundraising passed before Trinity broke ground for its new building in 1890 across the street from Old Trinity.

During late 1890 and early 1891, work on the Tudor Gothic–style church building progressed rapidly. The Reverend Hunter, Trinity's eighth rector, led the final Old Trinity service on the last Sunday in July 1891. Workmen moved the old bell across the street to the new tower and the next Sunday it pealed there—as it does today. The next spring, Bishop Cleland Nelson consecrated Trinity with pomp and ceremony.

Generations have followed in the founders' footsteps, supporting their beloved parish. Trinity women have participated in campaigns and opportunities for service—maintaining guilds; serving in the famous Cozy Tea Room opened in the 1910s to fund a new Rectory; buying Trinity bonds during the Great Depression; and assisting the Reverend Harry Walker with his nationally recognized mission—the Episcopal Service Men's Club—to Fort Benning's soldiers during World War II.

Trinity grew along with postwar Columbus, and its building grew with several additions. Many new faces have joined the long, silent procession of the saints to the altar, stretching through time for over 170 years, faithfully linking us to those who have worshipped here before.

As Rector Colin Campbell wrote for Trinity's 125th anniversary, "the true history of our parish is not the deeds that are recorded . . . or the buildings and adornments . . . but the stories of those souls who encompass us here as a cloud of witnesses. It is the prayers, the pain, the suffering, the forgiveness, the redemption, the faith, and the hope of those who have gathered here before which constitutes our real heritage. In short, it is their stories and the threads of their lives which make up our history."

Text submitted by John M. Sheftall. Photo from the Collins Collection, Diocese of Atlanta Archives.

GRACE-CALVARY EPISCOPAL CHURCH, CLARKESVILLE

✛

Clarkesville was North Georgia's first major mountain resort. Founded in 1823 after a treaty with the Cherokees, it quickly became a village of hotels and boarding houses for well-to-do families escaping the intense heat fevers during summers in Charleston and Savannah. The summer families stayed for an extended period each year, often as long as six months. The need for a church to serve seasonal Episcopalians was met in 1838 when E. B. Kellogg, a New York missionary, joined with three local families to establish a mission. The first service was on October 28, 1838. On April 15, 1839, Richard W. Habersham Jr. and George R. Jessup applied for parish status. The lot for the church was purchased on June 7, 1839. On May 4 and 5, 1840, the Clarkesville parish hosted the eighteenth annual Convention of the Diocese of Georgia. At that time there were only six parishes in the state: Christ Church, Savannah; St. Paul's Church, Augusta; Trinity Church, Columbus; Christ Church, St. Simon's Island; and Grace Church, Clarkesville.

The Convention elected the first Bishop of Georgia. The Reverend Stephen Elliott Jr. was installed as the thirty-seventh in succession of American bishops. The Convention was held in the Methodist Church, as drought had delayed completion of Grace Church. The sanctuary of Grace Church was consecrated on October 10, 1842, by Bishop Elliott. For the next few years the church thrived. Many of the summer visitors built homes and provided some stability for what was essentially a seasonal church. The Civil War changed the fortunes of the supporting families—many destitute and never to return after 1865—and for Grace Church. A few parishioners sold out in Savannah and Charleston and settled in their summer homes permanently. These few families kept the church alive well into the twentieth century.

Right: Grace-Calvary Episcopal Church, Clarkesville, consecrated in 1842.

The coming of the railroad after the Civil War brought new mission churches started in resorts along the line. Mt. Airy became another vacation destination. On October 24, 1882, Mr. and Mrs. Wilcox and Marie Elliott gave land for the site of a new Episcopal mission called Calvary Church. In 1951 Calvary Church in Mt. Airy was sold and the congregation moved to Cornelia on November 18. It remained a small active congregation during World War II. Grace Church suffered from isolation due to travel restrictions and the decline of older members, who had kept it alive. Services were infrequent and it was only through the concern of Calvary Church members that Grace continued to exist.

In the mid-1950s, retired Episcopalians began settling in the area. Membership increased, services were held regularly, and in 1964, a Parish House was completed. In 1971, Grace and Calvary Church's congregations were still undersized. In 1972, the two mission churches combined and in 1973 petitioned for parish status as Grace-Calvary Parish, granted on December 23, 1973. The Cornelia church building was sold two years later and the congregation began to restore the historic Clarkesville building. In 1977, a Parish House addition provided classrooms and a nursery. Adjacent property was acquired for a church office and choir room. In 1992, more additions were made to the building. In Father J. St. Julian M. Lachicotte's time, the growing congregation increased its interest in outreach. Grace-Calvary began sponsoring missionaries abroad and church missions in the diocese. Blairsville Mission became St. Clare's in 1990, and White County Mission became Church of the Resurrection in 1993.

Grace-Calvary is a beautiful example of Greek Revival architecture. The huge multipaned windows still retain much original hand-blown glass. The sanctuary's high pulpit and altar remain much the same. They express theology of the period—the centrality of the Word and Sacraments, with preaching occupying the rather more important place, as the size and height of the pulpit suggests. A small font was placed in front of the communion rail. Babies born during the summer months were baptized as soon as possible. Weddings were planned for the winter months back home during the social season. For this reason there is no center aisle. The boxed pews, a distinguishing feature in early churches, served to keep drafts off the parishioners. The Erben organ is one of the treasures of the church. It is the oldest working pipe organ of its kind in Georgia, commissioned in 1848 by a church ladies group—the Hope Society. The disassembled organ was transported from New York to Savannah, then upriver by steamboat to Augusta and by wagon to Clarkesville.

While electricity, air conditioning, and heat have been added, Grace-Calvary's sanctuary still remains the only basically unaltered Episcopal structure of the original six parishes in the state. It remains a constant reminder of the past, but the ever-changing congregation reflects movements of the church in new directions of stewardship. Like the ancient trees surrounding the sanctuary, there is always a unique feeling of deep roots amid fresh new growth. One of the early ministers referred to Grace as a "snap bean church," since the congregation lasted only until the last picking of the summer beans. The Reverend William Eppes noted in his report of 1862 to the Annual Convention of the Diocese: "On the whole, hard labor and late fruit are the prospects here. It could not be otherwise as things are situated. The people are personally kind and there is nothing to discourage patience and faith. May God grant His blessings to the work and the people."

God in his own time has brought us where we are today. Under the guidance of the Holy Spirit, we shall continue our mission and ministry in the foothills of the Appalachian Mountains.

Text submitted by John Kollock. Photo from the church archives.

GRACE EPISCOPAL CHURCH, GAINESVILLE

✛

Histories of Grace Church always mention the Reverend Ezra Kellogg who came from New York in October 1838 to build a parish in Clarkesville, according to Malone's *The Episcopal Church in Georgia*. In his 1839 annual report, Kellogg reported that he had officiated once in Gainesville: ". . . good Missionary ground for our Church . . . three Episcopal families residing in the place, and several others . . . resort thither for health during the summer. I design to commence services . . . about the first of next month, preaching every other Sunday until winter. . . . I hope a Missionary may be provided to labor and reside among them."

Early Gainesville Episcopalian Colonel George Hervey Hall, a transplant from Connecticut, bought land known as Mule Camp Springs. According to Hall County historian William Hosch, Hall built Grace Chapel on the property in 1857 or 1858.

The Reverend Matthew Henderson, Emmanuel Church, Athens, reported in 1859, "At Gainesville very considerable interest has been manifested to secure regular services and . . . we shall have a church there with a fine organ and bell in . . . months." Hall's Grace Chapel pipe organ was Gainesville's first, says Hosch. The Diocese reported in 1861 ". . . Gainesville is thriving with fourteen members."

The Civil War and Reconstruction left the fledgling congregation in disarray. Colonel Hall sold his property; left the country, and the small chapel was sold to the Presbyterians. The remaining members reestablished their worshiping community and by 1880 had eight members. Father T. G. Pond, missionary, reported in 1892 that Grace had seventeen communicants. By 1895 the number had grown to forty-one communicants and fifty-five services. A building

Left: Grace Episcopal Church, Gainesville.

Grace Church, circa 1952.

Members responded rapidly. Service was held April 12 in the Presbyterian Church, and a meeting was held in the Leslie Quinlan home to discuss rebuilding. Services were temporarily held in the Presbyterian Church, Brenau College, and the Quinlan home.

Atlanta architect Charles Hopson's church design was estimated to cost $6,000. Funds came from the Diocese, member donations, the community, other churches, and people around the country. Donations ranged from $1 to more than $500 from Trinity, Columbus. New York financier J. P. Morgan contributed $100. The cornerstone was laid on Easter Sunday, March 28, 1937. Bishop Mikell addressed the congregation in a late-afternoon ceremony. The building was consecrated in September.

Grace's growth in the late 1980s and early 1990s demanded expansion. After extensive study by the Vestry and committees, expansion from 11,800 square feet to 22,700 square feet at a cost of $2.4 million was made, including a new church seating four hundred. The cornerstone was laid December 6, 1992, and the buildings occupied in 1993. Architect Garland Reynolds Jr. said the early English Gothic period of about A.D. 1200 inspired the design. The 1937 church, now chapel, retained its unique features. A new Parish Hall, columbaria garden, and additional classrooms were added.

erected at College and Bradford Streets was moved to Grace's present location on Washington Street in 1913. It took three months to roll it on logs to the new site. Growth and stability followed. Grace was admitted as a parish at the Eighteenth Council of the Diocese of Atlanta.

During the Reverend Geoffrey Hinshelwood's service (1934–1938) Grace Church faced one of its biggest challenges. The tornado of April 6, 1936, blew through downtown, up Washington Street, and splintered the church. Members left a communion service shortly before it struck on Monday in Holy Week. The only person in the building was the sexton—one of over two hundred killed. The chalice and an altar cloth survived, but the church building and most contents were destroyed. Records were scattered, making it more difficult to trace Grace's early years.

The church has long been active in outreach programs such as Good News at Noon and Habitat for Humanity. Members have volunteered at Good News since its inception and were in the forefront of a new start for Habitat in January 2002. Children of Grace, the parish preschool started in 1979, serves the parish and community well.

Grace Church, grown from a few meeting in homes in the early 1800s to more than one thousand baptized members today, demonstrates an expanded ministry which can better serve the parish and community today and into the future.

Text submitted by the Reverend Douglas Dailey. Photos from the church archives.

St. Stephen's Episcopal Church, Milledgeville

✠

When viewed from its site on the west side of Statehouse Square on South Wayne Street, St. Stephen's may appear to be just one of the many antebellum structures in downtown Milledgeville. A brief look at its history, however, provides a much more interesting perception, for St. Stephen's history has always been inextricably intertwined with that of Baldwin County and the city itself, each unique in its own way.

Milledgeville was established in 1804 by act of the Georgia legislature to be the fourth capital of Georgia, with sites set aside on Statehouse Square for churches of four denominations. The earliest Episcopal services were not held until 1832 when two priests from Christ Church, Savannah, reported that the area presented "a field for missionary labor." Realizing that the new capital of the state lacked an Episcopal presence, the new Bishop of Georgia, the Right Reverend Stephen Elliott Jr., placed a high priority on establishing a parish in Milledgeville. Nine years after those first services, St. Stephen's took advantage of the free site, which it still occupies. Incorporation papers were signed by Governor Charles J. McDonald on April 4, 1841. In 1966 the most recent lease for ninety-nine years for the lot was signed.

Two years after incorporation, the church was constructed, with the Capitol literally in its back yard. The small, unpretentious structure, the oldest house of worship in continuous use in Baldwin County, featured a flat roof and contained no vestibule. The eighth oldest Episcopal Church in the state and the fifth oldest in the Diocese of Atlanta, it was dedicated by Bishop Elliott on December 12, 1843, with the Reverend Rufus White of Western New York as rector. It was one of the first dedicated by Elliott—in office only since 1840.

Historical highlights include an 1846 visit by the famous English geologist, Sir Charles Lyell, who described St. Stephen's as "neat and substantial." Surely he was invited by one of the incorporators, the state geologist, John Ruggles Cotting, who

became the first senior warden. When the Reverend William Johnson became rector in July of that year, St. Stephen's could count only eleven communicants. Two women teachers in the Sunday school are credited with preserving the church.

Originally pews were rented and continued to be for at least four years. A small Rectory, costing $1,200, was erected during the tenure of the Reverend Judson M. Curtis, 1859–1861, for membership in the antebellum years never exceeded twenty-one. St. Stephen's first historian, Mrs. Emma LeConte Furman, noted in 1877 that the

Exterior of St. Stephen's Episcopal Church, Milledgeville.

county was sparsely populated for many years because of its frontier position. In 1845 the population was 7,450 persons. In May of that year, with seventeen communicants, St. Stephen's hosted the Diocesan Annual Convention. The next year, the number of communicants dropped to fourteen—only two were men. The dozen women held what must have been the first of many fundraising projects, a fair, the equivalent of a modern bazaar. Membership declined to thirteen in 1850. Lay persons have always played a major role in the life of St. Stephen's, perhaps never more importantly than during the years 1861–1863 when the church lacked a rector. Georgia's adjutant general, Henry Wayne, conducted services and helped make St. Stephen's a welcoming home for refugees who were seeking to escape the invading Federal troops.

During General Sherman's forces brief occupation of Milledgeville in late November, 1864, soldiers from the 107th New York Infantry Regiment took shelter in St. Stephen's as well as other churches on Statehouse Square. The general himself spent the night in the nearby governor's mansion, which, along with the Capitol, had been deserted by state officials to avoid capture. To stay warm, the troops burned whatever came to hand, including pews, but their vandalism did not stop there. They also poured syrup into the pipes of the organ. Folklore says that indentations in the floor were left by the troops' horses. When the nearby magazine and arsenal were blown up as the troops left to continue their infamous March to the Sea, the roof was damaged and the windows blown out. The capital moved to Atlanta in 1867, but St. Stephen's claims as its senior warden the last elected governor to serve in Milledgeville, Charles J. Jenkins. His executive secretary, William H. Scott, served as junior warden.

Repairs to the building became affordable in 1871—but not to the organ. More work completed in the 1880s, produced an excellent example of Carpenter Gothic style with a beaded board interior. The Parish Hall, dedicated in 1970, echoes the Gothic tradition. Earlier, Harding Hall was constructed and named for the Reverend Frederick Harrison Harding, rector from 1924 to 1954 (the longest tenure of any rector), and houses the church offices. The main floor of the Parish Hall also holds a fully equipped kitchen and the Catherine Cline-Garner Memorial Library, the Virginia Herald Bowman Memorial Choir Room, and the Youth Room. The lower level accommodates the St. Stephen's Day School, founded by Director Carol Grant in 1985. The Food Pantry Program, the Warden's Hall addition, and membership growth occurred during the tenure of the Reverend A. Edward Sellers Jr. (1983–1998). The Reverend Dr. C. K.

St. Stephen's, Milledgeville, Day School program.

Robertson (1999–2004) added the Children's Chapel and innovative services. The church also supports a successful Veterans' Home outreach ministry.

In 1909 Nylic Bland, daughter of church organist and local agent for the New York Life Insurance Company, wrote her father's boss about the syrup-damaged organ. George W. Perkins responded with an offer, thankfully accepted, to pay for a new organ, which has since been replaced by a more modern one. Perkins' telegram is displayed in one of the specially built church memorabilia cases. The stained-glass altar window was a gift from Christ Church, Savannah, in appreciation for the hospitality extended during the Civil War days. The other lancet-arched windows in the church date from the turn of the last century and celebrate the lives of several communicants and that of the Reverend J. M. Stoney, rector from 1873 to 1884.

St. Stephen's is now under the guidance of its twenty-eighth rector. The Reverend Don Caron became rector in November 2005, and is continuing the varied ministries of the church, including study groups, children's and youth activities, and others as well as supporting a dozen outreach programs. In addition to two Holy Eucharist services on Sundays, a Saturday evening Eucharist using a Celtic liturgy is conducted, and a weekly worship service is also conducted at the Georgia War Veterans' Home.

Text submitted by Virginia C. Hinton, Ph.D. Photos by Dr. Walter Isaac.

St. James' Episcopal Church, Marietta

✠

The train approaches the crossing and the preacher stops until the whistle is far enough away that she can be heard. This is St. James', Marietta, founded in May 1842 by railroad engineers and local businessmen to be a center "whence missionaries shall emanate into the Cherokee country." The first building, seating 230, was consecrated on April 9, 1843, and named for the Philadelphia church of William Root, whose Sunday school classes in his home led to the founding of the church.

Established on twenty acres of land, given by Colonel S. H. Long, most of the property was sold over time to help finance the church. In 1849 the far corner was designated a "grave land" and remains a cemetery. The 1860s saw many parishioners moving south to avoid the war, and Rector Samuel Benedict, arrested for refusing to pray for the United States President, was banished to Canada. The Federal army used the church as a hospital, plundered it, and caused considerable damage. Legend says the 1860 Boston-built organ was thrown into the street and saved by a passing farmer who hid it in his barn. Confederate General Leonidas Polk, also Bishop of Louisiana, was brought to St. James' after being killed in the Battle of Pine Mountain. Polk Street next to the church was named in his honor.

Postwar restoration by the small congregation was slow. The church bell, donated to the Confederate army and later captured by Federal troops, was replaced. Parish women gave silver and jewelry to make a chalice—used every Sunday. Under Colonel Robert de Treville Lawrence's leadership in 1878, the parish men and boys brought rock and sand from Kennesaw Mountain to Polk Street to build a one-room Sunday School Building. At times classroom, soup kitchen, and storeroom, it was remodeled as a Chapel in 1952. During a 1962 renovation of St. James' Church, the Hook organ, a lectern, and Brumby Company chairs were moved to the Chapel. The restored Chapel is used for a weekly healing service, small weddings, funerals, and Bible study for the homeless who come to St. James' on Sundays for lunch.

Construction of the Bell Bomber Plant in World War II led to a population explosion in Marietta; seventy-five hundred to twenty-five thousand in two years. St. James' growth mirrored this community growth, and additional facilities were built, including a new Parish House. In 1957, Rector Joseph T. Walker started a day school which separated from the church and became the independent Joseph T. Walker School in 1972.

St James', Marietta, new Parish Hall and Courtyard.

only one of its kind in Georgia. The St. James' change-ringers have won numerous competitions and trained the ringers at St. Luke's (Atlanta) new tower.

In 2004 a new Parish Hall, playground, elevator, handicapped accessible facilities, renovated offices, and new classrooms for all ages were dedicated. Increased membership led to an expanded worship schedule: a 5:30 p.m. Saturday service with gospel music and Sunday services are 7:45, 9:00, and 11:15 a.m. Once a month, one of the choirs offers Evensong at 4:30 p.m.

St. James' has a long history of outreach. The World Missions Committee has worked with a community in Kenya and enabled construction of a church, maternal health clinic, and a preschool. St. James' provided funds for digging wells there and for operating a mill in Zambia. In Marietta, St. James' started a Sack Lunch program to feed the homeless; Reach Out Mental Health which provides monthly lunches and activities for persons with mental disabilities; the Wonderful Days Preschool for children from low-income families; and the local Habitat for Humanity. St. James' Charities provides financial assistance through the Center for Family Resources. The St. James' Thrift Shop, operated by the Episcopal Church Women, helps those in need.

St. James'—a lively and creative parish—began in 2000 The Pilgrimage at St. James', a center for spirituality. In 2005 the B. Fred Hannan Labyrinth was dedicated in memory of a recent associate rector. St. James' introduced the Workshop Rotation model for Church School to the area, as well as the Journey to Adulthood for youth. The Polk Street Players, an amateur theater group, recently celebrated its twenty-sixth anniversary. St. James' is poised for the next step in its community life. While discerning God's call to us, we rejoice in our worship and service to God and God's people, through Jesus Christ, our Lord.

Text submitted by the Reverend Karen Evans. Photos from the church archives.

St. James' Church Processional.

In January 1964, firefighters from Marietta and as far away as Atlanta battled a boiler room fire started under the church. St. James' Church was destroyed but the Chapel and the Parish House were saved. Rebuilding took two years, and on January 16, 1966, the larger new church was dedicated. A new school wing was built and the damaged bell recast in Holland by the Schilling family. The church was consecrated, and the mortgage burned, 150 years after its original consecration, in April 1963.

British expatriates' memories of change-ringing bells, led to the installation of an eight-bell peal in the tower in 1995. Consecrated in March of 1996, it was the

Emmanuel Episcopal Church, Athens, Georgia

✠

For more than 160 years, under eleven bishops and twenty rectors, the people of Emmanuel have served God by meeting the challenges of the times.

William Bacon Stephens, a Savannah physician and a founder of the Georgia Historical Society, visited Athens as a newly appointed member of the University of Georgia Board of Visitors. He liked the thriving young town, created in 1801 as home of the nation's first chartered university and soon also a manufacturing center. Bishop Stephen Elliot encouraged young Dr. Stephens to enter the Episcopal ministry and ordained him as deacon in 1843.

That same year, Dr. Richard Dudley Moore's young bride invited other Episcopalians to meet in her parlor to plan Athens' first Episcopal Church. Bishop Elliot appointed William Bacon Stephens their first rector. On March 17, 1843, Stephens conducted their first service in the Town Hall. By mid-November, on land donated by the University, they built at the corner of Lumpkin and Clayton Streets a white clapboard New England–style church, named Emmanuel for the church in Elizabeth Stockton Moore's hometown in Newcastle, Delaware.

Dynamic Athens businessmen and professors, some members of Baptist, Methodist, and Presbyterian Churches located on the University campus, served temporarily on Emmanuel's Vestry. These included John S. Linton and Young L. G. Harris. Members James Camak, R. L. Bloomfield, and Dr. Moore were among early lay leaders. Ministers Thomas L. Smith and J. H. Linebaugh followed Stevens who became Bishop of Pennsylvania.

Throughout its history, Emmanuel has viewed its physical property as an instrument of social outreach. Under the Reverend Matthew Henderson (1856–1872), Emmanuel became Athens' center for community meetings. With independent means, Henderson built a rectory with a spectacular garden directly across Lumpkin Street. He guided his flock through the war-torn 1860s. For over a century following his death Emmanuel children decorated his grave in Oconee Hill Cemetery with Easter flowers.

Right: Front view of Emmanuel Episcopal Church, Athens.

Members of Emmanuel Church, Athens, serving Thanksgiving dinner.

Rectors Alexander Drysdale, Frank Hallam, Thomas Boone, Edward Ingle, J. C. Davis, and Robert M. W. Black served from 1873 through 1896. Their Harvest Home celebrations evolved into the annual Thanksgiving offerings of food baskets for shut-ins and later into the annual Thanksgiving dinners for the homeless still prepared in the church's kitchen. The church was enlarged as membership increased.

When business expanded into their downtown area, the small congregation of fewer than a hundred members bought property to build a larger church at its present site at Prince Avenue and Pope Street. Boldly, they planned a church large enough to hold four hundred communicants. In 1891 they razed the old church, saved some of its timbers, built a temporary chapel behind the new site, and held their first service there in September.

On October 15, 1899, the first service was held in the Gothic Revival cruciform church. Today, Mrs. Moore's parlor table is in the Founder's Chapel in the north transept. In St. Matthew's Chapel in the south transept are the altar and the *Christus Rex* window brought from the original church. Glorious memorial stained-glass windows have been added through the years.

From 1893 until 1919, with advice from Thomas H. Nickerson, the Reverend Troy Beatty developed Emmanuel's fundraising and spiritual groups. The year the Diocese of Atlanta was created, the rector's family moved into a new Rectory, subsequently home to Rectors Glenn Richards, George Hiller, and David Cady Wright. Wright led Emmanuel from 1933 through World War II to 1947. From 1948 to 1967, the Reverend J. Earl Gilbreath created additional women's chapters and a Men's Club to accommodate parish growth. The Reverend Don Raby Edwards from 1968 to 1973 led Emmanuel-as-family in moving beyond themselves to address needs outside the parish and to sponsor a mission church, St. Gregory the Great. The Reverend Franklin Cole Ferguson from 1974 until advanced Parkinson's disease forced his retirement in 1988 centered his ministry on music, teaching, and worship. Communicants have worked with the University Episcopal Center since its creation in 1958.

To plan Emmanuel's postwar future, in 1944 six communicants incorporated a church endowment fund to finance a new Rectory, church offices, a church school addition, and gifts to reconstruct war-torn church properties abroad. With subsequent bequests, notably the Williams-Rhodes and Joelson funds and Thrift House earnings, Emmanuel has contributed significantly to Athens' nonprofit community and especially to a sister parish in Haiti. Under Rectors James Knox Yeary, Eddie Ard, and Peter Courtney, Emmanuel has continued to grow and to be made available to community groups.

As a parish, Emmanuel continues to welcome a steady diversity of communicants, intelligent study, progressive ideas and approaches to Christianity. Such is our joy. Such is our strength.

Text submitted by Mrs. Mary Ann Hodgson. Photos by Harry O. Yates III.

THE EPISCOPAL CHURCH OF THE ASCENSION, CARTERSVILLE

✠

On November 6, 1844, the Right Reverend Stephen Elliott, first Bishop of Georgia, visited the Etowah River, Cass County (later Bartow) area with the Reverend Thomas Scott of Marietta. Elliott preached on the morning of November 8 at the Pettit Creek Baptist Church to a small group of Episcopalians who were encouraged to erect a central church, a parsonage, and schoolhouse in the farming community. Fifty acres of land were acquired through gifts and purchase. Bishop Elliott's Convention address in 1844 said the Reverend Scott was "most active in this advancement of the Church into a country hitherto untrodden by an Episcopal clergyman."

The buildings were erected, and Bishop Elliott consecrated Ascension Church on June 22, 1845. The Reverend Owen P. Thackara, deacon, was the missionary in charge. By 1850, there were seven members. For the next fifteen years, the church was used mostly for summer visitors from Savannah. At one point, the Reverend R. W. B. Elliott (later Bishop of Western Texas) held services once a month at the Academy in Cartersville and in the evening at the William H. Stiles home in Euharlee.

As Cartersville grew, the county property was sold, and land bought in town. The profits, with contributions from parties in Macon, Augusta, Savannah, and New York, were used to erect the current church, located at the corner of Bartow Street and Cherokee Avenue. The first Eucharist was held during Easter in April 1874; and the church was consecrated by Bishop Beckwith on November 6, 1875. Ascension was built in the "early Carpenter Gothic" style on the earlier church's foundation beams. A triple panel of Tiffany-style arched stained-glass was installed behind the altar. The light colored plaster walls were accented with dark wainscoting. A wood stove near the pulpit heated the interior. W. H. Stiles, a founder, was known to get up and stir the fire in the pot-bellied stove when the sermon became too lengthy.

The Reverend W. R. McConnell, minister-in-charge, documented the history of Ascension in 1886. From 1886 until the 1930s, little of the history is known. Atlanta supply clergy provided occasional services. With few Episcopalians in the area, Ascension, without a minister, held infrequent services. The register records some services, especially baptisms, held in homes.

From 1936 to 1939, Father Jack Soper was vicar, and Ascension experienced growth and enthusiasm—a Sunday school organized and the stained-glass side windows

Episcopal Church of the Ascension, Cartersville, built 1874.

were acquired. In 1938, Bishop Mikell gave parishioners Susan and Robert Stiles permission to remove stained-glass windows from the nearby Cave Spring church closed by the Diocese. The windows, except *Jesus the Good Shepherd*, were smaller than the existing window openings. Father Soper requested family memorials to install extra glass to expand the seven small windows to fit.

During the 1940s, Ascension was without a resident priest and Father Roy Pettway came from Atlanta (1943–1945) every other Sunday to conduct an evening service. In 1946 stability came with the ministry of the Reverend Albert K. Mathews, D.D., of Atlanta, who served as vicar. Dr. Mathews traveled to Cartersville often during the week to minister to parishioners and provide leadership. Members experienced a sense of renewal and worship attendance, baptisms, and confirmations increased. The old (often rented) Rectory became the Sunday School Building. The parish picnic and outdoor service custom began, and continues as an annual event at Malbone, home of W. H. Stiles' descendants. The Parish House was built and dedicated in the fall of 1953. Dr. Mathews died tragically the next year in a car accident driving to Atlanta after Cartersville's Sunday services. After funeral services at Ascension, he was interred at Arlington National Cemetery, and General Douglas McArthur paid tribute.

For three years, the Reverend Douglas Winn, chaplain of Rome's Battey Hospital, served as priest-in-charge and in 1957, the parish called the Reverend Winn as full-time resident priest, the first in twenty years. A new Rectory was built on Granger Hill. With Father Winn's leadership, Ascension advanced from "aided parish" to full parish status by 1960. The old Rectory was raised, and a new Sunday school facility built, providing eight classrooms. The church interior was refurbished with new pews and chancel railing, given by generous members. After ten years of strong leadership at Ascension, Father Winn accepted a call to St. George's, Griffin.

On June 1, 1965, the Reverend Louis Tonsmeire became rector and many improvements occurred. In 1966 property at the church's rear was purchased for a parking lot. The church was air-conditioned in 1969, and a new sacristy built in 1970. In 1971 the vesting room was remodeled and named in honor of "C. Phillip Stiles." Father Tonsmeire led the Church into the broader community by sponsoring many programs. He organized the Retired Men's Group, which remains an active organization forty years later. Father Tonsmeire left Ascension in 1981 to nurture a new mission church.

In 1982, the Reverend Michael "Corky" Carlisle was called. The Rectory was sold, and a priest's housing allowance was added to the budget. The church experienced a period of renewal and growth; outreach became a focus; and Tuesday night suppers for the community began. The altar was moved away from the wall, and new prayer books and hymnals were introduced. A focus on music as an essential part of the liturgy revitalized the parish. Near the end of his service, Father Carlisle took a sabbatical to Kenya to establish a respite house for priests, introducing Ascension to the global community through his efforts. In 1988 Father Carlisle left to continue his Kenya work.

The Vestry called the Reverend Doris Graff Smith as rector and her leadership in Christian Education and Pastoral Care strengthened those ministries at Ascension. Vacation Bible School became an important program under her direction. She remained rector at Ascension until 1992.

For two years, Ascension underwent the discernment process again. In 1994, the current rector, the Reverend William Thomas Martin, was called. Under Father Tom's leadership, Ascension has begun moving towards a program-sized church. A new third Sunday service focuses on families and children. The Outreach Ministry has established a food pantry, which has been funded through additional money earned from the annual "Bane and Blessing" sale. A Healing Ministry was begun under Father Tom's direction; and Ascension had her first permanent deacon, the Reverend Emily P. Hatfield. Perhaps the greatest impact of his ministry has been guiding us forward with plans to build a Parish Life Center—a gathering place for future generations.

For 160 years Ascension has served the community, always opening her red doors to those in need. Her service will continue for generations to come, led by the vision and support of faithful parishioners who believe in Ascension's mission to "nurture and support each other, grow in community and faith, and welcome growth and change."

Text compiled and submitted by Kathi White, from the files of Carolyn Parmenter. Photo from the church archives.

ST. PETER'S EPISCOPAL CHURCH, ROME

✣

St. Peter's Church was organized on March 31, 1844. The Civil War brought hardships and Federal troops commandeered St. Peter's as a hospital in 1864. The parish entered a rebuilding period from 1865 to 1879. Parishioners offered family silver and jewelry to be made into a communion service still used today. Between 1885 and 1887 plans were made for a new stone chapel. The white Georgia marble cornerstone weighing approximately seventeen hundred pounds was laid for St. Peter's new church on St. Peter's Day—June 28, 1892. Sandstone veneer from Anniston, Alabama, was used. The organ, baptismal font, altar, lectern, benches, and other furnishings were moved to the new church (the present chapel). Soon the chapel could not hold the growing congregation. By June 1893 building plans began and materials were ordered.

By 1897 installation of memorial stained-glass windows began. A loan to cover church debt was secured from the estate of Anson Green Phelps Dodge Jr. and saved St. Peter's from foreclosure. A joyous service was held Christmas Day 1898 in the new church; on Christmas Day 1904 the mortgage was burned; and the church was consecrated December 25, 1905.

No Vestry minutes exist from 1915 to 1940 and the Parish Register was not updated. Women's organizations' records and a monthly tract provide glimpses of the state of the church during those years. After the Crash of 1929, the women bought property on East First Street for a proposed Parish House. The Guild sold the property next door to the new Parish House to the Jewish Synagogue.

During 1940–45, the almost fifty-year-old chapel foundation showed damage from extremes of weather. The front wall was removed and rebuilt ten feet back from the sidewalk. The surplus stone was reused for the Gothic vestibule at the East First Street entrance. The men's and women's organizations raised funds for restoring the chapel.

During World War II parishioners supported the Army and Navy Commission; the Red Cross used the buildings for training nurses, making bandages and medical supplies; servicemen were entertained; and clothing was sent to Europe. St. Peter's Centennial began on March 31, 1944, and centennial year outreach included support of local and worldwide missions. Battey Military Hospital, the USO, and Red Cross were aided. The rector served on the Bishop's Youth Commission helping plan Camp Mikell's programs.

Rectory property was acquired as St. Peter's entered a "Golden Era" (1946–1964) with 278 active communicants. Separate Boys' and Girls' Choirs were formed and Shorter and Berry Colleges continue to provide choirmasters, organists, and choristers to St. Peter's. The Willingham House was bought to serve as a parish office with the Ladies' Auxiliary Thrift Shop leading with their donations.

Integration of the parish was quietly achieved in 1953. A parishioner gave property along with money stipulating that the new Rectory would have an apartment for her lifetime. A generous memorial gift by parishioners provided the seed money for the building of a Parish Hall. As the parish grew, the need for an Episcopal Church in the Summerville,

St. Peter's Episcopal Church, Rome, Easter Service.

Trion, and LaFayette areas grew. St. Peter's assisted in the formation of St. Barnabus' Church in Trion. The arrival of the General Electric Plant in West Rome gave rise to a new mission there and St. Peter's played a vital part in establishing the Church of the Transfiguration.

A house next to the Willingham House was purchased for Sunday school space for 259 youths in the 1950s. A new Parish Hall was completed. Change was the watchword of the 1960s and 1970s and removal of barriers to women's service in all levels of ministry resulted in the election of its first Vestry woman and Janice Bracken Wright became assistant rector in 1983. Over the years St. Peter's has offered five candidates for Holy Orders. One is now in seminary. Resources (including Thrift Shop funds) were invested in the start of Steps to Alcoholic Rehabilitation House (STAR), Boy and Girl Scout troops, New Morning Day Care Center, Appleton Church Home, Youth for Christ, Sewanee, and Maple Street Center.

FISH was organized in 1972 and by 1983 the need for a men's overnight shelter became apparent and St. Peter's converted the Willingham House second floor to accommodate night guests. FISH continued to serve until 1988 when a Salvation Army facility opened and FISH transformed into Good Neighbors Ministries—an ecumenical aid center.

Good News, St. Peter's award-winning monthly parish newsletter, records support for Dick Wicker's Boys Home, New Morning Day Care Center, STAR House, Appalachian Poverty Program, Sewanee, Rebecca Blaylock Nursery, FISH, and Episcopal Charities Foundation. St. Peter's led a community-wide relief effort for the 1989 Hurricane Hugo and has provided support for three adult missioners and one youth missioner.

The Cornerstone Centennial Celebration (June 28, 1992) included dedication of eight new stained-glass chapel windows. Stained-glass windows later enhanced the bell tower and Daniel Hall. Needlepoint kneelers for the sanctuary pews and needlepoint kneelers for both altars are complete. St. Peter's closely followed its mission statement's outreach and parish efforts during 1999–2005. A capital fund drive provided for organ renovation, updating the Parish Hall, and restoring the exterior of the church. Among ongoing effective outreach projects are Bill Davies Homeless Shelters, Good Neighbor Ministries, Habitat for Humanity, Rome Urban Ministries, and the Shorter/Berry Canterbury Clubs. The soup kitchen provided sixty thousand meals! St. Peter's has stood "upon this rock" for 162 years and with God's grace we will continue.

Text and photos submitted by Mary and Curt Yarbrough.

Left: St. Peter's Episcopal Church—The St. Peter Window, Rome.

✠   ✠   ✠   ✠

St. George's Episcopal Church, Griffin

✠

General Lewis Lawrence Griffin, of Forsyth, founded Griffin in 1840 as a planned community, centrally located as a potential railroad hub so the abundant cotton crop could be shipped to market. Streets and public areas were platted and lots donated to each of the four principal Protestant denominations: Baptist, Methodist, Presbyterian, and Episcopal.

In August 1859, Bishop Elliott officiating in the Methodist Church, noted: "I found eight communicants. A parish by the name of St. George's had been organized two years prior, but having no shepherd to lead them the sheep have been scattered." The Civil War interrupted church growth and building plans. The unimproved lot was reclaimed by General Griffin's bankruptcy trustee, resulting in an ownership dispute. On May 3, 1864, the parish reorganized and was admitted to the Diocese of Georgia then meeting in Columbus.

Parishioners determined to build, the original lot was sold, and a new site at the corner of Tenth and Broad Streets was purchased June 6, 1869. Captain John McIntosh Kell, distinguished naval hero and Savannah native, returned to Griffin from recuperation, determined to construct a sanctuary.

Gray stone was quarried from Dr. George Beecher's farm and work began. Bishop Beckwith officiated at the cornerstone laying on November 14, 1869. Funds were raised and the building completed with first services held April 1871. Bishop Beckwith consecrated the church on November 12, 1874.

Right: Entrance to St. George's Episcopal Church, Griffin. The procession forms for the Seventh St. George's School graduation exercises, June 2006.

In 1893 the Rectory was built in "English Cottage" design to harmonize with the Gothic-style church. On February 26, 1893, the first vested choir was organized. In 1921 the Grantland Memorial Parish House was built and dedicated. In 1962 a new Church School Building was approved at a cost of $66,000. In 1995 a new organ was purchased. That same year, Griffin's St. Stephen's Episcopal Church—established in the early 1900s by and for Afro-Americans—finally joined forces with St. George's and their communion altar and pews were placed in the St. Stephen's Chapel.

In 1998 an anonymous donor gave the necessary funds to renovate the interior of the sanctuary: the floors were sanded, the reredos was recessed, and the communion table brought out to allow the officiant to face the congregation. The St. Stephen's Chapel and the Children's Chapel were relocated in 2005 to the former vesting rooms.

St. George's Parish has an admirable history of community service. During the tense days of integration its Vestry, under the leadership of then rector, the late Ray Averett, a biracial committee was formed which met weekly in the Parish Hall. This committee is credited with aiding the smooth integration of the schools, public accommodations, and judicial system in the county.

St. George's Parish has had a strong outreach ministry. During the 1950s the Play to Learn School for children with handicaps began using facilities at St. George's and remained there until moving to their own building in the 1980s. St. George's Court, a retirement center, was opened in October 1983 on land adjacent to the church; and an assisted living center—St. George's Woods—opened a decade later. In 1989, the assistant rector, now Bishop of Lexington, led the parish in establishing the Hope Health Clinic and the Five Loaves and Two Fish food pantry, which operate from parish properties. The former assists low-income patients without medical coverage. St. George's Episcopal School opened in 1995 and serves prekindergarten through eighth grade. In 2002 the Parish adopted the "Abundant Life Soup Kitchen" which serves nearly one hundred customers each weekday. Georgia's first Boy Scout troop was installed at St. George's and the members of its troop proudly wear the No. 1 unit designation to this day.

The legend of the triumph of St. George over the Dragon, depicting the triumph of Christians over the infidels of the Middle Ages, speaks to the continuing effort of St. George's Parish to witness to our Lord in this community through both worship and service.

Text and photo submitted by Howard Wallace.

THE EPISCOPAL CATHEDRAL OF ST. PHILIP

⊹

Growth of the Episcopal Church in Georgia gradually followed the natural development of Georgia to the northwest. By 1846 fourteen parishes existed, including in the now Diocese of Atlanta, a presence in Macon, Columbus, Clarkesville, Milledgeville, Marietta, Athens, and Rome, but no Episcopal Church in Marthasville—later to be renamed the City of Atlanta. In 1846 the entire Diocese of Georgia consisted of some six hundred communicants in fourteen parishes, including some one hundred slaves.

The Cathedral's story begins in May 1846, when the Diocese of Georgia, in Convention at Emmanuel Church, Athens, appointed the Reverend John J. Hunt to a mission station in the "Town of Atlanta," formerly Marthasville. The first meeting to organize St. Philip's Parish was held later that May at the Samuel G. Jones home, located at Mitchell and Forsyth Streets downtown. Present were C. F. N. Garnett, chief engineer of the Western Railroad; J. E. Thompson, chief engineer of the Georgia Railroad; Samuel G. Jones, railroad surveyor; William Stockton, civil engineer; and Nedom Angier, teacher and later mayor of Atlanta.

Over the summer and fall of 1846 "a few" would gather from time to time at the homes of Richard Peters, Samuel G. Jones, and others. On All Saints' Day, November 1, 1846, the first Episcopal service in Atlanta was conducted by Bishop Stephen Elliott (also reported as conducted by the Reverend John Mitchell) at the home of Samuel G. Jones. On May 6, 1847, at the Diocesan Convention in Savannah at St. John's Church, St Philip's Church was duly organized and admitted into communion. Its first building was to have been completed by Christmas 1847 and would have been the first church completed in Atlanta. But through the contractor's neglect, it was finished later and consecrated on May 28, 1848. The Methodist Church has the honor of being the first church built in the city. St. Philip's first building was constructed for $700 on Washington Street, across from the State Capitol, where the Agriculture Building now stands. "Wings" were added to the first "modest" structure in 1868 and a permanent church built in 1882.

Left: The Cathedral of St. Philip, Atlanta.

In 1894 Bishop Nelson, tenth Bishop of the Diocese of Georgia, moved his see from Savannah to Atlanta and named St Philip's as the Pro-Cathedral of the Diocese. A Cathedral "was to be erected" on St. Philip's property to be known as "The Cathedral of Holy Trinity," a name somehow lost to antiquity and not mentioned hence.

The 1907 division of the Diocese of Georgia into two parts allowed Bishop Nelson to choose to go with the new Diocese of Atlanta as its first Bishop and name St. Philip's as his cathedral, to be known as the "Cathedral of St. Philip." By 1933, the parish was 650 strong and well established as a downtown urban church active in its ministry. The church, however, was experiencing some attrition and losing members to churches "more favorably and centrally located." Many members left to attend St. Luke's and All Saints' downtown.

The Very Reverend Raimundo de Ovies, fifth dean of the Cathedral, in the spring of 1933 determined that St. Philip's future ministry should be to the residents of northside Atlanta. After many meetings the church proceeded, in May of 1933, to sell some of the downtown property and leased property (with a purchase option of

The new Great Hall at the Cathedral of St. Philip.

$45,000) at the intersection of Peachtree Road and Andrews Drive in Buckhead. On June 18, 1933, construction commenced on a church building known for years as the "Pro-Cathedral." The first service there was held September 10, 1933.

December 31, 1946, the Cathedral of St. Philip was securely ensconced in the Buckhead community, its structures sitting upon a prominent hill at the juncture of Peachtree Road and Andrews Drive. The narthex of the Pro-Cathedral opened out towards the south, down Peachtree Road, overlooking the rapidly growing skyline of the city of Atlanta. There were 1,103 communicants.

The only permanent structure on "Holy Hill" was Mikell Memorial Chapel completed in 1947 at a cost of $68,500 and dedicated to Bishop Henry Judah Mikell's ministry. Other temporary structures served as a Parish Hall, a Christian Education Department, a Youth Room, and a Scout Hut. Parking was generally in a parking lot constructed on the side of the hill fronting on Peachtree Road—what we now consider to be the Great Horseshoe Driveway.

Gradually, permanent buildings have replaced the temporary structures. First, a new Administration and Christian Education Building was completed in May of 1949 and named De Ovies Hall in honor of then retired Raimundo de Ovies. Next, a major structure including a large meeting area, kitchen, reception room, administrative offices, and classroom space was completed in August of 1955 and known as the Hall of Bishops—the original intent being a great hallway for display of portraits of the Bishops of the Diocese. And in 2004, a major Cathedral Complex renovation was completed, including a new three-story administration and church school wing, an entrance atrium, spacious access hallways to the Cathedral Nave, and remodeled Diocesan Offices for the Bishop.

St. Philip's was named after Philip, the deacon and evangelist; however, there was no Patronal Feast established in the Lectionary. The General Convention of the Church in 2000 established October 11 as the Feast Day of Philip, Deacon and Evangelist. The Parish had some sixty-three hundred communicants and an annual budget of over $3,5 million at the close of 2005.

Text submitted by Chancellor Richard Perry. Photos from the church archives.

✛   ✛   ✛   ✛

CHURCH OF THE ADVENT, MADISON

✠

Episcopalians came to Morgan County in 1807 and met in private homes or traveled to other towns for worship services. In 1846 the first Episcopal congregation was established and admitted to the Diocese of Georgia as a parish in 1847. The Reverend Dr. Colley came as rector in 1848, followed by the Reverend Mr. Habersham.

During the early 1850s a Greek revival–style building was erected off Academy Street in what is now the entrance to old Madison Cemetery. Called Church of the Advent, it was built upon a lot deeded to the Episcopal Church by the trustees of the Madison Male Academy. On August 7, 1853, the Right Reverend Stephen Elliott, Bishop of Georgia, came to Madison to consecrate the church. Records show that the church grew and prospered, especially during the years of Bishops Beckwith and Nelson.

In the 1920s the congregation had diminished so that it was unable to support and maintain the building. In 1927 it was closed and in 1938 ordered deconsecrated by Bishop Mikell. The Reverend David Cady Wright of Athens traveled to Madison for the deconsecration. The contents were given to Emmanuel Church, Athens, or church members. The property was sold to the city for $250; the building subsequently razed and the property sold for cemetery lots. The congregation donated the $250 to Appleton Home in Macon.

In 1953 a group of loyal Episcopalians met to reestablish the congregation and invited Bishop Claiborne and Canon Henry Albert Zinser to Madison to aid in the project. Canon Zinser became vicar and the congregation was renamed St. Michael and All Angels. The name was later changed back to Church of the Advent.

The congregation met first at City Hall in Madison, then reconstructed a building at Madison Graded School. The congregation grew and members began to think of finding a permanent church home. Bishop Claiborne declared in 1959 that Advent and St. Alban's, Monroe, would become yoked aided missions. For six months the Reverend Peyton Spane served the missions. Deacon Clyde M. Watson Jr. served the missions from June 1958 to June 1962.

Right: The Church of the Advent, Madison, during Advent.

With a great deal of pomp and circumstance, the newly renovated building was consecrated on February 10, 1963, by Bishop Randolph R. Claiborne Jr. The Reverend David Cady Wright Jr., who had deconsecrated the church in 1937, delivered the sermon.

The Nott Parker House next door was purchased September 7, 1965, for $7,500. The Victorian Queen Anne turrets and gingerbread were removed to return it to its former Federal appearance. The interior was adapted to serve as Parish House, Sunday school quarters, and an upstairs clergy apartment. Two rooms became one and formed a charming chapel. The building wasn't consecrated until June 12, 1977, because of indebtedness against the property. The church women sponsored home tours and raised money to pay the debt.

For twenty years, St. James' Roman Catholic Mission held services in Advent. For five years in the 1980s, St. James' had Mass at 8 a.m., Advent's congregation met at 11 a.m. and a local group of Lutherans had services at 2 p.m.

In 1986, Advent called its first full-time rector since 1899. He served until December 1989. Father James Edward James served as interim priest until

The Church of the Advent, Madison, interior view.

The old Methodist Church building was purchased on May 20, 1961, from the Christian Science Society of Madison for $7,000. The Vestry borrowed $2,400 and raised additional funds for payment. Mrs. Sue Reid Walton Manley gave $7,000 for payment and restoration of the building in memory of her sons, William Fletcher Manley and Reid Walton Manley. The Vestry hired restoration architect Thomas Little to draw plans for the renovation. At completion in 1963, the work cost in excess of $60,000.

A center aisle replaced the original two aisles. New pews, along with altar area furnishings were purchased. Two large chandeliers came from a church in Virginia and antique sconces were added. The balcony holds the old pews and new organ. The reredos was constructed to fit worship needs. Altar Guild members did the needlepoint at the altar rail.

August 1990. The Reverend Brian Charles Black assumed duties in September 1990, and during his term the communicants more than doubled, as did the budget and giving and the number of ministries and services increased.

Deterioration over the years to the Church of the Advent and Parish House dictated major renovations to the two buildings in 1991. A concrete-block house behind the Parish House was remodeled to accommodate the children's Sunday school. Among the church's many ministries is Joseph's Coat, a thrift store. The Reverend Loree Reed assumed the priest's duties in 2004 and is guiding an active and growing congregation.

Text submitted by Adelaide W. Ponder. Photos submitted by Anne P. Young and Lynne Roach.

ZION EPISCOPAL CHURCH, TALBOTTON

✠

Zion Episcopal Church, Talbotton, photo circa 1990.

Eleven persons met with the Reverend Richard Johnson, Monday, June 7, 1847, at his invitation, to establish an Episcopal Church in Talbotton. The original name of the congregation was Mount Zion Protestant Episcopal Church and it was located on land purchased early in 1848. The church was constructed in 1848 in wood native to the area. James D. Cottingham, a local carpenter and cabinetmaker, is credited with much of the expert craftsmanship in the country gothic structure.

The choir loft has a rare Pilcher organ installed in 1850. Fifteen decorative pipes carved of wood and gilded are above the console. The instrument remains operable with the aid of a hand pump. The church was consecrated in 1853 during the Episcopate of the Right Reverend Stephen Elliott Jr., and was used for regular services for more than 125 years.

Zion Episcopal Church is listed on the National Register of Historic Places and the Georgia Historical Commission placed a historical marker in back of the church at the roadside of U.S. Highway 80 in 1955. Occasionally, the Chattahoochee Convocation, where the church is located, has opened the doors of Zion for Evensong with a picnic on the grounds.

In the early 1990s, thanks to the efforts of the Reverend Charles M. Roper, then rector of St. Thomas, Columbus, a major renovation effort of Zion Church was undertaken to include the organ. Currently, several local families seek to reopen Zion for regular worship.

Text submitted by the Reverend William P. McLemore. Photo from the Collins Collection, Diocese of Atlanta Archives

✠   ✠   ✠   ✠

ST. LUKE'S EPISCOPAL CHURCH, ATLANTA

✠

St. Luke's began as Civil War Atlanta swelled with Confederate soldiers and refugees. St. Philip's was overflowing and with Bishop Elliot's permission, Dr. Charles Todd Quintard organized the new parish, preaching in various locations. Volunteer soldiers constructed his first church on Walton Street at a cost of $12,000 Confederate money. On April 22, 1864, Bishop Elliott consecrated the new building. Dr. Quintard did much to help the citizens face their daily wartime problems. The small church later burned. Little is known until 1870, except for the recording of two baptisms in 1865, as Atlanta rebuilt. A small group of original members met in June 1870 at the Masonic orphanage, adopting the name St. Stephen's; however, in January 1872 the Vestry restored the name St. Luke's. In 1875 the second St. Luke's opened at Spring and Walton.

In the early 1950s the actual founding date of St. Luke's, 1864, was questioned by an Atlanta church historian. Were the congregations of 1870 and 1864 one and the same? The question was raised again in 1964 as the Georgia Historical Commission considered placing a historical marker to commemorate the centennial of the Battle of Atlanta with a brief account of the parish and Dr. Quintard. After a review the commission's doubts were satisfied. It was determined that the 1870 congregation was a continuation of the 1864 congregation, and the historical marker was placed in front of the current St. Luke's.

Finances were so bleak in 1879 that the Reverend William C. Williams volunteered his services to keep the doors open. In April 1880 St. Luke's offered Bishop Beckwith the building as his cathedral. The Bishop assisted paying the debt and St. Luke's became the first cathedral of the Diocese of Georgia.

On Christmas Day 1882 the members occupied the basement of its third location at North Pryor and Houston and in February 1883 the first services were held "upstairs." In 1887, the Reverend Dr. Robert S. Barrett became dean of St. Luke's Cathedral and held that position until 1894, working to make Atlanta's largest Episcopal congregation known for its social outreach.

Cleland K. Nelson became Bishop on February 24, 1892, and soon questioned the use of St. Luke's as the cathedral. St. Philip's lot on Washington Street was determined a better location for a new cathedral to be called the Cathedral of the Holy Trinity. St. Luke's began to face the future as the century turned. Rector Cary B. Wilmer

Peachtree Street view of St. Luke's Episcopal Church, Atlanta.

served for twenty-four years. Dr. Wilmer, well known for his commitment to social justice, spoke out forcefully on the subjects of child labor, the Atlanta race riot, the innocence of Leo Frank, political corruption, and the streetcar workers strike.

In 1904 St. Luke's sold its third building and chose the current location on Peachtree Street. Thornton Marye, architect for the new church, drew plans in 1905 in English Gothic style. Three Mayer Studios of Germany windows were relocated from the third St. Luke's and Wilmer dreamed of windows representing the life of Christ. The congregation occupied the undercroft in 1906 until the nave was completed. Dr. Wilmer invited Rabbi David Marx of The Temple to participate in the cornerstone-laying service, an ecumenical act, new to Atlanta in 1906, which marked St. Luke's as a place of religious tolerance.

The new building accommodated all 686 communicants with room to spare. In 1911, St. Elizabeth's Guild undertook the project of providing an altarpiece and commissioned Edwin H. Blashfield to paint a mural for the huge sum then of $5,000. Soon the

Interior view from the balcony of St. Luke's, Atlanta.

Guild was hosting silver teas and opened a lunchroom to pay for it. On Easter Day 1913, *The Good Shepherd* mural was unveiled. It is believed to be the first work of art by a major artist commissioned for an Atlanta public building.

The Good Shepherd and St. Luke's soon became synonymous with caring for the physical needs of the less fortunate. The mortgage was paid in 1917 and Bishop Mikell consecrated the church. Dr. Wilmer left in 1924 and St. Luke's, at another crossroads, again considered its future, decided to stay and built a large new Parish House.

Dr. N. R. High Moor became the twelfth rector in 1925 and abolished pew rents. With fine preaching skills, administrative talent, and personality—his appeal doubled the membership to eighteen hundred by 1931. Hugh Hodgson became organist and master of the choristers in 1928 and gave forty-one years of service and music of the highest quality.

In 1931 the Reverend John Moore Walker became rector. The Great Depression impacted revenue but St. Luke's moved forward with live radio broadcast of services over WJTL. The church's financial future was secured with creation in 1934 of the St. Luke's Endowment. The Reverend Walker, after nine years as St. Luke's rector, was elected third Bishop of the Diocese of Atlanta with ordination at St. Luke's.

The Reverend J. Milton Richardson became rector in 1943, and with architect Francis P. Smith and former rector Wilmer refined the stained-glass window themes. New windows were dedicated during the late 1940s and 1950s; the Parish House remodeled; and new emphasis placed on Sunday school. In 1952 the Reverend Wilson W. Sneed became rector and the church swelled to twenty-two hundred members, largest in the Diocese; built Quintard-Sneed Hall, and gave generously for Diocesan expansion.

Societal changes in the 1960s as the Reverend Dr. Edward E. Tate became rector impacted the parish. The church lost membership but began embracing its wider community role. In January 1962 Mrs. Irwin T. Hyatt was elected the first woman Vestry member. The Alston Memorial Organ was dedicated in 1963 and Council met at St. Luke's in January 1964 to kick-off the parish's Centennial Year celebration, which included completion of the last large stained-glass window, *Peter's Confession*, and raising the $100,000 Centennial Thank You Offering to assist Episcopal seminaries and seminarians.

Two important joint projects with All Saints' Episcopal Church began in the 1960s: construction of Canterbury Court, a retirement home; and St. Jude's Recovery Center, a halfway house for battling alcoholism. In 1971 the Reverend Thomas D. Bowers became the eighteenth rector. New ministries included the Community Kitchen; the Training and Counseling Center (TACC); the Street Academy; and a Folk Mass. The first Holy Eucharist Service was broadcast on WSB Television in 1974.

The Reverend Dr. Daniel P. Matthews Sr. became the nineteenth rector in 1980; the parish grew under his leadership; and he called the Reverend Dr. Reynell Parkins— the first African American to serve in a majority white congregation in Atlanta. Parkins helped form St. Luke's Economic Development Corporation to provide job training to the homeless and began a Sunday service for the growing Hispanic community. Other outreach ministries were begun including the Mail Room and the St. Luke's Clinic; the

first annual Kanuga Retreat and stewardship became high priorities. Matthews resigned in 1987 and the Reverend Charles E. Bennison was called in 1988. Highlights of his ministry were mission trips to South America, liturgical change, and the formation of a Strategic Planning Committee. The Reverend Roger Ard served as interim rector in 1991.

The Reverend Dr. Spenser Simrill became rector in 1992 during a period of physical transformation. The Browne Decorating Company building was bought and razed. A memorial garden was built there and the stained-glass windows' glory was revealed, filling the nave with light. The Bell Tower was completed and the sound of ten English change bells now rings out over downtown. The Community Kitchen moved to another location on campus, renamed Crossroads Community Ministries, and expanded services.

The Reverend Daniel P. Matthews Jr. became rector in 2003. The Children's Sunday school and St. Joseph's Mercy Care Clinic were remodeled; programs of Christian Education, Stewardship, and Parish Care expanded; and the Downtown Connector speaker series launched.

The hundredth anniversary in 2006 of the move to the present church was celebrated with festive activities from January through St. Luke's Sunday in October as the congregation entered its second century of service from its 435 Peachtree Street home.

Text submitted by Robert L. Mays. Photos by Steven Purdon.

St. Mark's Episcopal Church, LaGrange

⁜

The Marquis de LaFayette, visiting Georgia in the early nineteenth century, remarked that the fertile hills of the Troup County area reminded him of his own home—"LaGrange"—in France. The farming community thus received its name. Like many southern cities, LaGrange attracted cotton mills. By the Civil War, the community also became the home of a few Episcopalians, called "foreigners" by the local residents. In 1864, at a Diocesan Convention in Columbus the congregation of St. Mark's was officially accepted as a mission of the Diocese of Georgia. For years, the small church had monthly services supplied by an itinerant priest, the Reverend Edward Denniston, from Opelika, Alabama. In 1886, he reported "this parish, though laboring under some disadvantages, is one of our most encouraging fields of labor . . . a few years of continued service will result under God in the establishing here of a strong growing Parish, services are held here on the third Sunday of the month."

The Reverend Henry Disbrow Phillips, later Bishop of Southern Virginia, took charge of St. Mark's in 1906 and remained for ten years. His energy took the congregation into a mill ministry that became one of the Diocese's unique efforts to minister to factory workers. The LaGrange Settlement, begun under his leadership, provided education and medical assistance to the men and women working in the textile mills. This Settlement later spawned two Episcopal congregations, Holy Comforter and Good Shepherd, which continued their ministry well into the mid-nineteen hundreds. Also, during Phillips' tenure, St. Elizabeth's, a black congregation, was formed in the southeast portion of LaGrange.

St. Mark's Episcopal Church, LaGrange.

Eight decades after its formation, St. Mark's struggled for survival and numbered only about eighty communicants. Like so many Southern Episcopal congregations, it failed to reach the larger population. However, the members realized that their small wooden Gothic building seating less than forty worshippers, didn't promote growth. After World War II, the church sold its building to a Jewish congregation and it remains their worship center today. The Episcopalians purchased property three blocks west and built a large brick facility on South Greenwood Street, where the parish continues its life and worship. In 1952, with over one hundred members, the Diocesan Council formally elevated St. Mark's to parish status.

In the early sixties, the congregation had grown to 250 members and built a large Parish Hall and offices to accommodate the church needs. The Reverend William Augustus Jones, later Bishop of Missouri, became rector in 1958 and assisted the congregation in this building project. Additions included a unique carved Celtic cross designed by Atlanta architect Preston McIntosh and carved by German sculptor Fred Schoenfeld. The side of the cross facing away from the church contains the traditional symbols of the apostles. The side facing the church portrays contemporary symbols and poses the questions: "Who are you? Where are you going? Why?" During Jones' tenure, the parish developed a relationship with the Diocese of Chota Nagpur in India and received a visit from their Bishop, the Right Reverend Dilbar Hans. This relationship resulted in the parish helping to build a church in his diocese in 1963. During these years the Diocese closed St. Elizabeth's Parish and many of the members joined St. Mark's.

Clergy following Bill Jones were the Reverend Cecil Locke Alligood (1965–1969), the Reverend Thomas Davies Clay (1969–1978), the Reverend James Knox Yeary (1978–1989), the Reverend William Andrew Waldo (1990–1994), and presently the Reverend Lori Marleen Lowe who began her service in 1995 as Rector.

St. Mark's provides a "Meals on Wheels" program; youth missions to Hurley, Virginia; community outreach through the Chattahoochee Valley Episcopal Ministry;

St. Mark's Episcopal Church, LaGrange, Palm Sunday processional begins.

on-going Education for Ministry (EFM) classes; and cooperates with the local Advent Lutheran Church for a number of liturgical events.

The congregation worships at 8:00 and 10:30 a.m. on Sunday, with a traditional early service and a contemporary service later. The Vestry recently adopted the mission statement: "St. Mark's is a Christian community with a radical welcome for all." It reflects the diversity of the only Episcopal congregation in LaGrange, which comprises a good cross-section of the community. The mother of a family recently joining the parish commented, "This church is a treasure. . . . I believe Jesus accepted people as they were and I certainly feel this to be true about St. Mark's."

Text and photos submitted by the Reverend William P. McLemore.

St. Mark's Episcopal Church, Dalton

✛

When Sherman's army captured Dalton in the spring of 1864, only one Episcopalian resided in the town. By 1866, however, Colonel Benjamin Green had arrived from Washington, D.C., and was holding Sunday school in his law offices in the Courthouse. St. Mark's mission was founded and assigned to the Reverend John J. Hunt, a North Georgia missionary since the 1830s. Petitioning the Diocese of Georgia in 1867 for aid, the Vestry noted that "our little town and its vicinity were the theatre of military operations and were swept by both armies. War and the torch have left us very poor." With Colonel Green's donated lot and a Diocesan loan of $500 for construction, the church cornerstone was laid in 1869 and the first service held in the structure in 1871. Optimism clearly abounded, however, for with only eleven communicants, the building seated three hundred. Ten years later the Diocese was told that St. Mark's, though having a membership of only sixty, was in "a very healthy and hopeful condition."

Despite significant growth in the later 1880s, the following decade saw a decline, and in 1896 a smaller church, seating about a hundred, was built several blocks from the earlier one. By 1907 the church had reverted from parish to organized mission status. Not until 1946 was there a resident minister, and as the number of communicants fell below fifty, evaluators from the national Episcopal Church recommended the church close.

The turning point came in 1952, during the brief episcopate of Bishop John Walthour. His "gravest concern" before his untimely death was "the work of the Church in the smaller cities and towns of the Diocese," and seeing in St. Mark's a promise that had escaped the notice of others he assigned the Reverend Donald G. Mitchell Jr. as the third resident clergyman. Grandson of a priest who had served St. Mark's from 1878 to 1880, Father Mitchell provided inspiration and guidance that sparked new growth, and at the end of 1956 the congregation included 119 baptized persons, with 78 communicants. In 1957 the mission was designated an aided parish, and in 1958 became a self-supporting parish.

Interior of St. Mark's Episcopal Church, Dalton, at Christmas.

St. Mark's size more than tripled during the next decade. In 1959 the Reverend Frank Allan undertook his first ministry by succeeding Father Mitchell. Plans began for a larger modern building, and the third and current church was occupied in 1965, its cornerstone joined to that of 1869. As 1966 began, there were 356 baptized members and 220 communicants. The Reverend Allan was succeeded by the Reverend George H. Sparks (1967–1974), the Reverend Albert H. Hatch (1975–1978), the Reverend Donald L. Cramer (1979–1983), and the Reverend James Edwin Bacon Jr. (1984–1989).

The 1960s growth reflected Dalton's transformation into the world's greatest concentration of carpet production. With increased numbers came diversification, and the congregation lost some of the close-knit familial bonds that had held it together during the lean years, prompting frustrations and confused expectations that led many parishioners to feel unfulfilled. Much was accomplished—including reconstruction and enlargement of the Parish House after a devastating 1978 fire destroyed the church office and most early records. The clerical vacancy in 1983 led the congregation to its most intensive self-scrutiny.

St. Mark's members mobilized talents and resources to achieve formidable goals. An addition doubled the Parish House size and a new organ necessitated construction of a new sacristy. Completed in 1988, these projects were but the material expressions and symbols of a remarkable spiritual revitalization that enhanced worship, study, and pastoral activities within the parish. Simultaneously, outreach programs to deal with illiteracy, teen pregnancy, indigent and transient assistance, provision of low-cost housing, and support for the addicted, cancer patients, diabetics, HIV victims, and their families began and have continued during the current ministry of the Reverend C. Dean Taylor, who arrived in 1990. Noteworthy undertakings are the annual Lenten speaker series, including internationally recognized figures Marcus Borg, Rabbi Harold Kushner, and John Shelby Spong; youth missions to South Dakota, Arkansas, Costa Rica, and Jamaica; and outreach to the burgeoning Hispanic population. Now nearly halfway through its second century, St. Mark's continues to be sustained by the love and loyalty of its people and their pastors, ready to offer to God its worship and witness in the name of Jesus Christ.

Text submitted by John A. Hutcheson Jr. Photo from the church archives.

THE EPISCOPAL CHURCH OF THE MEDIATOR, WASHINGTON

☩

Continuing the historic and catholic witness of the Church of England, Anglican worship has been a part of the Washington experience from the city's earliest days, when families gathered in homes to share Morning and Evening Prayer, and to celebrate the Holy Communion when a priest was available. Established in 1780, the City of Washington was the first city in the United States named for George Washington, and is ten years older than Washington, D.C.

The Church of the Mediator, founded as a worshipping community in 1868, led by the Reverend Joshua Knowles, a missionary priest from Massachusetts, first held services in the Masonic Hall. Bishop John W. Beckwith presided over his first council of the Diocese of Georgia in Savannah in May 1868, and Mediator was admitted to membership. At that event, Mr. Knowles observed, "a respectable congregation, including eleven communicants, were active." The first trustees of the parish included Robert Toombs, secretary of state of the Confederacy. The first church building of 1872 on West Main Street (now Robert Toombs Avenue), was destroyed in the great town fire of 1895. The pine pews, the nineteenth-century altar, and baptismal font were saved and are in use in the present facilities.

The new church building, situated on property once part of the Robert Toombs estate, is next door to the historic Toombs' home. Many felt that it was "too far out of town," though only three blocks from the square! An exquisite example of the Victorian Gothic style, it was consecrated by Bishop Nelson on June 21, 1896. Remarkable stained-glass windows designed and executed in the studio of the internationally recognized Wilbur Burnham during the 1960s grace the church. Between 1919 and 1949 a small band of loyal Episcopalians supported the church, though it was an unorganized mission for part of the period.

After World War II the parish had a resurgence, and on July 3, 1949, Bishop John Moore Walker presided at a service of baptism, confirmation, and the Holy Eucharist. In 1951 Mediator became an organized mission again under the leadership of Jay Victor Nickelson. A report to the Forty-fifth Council stated: "Two missions of long standing whose status has waxed and waned for many years were now so revitalized that a resident minister was being provided for in one of the towns to serve only the two towns." The Reverend John Paul Jones served both Washington's Mediator and Greensboro's Redeemer from 1952 to 1954. Clergy serving the Church of the Mediator after the Reverend Mr. Jones were Corvin C. Von Miller, 1955–56; Robert E. Burgreen, 1956–59; Clifton Banks, 1959–61; Henry J. Miller Jr., 1962–64; Cecil Alligood, 1965–66; Ronald Gibson, 1966–71; William O. Boyd, 1972–1989; and John A. Via, 1990–2006. Mediator was formally yoked with Redeemer, Greensboro, from 1990 through 2003, and now yoked with the Church of St. Alban, Elberton.

A vigorous congregation with powerful lay leadership carries on the work of Christ here today, guided by firm devotion to the affirmations of the baptismal covenant: to continue in the apostles' teaching and fellowship, in the breaking of the bread, and in the prayers; to proclaim by word and example the Good News of God in Christ; to seek and serve Christ in all persons; to strive for justice and peace among all people; and to respect the dignity of every human being. The Old Vicarage houses the Faith in Action program offices. The Parish House is a community center, where more than ten community organizations hold their meetings and Learning in Retirement and Athens Tech extension courses are taught. The kitchen is a drop-off point, where many people leave and pick up items as a convenience—a matter of great curiosity and some amusement. Major parish events include the ECW Teahouse during the Tour of Homes in April and the Gift Bazaar and Holiday Luncheon in December.

All sorts and conditions of persons make up the fellowship. The Church of the Mediator is a strong intergenerational and interracial voice in the heart of old colonial Georgia.

Text submitted by Betty Slaton and the Reverend John Via. Photo by the Reverend John Via.
Opposite page: Church of the Mediator, Washington, built in the Gothic Victorian style.

☩   ☩   ☩   ☩

THE EPISCOPAL CHURCH OF THE REDEEMER, GREENSBORO

⁜

The story of the Church of the Redeemer and its role in Greensboro, the seat of Greene County, is one that tracks closely with the history of the South. The church was bred from the ravages of the Civil War, grew, and then declined with the ravages of the boll weevil and the Great Depression. Persistence and faith kept the small church alive for decades until the creation of a thriving resort, retirement, and tourism economy marked the beginning of a new life for this growing parish.

The Church of the Redeemer was organized as an Episcopal parish in 1863. The first members included several churchwomen who had fled from Charleston and Savannah during the Civil War. The Right Reverend Stephen Elliott, the first Bishop of Georgia, met with the group on September 21, 1863, for the first parish communion in the family home of Mrs. Philip Clayton. Mr. Clayton had the distinction of serving as assistant secretary of the treasury during the administration of President Buchanan, and he held the same position in the government of the Confederate States of America. After the war, he was so well thought of as a person of great integrity that he served as United States Ambassador to Peru.

As the congregation grew, a building fund was started under the guidance of the Reverend Stephen Elliott, and Miss Elizabeth Gilby, an English governess, contributed one hundred dollars toward the effort. Other gifts came from as far away as Washington, D.C. The congregation continued to meet in homes, and it finally rented the Town Hall to accommodate its growing numbers. On February 9, 1867, the wardens of the church purchased a lot for $100 from Mr. Holcomb G. Harper, Mrs. Clayton's father. They hired J. G. Barnwell of Rome, Georgia, as builder and architect. The building was completed in four months, and was consecrated on June 14, 1868, by the

Right Reverend John Beckwith, Bishop of Georgia. The first rector to celebrate in the new church was the beloved and influential Father Joshua Knowles. He served for nineteen years, and is buried with his wife in the churchyard.

In 1987 the church was entered onto the National Register of Historic Places, and in 1989 and 1990 the aging building was restored. The original red color was uncovered, and the church was returned to its 1868 appearance.

Episcopal Church of the Redeemer, Greensboro.

The church design is Carpenter Gothic, featuring the unusual curved roof and intricate beam-work of that style. To achieve the vertical emphasis of the Gothic style, the distinctive "board and batten" construction technique was used. Diamond-shaped panes in the rectangular windows also draw the eye upward. The window behind the altar—with its intricately mullioned handmade stained glass—is embedded in a Gothic arch. The bell tower, added only a few years after the church was finished, features a large round window with an intricate window pane design. The original oil chandeliers remain in place, now wired for electricity.

The congregation declined in numbers during the twentieth century, but never closed its doors. It is the oldest continuing worshipping community amongst all of the many churches in Greene County. Although a small number of churches are older, services at Church of the Redeemer have never ceased. By the late 1970s membership had

Parishioners of Church of the Redeemer, Greensboro, at Washington Grass Inn, June 5, 2005.

dwindled to only three or four families. With the creation of Lake Oconee in 1980 and the rapid growth in golf and retirement lake communities, membership began to increase. For many years yoked with other parishes, in 2003, the wardens of the church determined that they had grown sufficiently to call the first full-time rector in nearly twenty years.

The church, which holds approximately 80 people, now boasts a membership in excess of 140, and holds two Sunday services to accommodate that growth. The Church of the Redeemer has a three-fold ministry of worship, hospitality, and outreach. The church provides space and volunteers for the Good Samaritan Clinic, a health-care facility for the indigent; operates the growing Redeemer Employment Advocacy Program (REAP); and contributes in excess of $50,000 each year to various social programs and nonprofits in the Greene County area. Nearly half of that money comes from the Episcopal Church Women's very successful annual Tour of Extraordinary Homes at Reynolds Plantation—the largest of the lake communities.

Text and photos submitted by the Reverend D. Geoffrey Taylor, rector.

APPLETON CHURCH HOME AND APPLETON MINISTRIES, MACON

✠

Appleton Church Home was founded in the Diocese of Georgia in 1868, and inherited by the Diocese of Atlanta in 1907. Like human lives, this living entity of ministry has had its ups and downs over the past 140 years.

Mr. William Henry Appleton, owner of the Appleton Publishing Company of New York, told his friend, John W. Beckwith, Bishop of Georgia: "I will aid you, and when you have selected your residence I will build you a church that shall belong to you." Beckwith said that his heart was full of sympathy for the destitute orphans of the Confederate soldiers, and wished instead to establish a home for them. It was operated by an order of deaconesses called the Order of St. Katherine, in memory of Appleton's daughter Katherine, who had gone to Hong Kong and died there.

Appleton Church Home started as an orphanage, in a building which is now part of the St. Paul's Parish Hall. About 1929, land was purchased on the outskirts of Macon, on Forest Hill Road, now home of St. Francis Church. Former dorms are used as offices and Sunday school rooms and the Chapel has been expanded into the sanctuary. Appleton was reestablished as a self-sustaining community in which

Left: Original Appleton Church Home, now part of St. Paul's Parish Hall, Macon.

A dormitory at Appleton Church Home, Macon, now part of the campus of St. Francis' Episcopal Church.

So, prayerfully and under consultation with the University of North Carolina's residential childcare experts, the Bishop of Atlanta and Board refocused the mission. The program was restructured to minister to teenage girls. The old campus was sold to St. Francis and group homes were purchased in North Macon. Each housed six to eight girls who were cared for by a housemother. Intense professional counseling services were provided in addition to tutoring and spiritual nurturing. Although many girls thrived in this setting, the girls of the 1980s who were being referred needed a much more restrictive environment—away from drugs and negative peer influence found in the regular community.

Again, after prayerful consultation with experts, an outdoor therapeutic program was established. Appleton bought land in rural Jones County and created an Appleton School, which was built by the students and administered by well-qualified teachers. Family counseling services became an integral part of this program, and the name changed to Appleton Family Ministries. Eighty-five percent of the girls served rejoined society as fully contributing citizens—a percentage far above expectations for troubled teenagers.

the residents could provide for themselves by farming, canning, and sewing their own clothes. During the 1940s, Appleton's ministry once again stepped forward to meet a critical need. Many girls remained in care until they graduated from high school or college. Episcopal Church Women's (ECW) organizations all around the diocese would "sponsor" a girl who became very special to them.

In the late 1960s, a different type of need appeared. These girls were victims of family violence from which they were running away only to find themselves further victimized by the emerging drug culture and all of the inherent problems that came with living on the street. They needed, in addition to love and basic care, a much deeper level of professional counseling that could not be provided in a large institutional setting.

Funding decreased in the late 1980s, Appleton was closed, and the oldest social ministry of the Diocese changed its focus. It continues to function as an after-school program for disadvantaged children, operated in conjunction with St. James Parish, Macon. Those who served and those who were served yearn and pray that Appleton may continue to grow and meet the challenge of ministry to youth, in behalf of the Diocese of Atlanta.

Text submitted by Marty Banks and Bruce Bridges. Photos by Dale and Susan Myers.

ST. PAUL'S EPISCOPAL CHURCH, MACON

✠

The Gothic landmark at the corner of College and Forsyth Streets in Macon has been home to generations of members of St. Paul's Parish. From humble beginning in 1869 in a brick warehouse used for Civil War munitions storage, St. Paul's has grown into a complex including the present church, designed by John J. Nevitt of Savannah and built in 1881–84; the Rectory built in 1910; and the Parish House, built in 1868 as the original Appleton Home for Girls. Retaining the historical flavor of the properties has been integral to its maintenance through the years.

St. Paul's was started as a Sunday school mission of Christ Church, Macon's original Episcopal Church. Its establishment as a parish came from the need for a church on the hill above downtown Macon and a controversy involving the longtime rector of Christ Church, the Reverend Henry Kollock Rees. Inspired by the Oxford movement during an 1868 New Jersey visit, Rees initiated some of its rituals at Christ Church and St. Paul's Mission. These included a full musical and choral service, the placement of flowers and lighted candles on the altar and the celebrant facing the cross on the altar while reciting the creed. Christ Church's congregation was not pleased with these reminders of Rome.

The ensuing dispute, though conducted with admirable courtesy, resulted in the formation of St. Paul's Parish on May 25, 1869, with Rees as rector and seventy-five communicants of Christ Church among its founding members. There were three objectives for the new parish: a weekly Eucharist as the highest act of worship; the weekly offertory as an act of worship; and an open church with free seats for all worshippers.

The congregation of St. Paul's grew from 84 in 1869 to as many as 710 in 1968, with the greatest period of growth coming after World War II. Since 1968 membership levels fluctuated around 300 to 400. Through the years St. Paul's image has transformed from the comfortable church filled with Macon's upper classes, to a diverse mix that challenges the status quo while trying to retain tradition.

Right: Entrance to St. Paul's Episcopal Church, built in 1881, Macon.

St. Paul's has a history of strong commitment to service to others. A new focus on community involvement began in the late 1960s. The concept of retirement living facilities was new to Macon, and St. Paul's pioneered by building St. Paul Apartments and Village for retired and disabled persons. The high-rise was built on St. Paul's original church site, a former warehouse from which the bricks were taken and used in building the present church. The facilities have been in continuous operation since opening in 1972. Ministry to residents is a part of St. Paul's outreach.

St. Paul's participates in: a weekend lunch program for the needy and homeless; Rebuilding Together, an annual citywide project to refurbish and repair homes of the needy and elderly; the Macon Volunteer Clinic, serving the medical needs of the working poor and uninsured; Habitat for Humanity; and Alternative Christmas and Salvation Army Stockings. St. Paul's contributes substantial funding to Loaves and Fishes, and an ecumenical agency ministering to those in need in the community. In the past thirty years, St. Paul's has sponsored relocation to Macon of three families from war-torn countries.

St. Paul's contribution to the Episcopal Church by sponsoring of several young members of the parish to attend seminary and as postulants to enter the ministry has been a source of great joy. Two of St. Paul's notable rectors have become bishops—the Right Reverend John VanderHorst of the Diocese of Tennessee, and the Right Reverend Frank K. Allan of Atlanta.

St. Paul's has much for which to be thankful, as well as proud. A legacy of service and beauty has been passed down through the generations. The stained-glass windows include two memorial windows in the chancel that are documented Tiffany glass, two of the few examples of this art form in Georgia. The rose window in the west wall of the nave was first located over the altar in the original church and moved to the present church with symbols of the apostles added to surround it. New stained-glass windows representing the sacraments of the church are being installed in the historic Beckwith Chapel in the Parish House, which was built for the use of the residents of the Appleton Church Home. It has been beautifully preserved and continues to serve as worship space.

Text submitted by Cynthia Patterson. Photos by Dale and Susan Myers.

Left: Stained-glass window in St. Paul's Episcopal Church, Macon.

✜   ✜   ✜   ✜

CHAPTER TWO

GROWING PAINS AND THE DIOCESE OF ATLANTA IS FORMED

B Y THE 1870S, GEORGIA'S ECONOMY HAD BEGUN TO RECOVER FROM THE DEVASTATION OF THE CIVIL WAR AND THE TERRIBLE ECONOMIC CONDITIONS—RECONSTRUCTION— which followed. New churches had miraculously begun to form at the close of the war. Twenty-eight congregations reported to the 1870 Diocesan Convention at St. Paul's, Albany. Christ Church, Savannah, held the highest membership at 413. However, it could no longer rule supreme. The Georgia churches were growing. St. Philip's, Atlanta, numbered 217; Christ Church, Macon, had 233; Trinity, Columbus, listed 227; and Emmanuel, Athens, 115. Within six years, Bishop Beckwith moved his office to Atlanta. Bishop Beckwith died on Sunday, November 23, 1890. His old friend, Mississippi Bishop Hugh Miller Thompson, eulogized Beckwith: "He loved not new methods, nor new ways, any new manner of speech; his position on any question was never doubtful. The whole temper of the man was of one loyal to traditions, reverential of the Church's past, fixed in his faith, settled in his convictions."

Replacing Beckwith challenged the young diocese. The first person elected, the Reverend Dr. Thomas F. Gailor, vice-chancellor of the University of the South, declined the position. An adjourned meeting over a month later elected the Right Reverend Ethelbert Talbot, Missionary Bishop of Wyoming, who also declined. This same Convention met a third time in Macon, November 11, 1891, and the Reverend Cleland Kinloch Nelson, rector of the Church of the Nativity, South Bethlehem, Pennsylvania, was elected and accepted the position of third Bishop of Georgia. He assumed his duties upon consecration at St. Luke's, Atlanta, February 24, 1892. Believing a diocese should be in a state's capital, Nelson selected Atlanta for both his home and office.

By Nelson's tenth anniversary leading the Diocese of Georgia, nine new parishes had formed and his responsibilities included visitations to over ninety congregations and missions in every corner of the state. He most often traveled from Atlanta by railroad. Certainly, as he peered out of the windows of these trains looking at the passing countryside, he undoubtedly wondered how much longer he could humanly serve so many places in such a large area. Atlanta's thirteen parishes now had more congregations than any other city in Georgia and well over two thousand communicants. Many clergy and laity were already talking about the possibility of separating the state into two dioceses. The overriding question remained, "Who would go where?"

✠   ✠   ✠   ✠

The New Diocese of Atlanta is Created

✠

By 1907, the Diocese of Georgia, which had less than a dozen clergy and parishes in 1823, found itself sprawled over fifty-nine thousand square miles of territory from the Appalachian Ridge to the Coastal Plain with twenty-seven parishes, 108 missions, and just under ten thousand communicants. After years of often heated debate and preparation, Georgia's Episcopal community unanimously voted to divide itself into two geographical areas on May 15, 1907, at Christ Church, Savannah. As the incumbent authority, having served as Bishop of Georgia since February 1892, the Right Reverend Cleland Kinloch Nelson had the choice of which diocese he wished to serve. On All Saints Day, 1907, his letter to the clergy and laity included the following: "For reasons and by arguments which appear to me valid and unanswerable, I conceive it to be wise that I make choice of the northern Diocese as the field of my future administration, and most regretfully throw upon the southern Diocese the obligation to elect a Bishop. . . .'"

This new Diocese of Atlanta now included five thousand communicants with about two dozen congregations—with St. Luke's, Atlanta, the largest with 686 members. The new jurisdiction included Athens, Atlanta, Columbus, and Macon. Nelson focused on strengthening the existing work rather than developing new congregations. He addressed this at Council, St. Luke's, Atlanta, December 7, 1909: "True it is that we have not built many churches or opened many new missions or added a large number of clergy. But some of these things are not features of a settled policy. My own endeavor has been to give more personal attention to each Parish and Mission, and rather to strengthen than to enlarge."

Bishop Nelson was a man of great character and persistence. One crisis, which consumed his later episcopate, stemmed from a decision by the City of Atlanta to build a new highway right near St. Philip's Cathedral, located then at 16 Washington Street. The roadway seriously compromised the Cathedral property and the Diocese took the city to court. He wrote in his journal, January 9–14, 1911: "Spent most of the time in Judge Pendleton's court in damage suit brought as Trustee for the Diocese of Atlanta and St. Philip's Church against the city of Atlanta for erection of the viaduct approach in front of our property. The verdict of the jury was against us." This, among other issues, would prompt the congregation to eventually resettle on its present prominent location on Peachtree Street.

Bishop Nelson died on February 13, 1917. In a memorial to him, a friend said: "For fifteen years his devoted initiative, tireless, ceaseless efforts caused the work of the Diocese to become so large that it was deemed necessary to create a new Diocese. . . . Nelson selected the newly created Diocese, wherein, for ten years he continued his unswerving devotion and fruitful service daily increasing, deepening and broadening in spiritual grace and human sympathy."

During his tenure as Bishop of the Diocese of Atlanta, thirteen new congregations were added to the Diocese, of which only two remain open today: St. Timothy's, Decatur, and St. James', Macon—both organized in 1910. The other churches formed during the later Nelson years, which since closed their doors are: St. Mark's, Macon (1907); St. Stephen's, Montezuma (1908); St. John's, Norcross (1908); Good Shepherd, LaGrange (1909); Christ Church, Hapeville (1912); Transfiguration, Helen (1914); St. Elizabeth's, LaGrange (1914); St. Stephen's, Macon (1914); an unnamed mission in Dahlonega (1916); St. Stephen's, Griffin (1916); and Holy Comforter, LaGrange (1916). There were, in 1917, only three parishes with over 500 communicants: All Saints, Atlanta (573); St. Luke's, Atlanta (880); and Trinity, Columbus (575).

In Nelson's final address, at St. Peter's Church, Rome, May 24, 1916, he talked about issues of law and order, the contributions of women to diocesan life, and the national efforts at mission. His thoughts included guidance regarding the use of the Prayer Book and observance of the rubrics. However, he encouraged compliance out of respect—not subservience: "Obedience should be a privilege, not an obligation; it should be stimulated by confidence not imposed by law and penalty. Neither a titular head, nor an absolute sway are proper to a Bishop in the Church of God. It is his feeling that he is touched with the feelings of the infirmities of other men, which will make him strong among men." A firm foundation was laid for the Diocese of Atlanta by Cleland Kinloch Nelson.

Text submitted by the Reverend William P. McLemore.

✠   ✠   ✠   ✠

St. James' Episcopal Church, Cedartown

✠

St. James' Church dates from 1878 when a small group of Episcopalians met for services in the tiny northwest Georgia village of Cedartown. The Reverend W. E. Epps of Cave Spring, Georgia, approximately eight miles away, officiated. Their call to meet was likely through the voices of Mr. and Mrs. Amos N. West, Episcopalians who had recently come to Cedartown from Pittsburgh by way of Richmond, Virginia, to establish Cherokee Iron Works. The 1880 *Diocesan Journal* lists the congregation as "Cedartown Mission" with seven members. Within five years, largely as a result of the challenges and generosity of the West family, a lovely frame building of classic Carpenter Gothic style was constructed. The steeple bell is said to have come from a locomotive of the East and West Railroad, and the name St. James' from Mrs. West's former and much-loved parish, St. James', Manhattan, New York. The church seats 120 and is a historic landmark of Polk County.

The 1902 Parochial Report lists thirty-four members with an annual budget of $572. In 1927, St. James' hosted the twentieth Council of the Diocese of Atlanta. Bishop Mikell took the occasion to note that Cedartown appeared to be a developing small parish and urged the priest "to take charge, and in spite of temptations to move elsewhere, remain with the smaller Parish, gaining the love of his own people and the confidence and respect of the community." History bears out that throughout the congregation's 127 years, over eighteen priests have served the parish, averaging about two to five years each. With tenure from 1945 to 1961, the Reverend John Hunt Jr. holds the record as the longest serving cleric.

Over these years a number of changes and improvements have been made, although nothing has been done to change the integrity of the original building. A former residence next door was acquired and remodeled around 1958 and serves as a genuine Parish House containing offices, meeting and dining space. The congregation has faithfully maintained an Episcopal presence in Cedartown over the years. Although there have been good times and some bad times, the continuing faithfulness of its people have brought it to this day with renewed strength and vigor. The future, by God's grace, will find the congregation still pursuing the mission, in prayer and worship, in proclaiming the Gospel, and promoting justice, peace, and love.

Submitted by the Reverends Donald Black and William McLemore. Photo from the church archives.
Left: St. James' Episcopal Church, Cedartown.

✠   ✠   ✠   ✠

ST. PAUL'S EPISCOPAL CHURCH, ATLANTA

✝

In 1880, eighteen years after The Emancipation Proclamation, a small group of blacks organized a Sunday school in Atlanta. Worship service classes were convened in a loft at the corner of Lee and Gordon Streets in the West End of town. This was the first black Episcopal Sunday school established in Atlanta. A few elders (Mr. Hunt and Mesdames Bellamy and Dozier) petitioned Bishop Beckwith and the Diocese of Georgia to establish a mission. The petition was granted and St. Paul's was born.

In 1895, the Reverend William A. Green was minister-in-charge and moved the church to a new building in the heart of the black community on Auburn Avenue. During the next decade, membership expanded continuously. In 1898, Father Green established a second black mission in the city—St. Matthias' on Lawshe Street. The two missions grew and prospered under the Reverend Henry Simons (who succeeded Father Green) and the Reverend Albert Eustace Day. Under his leadership, St. Paul's acquired a valuable tract of land (three-quarters of a city block) on Auburn Avenue and Fort Street. During this time, the church operated an organized and well-staffed parochial school. In 1906, when the city found itself gripped in a race riot, Father Day and some of his parishioners worked untiringly in the community to reestablish racial harmony.

In 1917, the Reverend Aubrey Anson Hewitt became vicar after the death of Father Day. That year, a fire engulfed a seventy-three-block radius in Atlanta consuming the church building and destroying records. The parishioners were forced to worship wherever they could. In desperation, Father Hewitt called upon the Diocese for help. In response, an old Sunday School Building was given by the Cathedral of St. Philip and moved to the Auburn Avenue location providing temporary housing for St. Paul's.

In 1918, the Reverend E. L. Braithwaite was called from St. Stephen's, Griffin. During the interim, Father W. Q. Rogers, in charge of St. Matthias, supervised St. Paul's. Father Rogers moved the church to Ashby Street and Mason/Turner

Left: The altar at St. Paul's Episcopal Church, Atlanta.

Avenue. In 1926, the Reverend H. Randolph Moore succeeded Braithwaite as archdeacon for Negro work and priest-in-charge of St. Paul's. Under Father Moore's leadership in 1929, the St. Matthias and St. Paul's missions were combined as a single mission and operated under the title—St. Paul's Episcopal Church. In 1932, the St. Matthias building at 135 Ashby Street was remodeled and became the new home of St. Paul's. On September 30, 1933, Father Moore welcomed Bishop Mikell back to St. Paul's to dedicate and consecrate the new Ashby Street sanctuary.

In May of 1934, the Reverend Henry J. C. Bowden (1934–1943) was appointed priest-in-charge and became vicar in 1935. On December 20, 1935, a new Parish House/Rectory Building was dedicated. During World War II St. Paul's was served by two priests, the Reverend George Harper (1943–1944) and the Reverend Frederick J. Hunter (1945–1947).

In 1947, the Reverend Samuel C. Usher became priest-in-charge. The church had achieved status as a self-supporting parish. St. Paul's membership would increase and St. Paul's would become a full-fledged parish at the forty-seventh Diocesan Council in January 1954. The title of the priest-in-charge became rector. In 1961, the Reverend Adolphus Carty (1961–1963) followed Father Usher as rector.

On September 1, 1964, the Reverend Robert Boyd Hunter (1964–1975) of Nashville, Tennessee, became rector of St. Paul's. Under his leadership, ground was broken for a new building on June 16, 1968. On June 22, 1969, St. Paul's moved to its current location on Peyton Road.

In April 1977, the Reverend Edward L. Warner (1977–2000) became rector. At St. Paul's Centennial Celebration the mortgage was burned. Early in the 1980s, St. Paul's had begun to discuss proposals to complete the church on Peyton Road. A beautiful, new sanctuary was dedicated and blessed by Bishop Frank Allan in 1994.

In 2001, the Reverend Bernard Rosser became priest-in-charge of St. Paul's. In July of 2002, the Vestry of St. Paul's called the Reverend Canon Robert C. Wright as rector. Father Wright is a visionary and a strong advocate of outreach and the youth of the church. Outreach at St. Paul's is both local and international. The first international missionaries of St. Paul's were teens sent to Jamaica to serve children with AIDS. The adults of the parish responded to their example by traveling to Blue Fields, Nicaragua, to build buildings, sing songs, and share the Good News of God in Christ. In 2006 an adult group will be sent to Rwanda, East Africa.

Membership has increased from 400 to 550; average Sunday attendance has increased from 165 to 350; and the annual budget has increased from $200,000 to $500,000. Worship at St. Paul's accommodates the diversity of the congregation and community. The first Sunday is the customary "High Church" with incense, anthems, and traditional Episcopal hymns; the second Sunday has been appointed as the "Gospel/ Jazz" Sunday replete with a Jazz Quartet; the third Sunday is singing of traditional Negro spirituals and from the LEVAS hymnal; the fourth Sunday encompasses all; and the fifth Sunday has been designated for the youth of the church. Father Wright has instituted Children's Sunday Sermon on the fourth Sunday. Two priests recently emerged from the congregation.

On September 17, 2005, the church celebrated its 125th anniversary and retired the mortgage on the sanctuary. St. Paul's Vision Statement is: "We are a growing church with dynamic worship that: encourages a warm and welcoming community; is knowledgeable of our faith and tradition; reaches out to those who may or may not believe; and increases in service to our local and world communities in Jesus' name."

Text submitted by Mrs. Harriett Witsell Bowens. Photo by Anderson Scott.

THE CHURCH OF THE INCARNATION, ATLANTA

✠

The Church of the Incarnation is the third oldest worshipping Episcopal community in Atlanta. In October of 1882, Mrs. Nellie Peters Black requested a meeting of all Episcopal ladies in West End at the home of Mrs. Benjamin Conley, wife of the former governor. The residence was located where Brown High School now stands. Those present were Mrs. Conley, Mrs. Charles Goodman, Mrs. Mary J. Van Dyke, Mrs. Joe Hunnicutt, and Mrs. E. M. Haunson.

Between 1882 and 1892 regular services were held in the Masonic Hall at Gordon and Lee Streets. Services moved to Ashby Street Presbyterian Chapel (later West End Presbyterian Church). In 1880 the Diocese of Georgia established a Board of Missions responsible for all Diocesan missionary operations. Until 1885 the clergy serving Incarnation were city missionaries in charge of several missions. In Atlanta, only St. Philip's and St. Luke's had parish status.

Through Mrs. Van Dyke's generosity, a Lee Street lot was donated as the building site. Mr. C. Walter Smith prepared the church's structural plans. On January 13, 1896, the groundbreaking was held, followed two weeks later by laying the cornerstone. Despite a monthly treasurer's report of $3.00 in income, canceled by $3.00 expenses, the congregation boldly borrowed funds and the church was built for $3,671.80.

On April 30, 1896, the Right Reverend C. K. Nelson, Bishop of Georgia, opened the church for worship. Incarnation received parish status on May 6, 1896, at Council in St. Paul's, Augusta, with seventy-three communicants. In 1907, Incarnation became a viable part of the new Diocese of Atlanta. In 1927, Dr. G. Wallace Gasque filled the pulpit of Incarnation "temporarily." So impressive were his preaching and teaching abilities that his service lasted eleven years. He originated the idea for Camp Mikell, near Toccoa.

In 1945, the Reverend Cecil L. Alligood agreed to stay a few months and stayed eighteen years. The congregation grew rapidly, reflecting the nation's post–World War II boom in church membership.

As West End became commercial and Cascade Heights developed into a prospering community, plans to move were considered, became a reality, and the church relocated to Cascade Heights, at the time very suburban, before completion of the expressway system. First services were held in the new church on August 24, 1958.

Father Harry Harper came in 1963 from the New Zealand mission field. Community social and racial changes presented the need for a different outreach. Father Harper worked to prepare the congregation and vestry for the challenge. Frustration, fear, guilt, and anxiety brought a decline in membership. Incarnation began reaching out to the

Front view of the Church of the Incarnation, Atlanta.

Church of the Incarnation, Atlanta, Easter Sunday 2005.

community and although pressure grew to relocate, the church successfully integrated. A Bargain Shop (originally "Harper's Bazaar") in the West End was successfully operated by the church women. Shepherd's Gate, a community center, opened as a church school program for "latch-key" children, then expanded to include a youth group, tutoring, arts and crafts, adult instruction, but most importantly a second "home" for children needing attention and affection.

On July 21, 1968, the Reverend Carlisle Ramcharan became rector. The courtyard was completed during this period as a memorial gift from Miss Louise Hames. Father Ramcharan resigned in June 1972. In March of 1973, the Reverend Albert R. Dreisbach Jr. was called as rector. A former advisor to the Bishop of Delaware on intergroup relations as last executive director of the Episcopal Society of Cultural

and Racial Unity, he came with full credentials to meet the challenges of the time. A new two-story Educational Building was constructed; the parish acquired beautiful forty-year-old silks and appliqués from the National Cathedral Altar Guild, which were transformed into stunning vestments, altar hangings, and a pall. Banners, Stations of the Cross, and backlighting the stained-glass windows from the Lee Street Church were added to enhance the sanctuary's beauty.

In the late 1970s, Father Dreisbach founded the Atlanta Center of the Continuing Study of the Shroud of Turin, and resigned effective May 31, 1985, to assume its directorship. The Reverend Richard A. Williams became rector in 1986 and remained for two years. He held weekly services for residents of Epworth Towers, a senior citizen's residence. The Reverend Dreisbach served as an interim priest and pastor until the next rector was called to the parish.

The Reverend Richard C. Britton was installed on May 5, 1990. With his leadership, the parish developed a viable mission statement and began a strategy for mission planning; the articles of incorporation and bylaws were revised; a Bible Study Group was reestablished; and for the first time a Youth Eucharistic Ministry Program began. He remained until August 1996. Again, the Reverend Dreisbach consented to serve as interim rector. In 1998 Father James Williams was called as rector and remained until his resignation in November 2004. Programs he started included Safe Harbor, which provided respite for Alzheimer's patients' caregivers.

In 2005 the Reverend Canon Dr. O. Gordon A. Okunsanya was called as the interim rector. His years of experience have proven to be a stabilizing influence for the church in its search for a new rector. His service has been exemplary as priest developer. The parish continues to seek the guidance of the Holy Spirit to strengthen its life together as a church, to guide its direction in mission in the name of Jesus Christ, and to renew itself as the people of God.

Text and photos submitted by Rolando Thorne.

✠   ✠   ✠   ✠

St. Margaret's Church, Carrollton

✠

St. Margaret's Church in Carrollton is known as the "church that helps people." A congregation of only three hundred families, this proud 118-year-old church has been an effective witness of compassion for the poor and needy since it started its outreach as an aided parish in 1952 under the inspired leadership of the Reverend Dewey Gable, first resident priest.

St. Margaret's was dormant for sixty years. From 1887 a few communicants loyally held services in each others' homes; then, as a mission, in a tiny chapel they built on South White Street. This quaint, wooden church with its steep roof, interior of beaded wood paneling and pump organ, rested so lightly on its foundation that it was literally blown over on its side in a storm in the 1930s. It was tilted back in place without serious damage.

The church building seemed to take on ballast after World War II as the town acquired gravitas from new industries, especially a prospering local start-up company called Southwire, which brought more Episcopalians into town.

A new Williamsburg-style church was built in 1953 on Newman Street, two blocks from Carrollton's Town Square. The Reverend Gable had the idea to link the church with its patron saint, the Scottish Queen Margaret, who restored a sixth-century monastery on the holy isle of Iona in the eleventh century.

Father Gable arranged for a piece of green and white marble from the Ionian chapel ruins to be set in the altar of St. Margaret's new church as a reminder of the Living Word.

St. Margaret's namesake became increasingly significant as the church grew. Queen Margaret was legendary as one whose generosity in feeding the poor extended to serving them first at her own table. By the 1950s the little aided parish, like its patron saint, reached out to the "least of these." The former chapel was then deconsecrated and in 1964 moved to the West Georgia College campus to be an interfaith chapel.

St. Margaret's Episcopal Church, Carrollton.

The Reverend Gable left in 1956 for studies at Oxford, England. The priestless flock carried on services and the work of the church with a fervor that set a pattern for five such stressful times in the future. In the periods without priests members of the congregation stepped forward and demonstrated the church's strength and adaptability. Lay readers handled the services, others the fundraising so well that the new Thrift Shop brought in $1,405 and facilities expanded to two neighboring houses used for Sunday school, bazaars, and suppers.

After Father Gable, the priests were E. Stuart Wood (1956–1959); Donald Harrison (1960–1965)—full parish status; Charles C. Green (1965–1969)—Parish Hall was added; Gene Britton (1970–1976)—first St. Margaret's birthday festival with bagpipes, the wearing of kilts and plaids, and serving tea with scones; and John Boucher (1977–1991)—stressful time of unpaid bills, falling attendance, trial Prayer Book fuss, and a divergent group holding separate Bible class. In four years Father Boucher restored the church's spiritual and economic health.

The Reverend James Callahan's dynamic ministry of nineteen years (1981–2000) followed, with the congregation tripling and the start of the first major Community Outreach program: the soup kitchen in 1983. Barry Staples was hired as director of all outreach. She helped the desperately needy with money, guidance, shelter, and legal support. Other programs such as Homework Helper for children in public housing and the Paper Pantry for new mothers without support began. The climax of Father Callahan's tenure was the celebration of St. Margaret's Centennial on November 21, 1983. It created a spirit of revival, with glad-hearted reveling, Scottish games, Highland dances, and services augmented with bagpipes and trumpets.

Following Father Callahan's retirement in 2000, the Reverend David W. Perkins served for a year as interim rector. He steadied the congregation with his Biblical scholarship, making scripture and literature shine forth. St. Margaret's current priest, the Reverend Hazel Glover, arrived in 2002 and comforted the congregation with her informal, motherly warmth. Her all-embracing spirit is well symbolized in the new landscaping of the grounds—a unifying presence with new paths and paint. Her calm faith is a balm for the current disaffection rattling the Anglican Communion.

Text submitted by Emily Cumming. Photos from the church archives.

✠   ✠   ✠   ✠

Bagpipes enrich the service at St. Margaret's Episcopal Church, Carrollton.

THE ORDER OF DAUGHTERS OF THE KING

✛

The Order of the Daughters of the King is a lay Order for women, which was started in 1865 by a group of women from a Bible class at the Church of the Holy Sepulchre in New York. The first chapter in this Diocese was chartered in 1892 at St. Luke's Church, Atlanta, and was followed in 1894 by one at St. Stephen's, Milledgeville, and one at the Church of the Incarnation in 1897. The Cathedral's chapter began in 1898. Today there are chapters in over sixty-four parishes along with several junior chapters for girls aged eight to eighteen. At the present time there are over fourteen hundred senior and junior daughters and more women are joining the Order every month.

The Order is open to all women who wish to pursue a spiritual way of life. Each woman, after a period of study, takes a vow to follow a Rule of Life, which includes prayer, service, and evangelism. They serve at the discretion of the rector in the church and assist him or her in many ways. Among their duties they pray for the sick, visit shut-ins, help with wedding and funeral services, and perform outreach in endless ways.

Every year an annual Assembly is held at the Cathedral, usually in February, which consists of a business meeting, a speaker, Holy Eucharist, and lunch, which is attended by daughters from all over the Diocese. At the end of April a weekend retreat is held at Camp Mikell, which has become the spiritual renewal of the year. Both of these events are always well attended. The Diocese and various chapters hold Quiet Days during the course of the year.

The Order of the Daughters of the King is not only alive in the Diocese of Atlanta but all over this nation, with over twenty-four thousand members. It has also spread internationally with daughters in many parts of the world. This Diocese is privileged to have the national office and its headquarters situated in Woodstock, Georgia.

Text submitted by Aileen Hiscutt.

✛   ✛   ✛   ✛

HOLY TRINITY PARISH, DECATUR

✛

For all its 115 years, Holy Trinity has been located in the City of Decatur. In 1892 a small congregation of thirteen families established the first Episcopal Church in the area. In 1893, a small frame church was built for a total of $1,600. The mission flourished with services conducted by visiting clergy or lay readers. The Reverend John James Patrick Perry was the first resident priest in 1909–10. Parish status was attained in 1920 with 128 communicants.

In 1925, the Reverend Charles Holding became rector and led the church for nineteen years. Although the original church was enlarged, it was outgrown and in 1928, Holy Trinity purchased its present site at 515 East Ponce de Leon Avenue. A parish house was built, the second floor to serve temporarily as a place of worship until a church could be erected. Difficult times during the 1930s made it seem doubtful whether

Holy Trinity Parish, Decatur, 1908 photo.

the parish would survive. Through sacrificial giving and with a manageable mortgage, the fear of losing the property was removed and all thought of construction postponed.

The fiftieth anniversary was celebrated on Sunday, October 11, 1942, with a vesper service led by Bishop Walker. Holy Trinity hosted its first Council in May 1944. The next long-term rector, the Reverend Charles Tisdale, provided dynamic leadership, and the church grew rapidly. On September 9, 1951, the first services were held in the new brick church (now Tisdale Hall dedicated in 2002). During the 1950s, Holy Trinity sponsored three missions: St. Michael and All Angels; Holy Cross; and St. Bartholomew's. By the mid-1950s, classes and services were overflowing and a more space was planned. Several neighboring lots were purchased and in 1957, a chapel and eight classrooms were built. With Tisdale's guidance, seven young men entered the priesthood, inspired by his example. Crippling arthritis forced Tisdale, age forty-eight, to resign in 1963. The Reverend William Littleton, the next rector, served two years. Women first served on the Vestry during his ministry.

Six months into the Reverend J. F. G. Hopper's tenure, on July 9, 1967, fire gutted the Parish House and seriously damaged the church. The parish accepted Decatur First United Methodist Church's offer to use their old sanctuary and Sunday school classes met in Glennwood School. All agreed to rebuild on the same property. On November 1, 1970, after more than three years' absence, the congregation again worshiped in its own church.

Father Hopper retired in 1975, and the Reverend Richard Milner, who came to the parish as curate in 1972, became rector and served until 1979, guiding the parish through many changes including use of the 1979 *Book of Common Prayer*. Women were

Holy Trinity Parish, Decatur, fall 2005.

included in the lay reader/chalice bearer program and underwent rigorous training to serve as lay pastoral ministers. Another of Milner's legacies was the Counseling Center, created to serve parishioners and the community.

The Reverend Francis T. Daunt arrived in September 1980, and began the practice of members approaching the altar during the "Prayers of the People" for prayers on their behalf. Outreach grew under Daunt's guidance. A women and children's shelter, under the Decatur Cooperative Ministry, was opened in the 1957 Educational Building. The Decatur Emergency Assistance Ministry housed its offices there also. In May 1986, Holy Trinity celebrated consecration of the debt-free church. Father Daunt was called to Baton Rouge in 1989. Since the 1980s, signers have interpreted the main services and events and large print books have become available. An elevator was dedicated in 1990 and an automatic entry door makes the church accessible to all.

The Reverend Philip C. Linder became rector in November 1990. His leadership brought renewed parish vitality and attracted many young families. Finances were put on a firm foundation and needed repairs completed. The church celebrated its centennial in 1992 with pomp, ceremony, and fun, with participation by the Most Reverend John M. Allin and the Right Reverend Frank Allan. A centennial scholarship trust to provide grants for the pursuit of theological education was established. Father Linder called the first woman priest as his assistant, a practice that has continued. The parish was the first in the area to build a labyrinth. The 1998 Capital Campaign exceeded expectations and many renovations and improvements began. Father Linder was called to become dean of Trinity Cathedral, Columbia, South Carolina.

With the new century, the Reverend William T. Deneke became rector, with the request to encourage spiritual growth. His teaching on iconography has enriched our worship. Strong lay leadership continues to be encouraged. A friendly Holy Trinity reaches out to the community and beyond. The Capital Campaign was extended in order to renovate the 1957 Educational Building, named in honor of the late Father Hunt Comer. Father Deneke welcomes the many new attendees who come to Holy Trinity from other denominations or who are unchurched. We are working to teach them the wonderful traditions and history of the Anglican tradition. A greater focus on children's ministries has led to innovative programs and a new playground. Life at Holy Trinity goes on at a busy and enthusiastic pace.

Text submitted by Belinda O. Watkins. Photos from the church archives.

✠   ✠   ✠   ✠

St. Andrew's Episcopal Church, Fort Valley

✠

In 1892, during the tenure of Bishop Nelson, an English cabinetmaker by the name of George H. Harrison came with his family to Fort Valley, Georgia. There were a few Episcopalians, but no church. Mr. Harrison, as a loyal churchman with a great love for England, felt that he could not bring up his family outside the Episcopal Church.

Accordingly, Bishop Nelson bought a lot on Central Avenue in Fort Valley, the present site of the church and, with Mr. Harrison in charge, built the little chancel which for many years kept the small, but devoted congregation together. The chancel, built largely by Mr. Harrison, was designed in the Gothic style, with the altar facing east as altars had in the old country.

In 1897, the church building was completed. It was named St. Andrew's after the parish church in Uxbridge, Middlesex, England, where Mr. Harrison and his family had worshiped. The first priest who served St. Andrew's, the Reverend Edward Denniston, lived on a farm west of Phenix City, Alabama, and made his living by farming. Having no conveyance, he walked from his home to St. Andrew's and back again, serving Zion Church in Talbotton, Georgia, while en route. Since it was a long way and consumed so much time, it is not strange that these two churches received his ministrations but once a month.

In 1893, it was decided that if the church should open every Sunday instead of only once a month, it might make more progress. Bishop Nelson approving, Mr. Charles T. Eberhardt was appointed lay reader, and Mr. Eberhardt and Mr. Harrison

alternated in reading the services. Through the efforts of the Women's Auxiliary, pews, a new carpet, a lectern, and other furnishings were added bit by bit. Finally, a new church was built in 1920. The old altar was placed in the new sanctuary beneath the beautiful window, which was given by Mrs. Alice Shepard Crandall, in memory of George and Emily Harrison.

Many missionaries have served St. Andrew's, but up to 1942, only three resident priests served the church. The Reverend E. J. Saywell came in 1924, and was succeeded

Sketch of St. Andrew's Episcopal Church in Fort Valley.

by the Reverend Lawton Riley in 1926. From 1926 until 1942, St. Andrew's was served periodically by the priests of the various Macon, Georgia, churches, and by the lay readers, Mr. Frank Harrison (son of the founder) and Mr. Billy Wood.

In the spring of 1942, St. Andrew's took another step forward when it decided once more to have a resident priest. The budget was increased accordingly, an adjoining lot was purchased and paid for, twelve stained-glass windows in the church were installed, and a $1,500 debt of twenty-three-years standing was wiped out completely. With the erasure of this debt, it was possible for St. Andrew's to be consecrated on its fiftieth anniversary.

During World War II, nearby Warner Robins Air Base came into being. Due to that community's rapid growth, it soon became apparent that a mission should be founded there. St. Andrew's priest, the Reverend J. F. G. Hopper, organized such a mission in 1943, and preached there each week, as did priests who followed him. In 1956, the new mission, All Saints, had become so large that another priest was assigned to serve there.

St. Andrew's continued to grow and, in 1950, a fine brick rectory was erected on the lot adjoining the church. In 1954, a handsome brick Parish Hall was built, consisting of three classrooms, an assembly room, and a kitchen. In December of 1956 the Right Reverend R. R. Claiborne, Bishop of Atlanta, granted St. Andrew's full-parish status.

Text submitted by the church based on information provided by Miss Parmalee Cheves and Mrs. Lou Smith. Photos from the church archives.

Right: Altar in St. Andrew's, Fort Valley.

of this church provided space for a variety of new activities. By this time St. Matthias' had active youth and senior choirs and Sunday school classes for young people. In 1951 St. Matthias' became an aided parish.

In 1948 the Vestry purchased a brick home across the street from the church to serve as a Rectory, but failed to budget for the mortgage. The Woman's Auxiliary organized monthly suppers and used the proceeds to pay the mortgage. Typical menu items were spaghetti, casseroles, and the fondly remembered "Episcopal Chicken Pie." For many years during the 1950s the Auxiliary provided additional funds with their annual bazaar featuring handmade items and baked goods.

By the mid-1960s the parish had about ninety communicants. Around this time the still ongoing tradition of a First Sunday potluck lunch began. A young people's group met each Sunday evening. In 1961 the parish added a church school building that is still used. At the Diocesan Council of 1975 St. Matthias' was granted full-parish status. The present St. Matthias' complex includes a spacious Parish Hall

Communion at St. Matthias' Episcopal Church, Toccoa.

built in 1997 and a sanctuary built in 2001. The old church, largely destroyed by fire in 1998, has been renovated to contain a labyrinth and library. Adjacent residences purchased in 1983 and 2000 contain offices and meeting space.

Today St. Matthias' has 233 communicants. Two Sunday services attract an average attendance of 96. Sunday school classes are attended by an average of 26 children and adults. The Daughters of the King chapter was reestablished in 2001 and now has 8 members. Thirty-one youth and adults serve as acolytes and lay readers. Youth participate in Rite 13 and J2A activities and organize an overseas pilgrimage every other year. Senior members meet monthly for fellowship and dinner. Each Lent and Advent Wednesday study groups are held with a soup and cornbread supper, a tradition that goes back, somewhat irregularly, for decades. Programs for youth attract new members with children and, as in the last century, St. Matthias' grows as Episcopalians from other areas move to Toccoa.

Text submitted by Bonnie Finne Churchill. Photos by Bonnie Finne Churchill and Jerry Rose.

St. Timothy's Episcopal Church, Decatur

✝

The history of St. Timothy's began in 1898 when a group of women in the Kirkwood community petitioned the Bishop for Episcopal services. In 1902 a small chapel was built that seated approximately sixty people. In 1933, the Bishop assigned the Reverend Wesley E. Couch from St. George's in College Park to conduct services. The period of 1951–1952 brought the construction of a new church behind the Chapel. The Reverend C. B. Lucas (1950–1956) became vicar. In 1959, St. Timothy's became a self-supporting parish and it was decided that St. Timothy's best chance for growth was to relocate. The Kirkwood property was sold. A new site was acquired at the corner of Flat Shoals and Clifton Church Roads. The new building was completed in 1966. The first official service was held on May 15, 1966. The 1970s brought further changes to St. Timothy's resulting in the parish being integrated. In 1981, Senior Warden Ronald Wiggins and the Reverend Palmer Temple burned the mortgage. In March 1982, the Reverend Isaac Miller became the parish's first African American rector. During the years that followed the surrounding communities continued the racial transition, and eventually the parish became predominately African American.

St. Timothy's records presently list eighty-seven households with ethnic backgrounds from the United States, South America, the Caribbean, and Africa. The members serve on the following committees: Finance, Building and Grounds, Christian Education, Outreach, Worship, and Stewardship. The church also has chapters of Episcopal Church Women, Daughters of the King, MOST (Men of St. Timothy's), and The Brotherhood of St. Andrew.

St. Timothy's worship service includes prayer, praise, and music, which support the liturgy and Holy Word. Worship is in the High Mass tradition, which unites Christ's Church in one foundation. The Holy Eucharist is celebrated in the Anglican tradition. The Good News is proclaimed in all gatherings at St. Timothy's, and Christ is made known to all in the breaking of the bread. Special services are offered during Lent, Holy Week, Easter, Thanksgiving, Christmas, and other occasions during the year. St. Timothy's currently holds a Sunday and Tuesday worship service and Christian Education classes on Sunday and Wednesday.

Liturgical ministries include Lay Eucharistic Ministers, Music, Altar Guild, Acolytes, Greeters, Wardens, Ushers, and The Verger. Through the committees and organizations listed, the parish life at St. Timothy's has been greatly enhanced and fellowship continues to grow under the leadership of the Reverend Brian A. Jemmott, vicar. Outreach includes assistance to Holy Comforter, sister church to St. Timothy's, in preparing and serving suppers and preparing and delivering hot meals to families in need on Thanksgiving. During Christmas these families are invited to Christmas dinner and given gifts. During Christmas the Episcopal Church Women donate gifts and money to Emmaus House Christmas program.

The Caribbean-American Festival was initiated in 1995 by the Reverend Angela Boatwright, former vicar, to celebrate the richness and diversity of the African American, Caribbean, African, South American, Indian, and British cultures worshiping at St. Timothy's. Other annual events include Harvest Meal, Homecoming Celebration, Black History series during the month of February, Children's Christmas Pageant, Holiday Christmas Dinner Dance, Women's Day Celebration and Pastor's Appreciation Day. Since 1902 St. Timothy's Episcopal Church has had thirty priests providing service to the parishioners with the Reverend Brian Jemmott having begun his service in 2003.

Text and photos submitted by Mr. Ronald Wiggins, Mrs. Gwen Hyman, and Mrs. Elnora Robinson.
Opposite page: Entrance of St. Timothy's Episcopal Church, Decatur.

✝   ✝   ✝   ✝

Members of St. Timothy's participate in the annual Hunger Walk at Turner Field.

EPISCOPAL CHURCH OF THE EPIPHANY, ATLANTA

✢

The Church of the Epiphany began in 1893 when Mr. and Mrs. D. P. Holland, residents of Inman Park, Atlanta's first planned suburb, asked a lay reader from St. Luke's Episcopal Church to lead Evening Prayer in their home. By 1898, attendance at services and Sunday school had grown significantly. The Right Reverend C. K. Nelson, then Bishop of Georgia, granted mission status. He suggested the name *Epiphany*, the same as his home church in Bethlehem, Pennsylvania, and because the new church was in the easternmost part of Atlanta, evoking connections with the Magi. Epiphany's logo—a five-pointed star—serves as an apt reminder of the church's first location—on a lot, purchased for $300, at the convergence of Little Five Points. Ground was broken for that first small building in February 1898, the cornerstone of Stone Mountain granite was laid in March, and the first service was held on May 15.

In December of 1908, the Church of the Epiphany was admitted to the Diocese of Atlanta as a parish and called its first rector the Reverend Russell K. Smith. The original building was only twenty-one by thirty-two feet. Despite an expansion in 1906, the congregation quickly outgrew the church and in 1922 sold the property at Little Five Points and moved to nearby Seminole Avenue. Epiphany flourished in this location, growing to 667 communicants in the next seventeen years. There is still one member, Silvia Ethridge, who was born in that neighborhood, baptized, confirmed, and married at Epiphany during the Seminole Avenue years, and continues to sing in the choir every Sunday.

The city's outward expansion and social dislocations following World War

Church of the Epiphany, Atlanta, original front in foreground with new entry beyond.

II brought demographic transition to Inman Park and by 1953 the number of communicants was 165. That year, the Reverend Dr. Norman Gore was called as Epiphany's sixth rector. Under his leadership, the congregation made its third move, purchasing the current property on Ponce de Leon Avenue from Emory University in 1956. The first services were held in the new Chapel in October 1957. An expansion of the church in 1961 increased the length of the nave; and, in 1963, an addition was built to house additional classrooms and a larger Parish Hall.

The parish continued to grow under the leadership of the Reverend Stan McGraw (1971–79) and the Reverend Benjamin Turnage (1980–1984). A milestone of this period was the election to the Vestry in 1971 of the first woman, Betty Walton. In 1973, Betty became the first female senior warden. By 1984, there were 130 households, representing about three hundred adults and children.

In the spring of 1985, at a time when women were only slowly gaining acceptance in the Episcopal priesthood, the Reverend Elizabeth Claiborne Jones accepted the call to serve as the first female rector of an Episcopal church in the Diocese and the ninth rector of Epiphany. Under her leadership, the parish undertook two major building projects. The first project, in 1988–89, was in the church itself. The renovation reversed the orientation of the church, creating a free-standing altar at the south end of the building, adding a new pipe organ to the choir and adding side aisles to allow for more flexibility with liturgical processions and easier access to the pews. A baptistery and a memorial garden were included. Peter Schneider, a parishioner, made a beautiful wood and brass cross that hangs on the wooden reredos behind the 1898 white marble altar used in every incarnation of Epiphany. The altar rail is now an oval that allows the congregation to gather around the altar during the Eucharist.

Following extensive long-range planning, in 2001, the parish undertook a capital campaign: "Building Our Vision." The Parish Hall was greatly expanded; classrooms, choir suite, restrooms, and a gallery were added; and the office area was completely remodeled. Landscaping undertaken at the same time created a courtyard between the church and the Parish Hall and a meditation garden. During this enormous project, the house next door became available. As this is the only possible property for future expansion, the house was bought and is presently being rented.

In the past twenty years, the ministries of the Church of the Epiphany have expanded: several mission trips to Central America; an annual Jumble Sale; an exhibit of over two hundred nativity scenes bequeathed to the church; involvement with the

The altar in Church of the Epiphany, Atlanta.

Peachtree-Pine Shelter and Hagar's House; participation in Habitat for Humanity; shopping for needy families at Christmas time; sponsoring several refugee families; sponsoring a popular and lively Vacation Bible School every summer; offering space to the community for AA and other meetings; offering Education for Ministry and Disciples of Christ; has a running art exhibit in the gallery; and many other activities in addition to three Sunday and a mid-week worship service and Sunday classes for children and adults.

The full-time staff has grown to include an assistant to the rector, an organist/choirmaster, and parish administrator as well as a part-time special events coordinator and a sexton. The Reverend Claiborne Jones left Epiphany in December of 2004 to answer a call to Emmaus House and a search is underway for the tenth rector. This is an exciting time for Epiphany as we wait for what comes next.

Text abstracted by members from work of the Church of the Epiphany Parish Profile Nominating Committee. Photos by James P. Marshall Jr. and Anderson Scott.

ALL ANGELS EPISCOPAL CHURCH, EATONTON

✛

All Angels Episcopal Church was built in the Queen Anne Victorian style in 1899 on North Jefferson Avenue, as a mission of St. Stephen's Church, Milledgeville. Bishop Nelson's diaries note as early as 1895 his visits and celebration of the Holy Eucharist in Eatonton. The Reverend John Jabez Lanier, rector of St. Stephen's from 1899 to 1908 was first missioner to All Angels.

All Angels prospered under Nelson's and Lanier's leadership. However, by 1917 the boll weevil had devastated the cotton economy in Putnam County, and the church was forced to close its doors. Bishop Mikell sold the property in December 1919. The church was then converted to a private dwelling and remained so with several owners until August of 1999. Four Eatonton Episcopalians met together for Evening Prayer on the first Sunday of Lent in February of 1999, at the Bronson House, headquarters of the Eatonton-Putnam County Historical Society, Inc. The Reverend Roger Ard, interim rector at St. Stephen's, Milledgeville, provided organizational and spiritual support to the new group and officiated at its first Holy Eucharist at the Bronson House. By August, fourteen eager Putnam County Episcopalians purchased the 1899 All Angels Church building and began restoration. Bishop Frank Allan granted permission to use the original name of "All Angels" and to form a Steering Committee.

Between August and December 24, 1999, the Steering Committee, members, and friends removed nearly eighty years worth of added interior walls, a loft area, kitchen, and other additions. The original heart pine wallboards, scissor-truss beams, and flooring were all intact. Holy Eucharist Service on Christmas Eve 1999 was attended by a standing-room only crowd of members and well-wishers. "Angels" from other churches in Eatonton, Athens, Gainesville, Madison, Milledgeville, Monroe, Atlanta, and New Jersey aided the restoration with their labor, money, and in-kind gifts and the restoration and furnishings were all paid for by December 24, 1999. A pair of circa 1810 gilded carved wooden angels were placed on loan by a supporter and flank the altar.

Bishop Allan soon granted status as a Chapel of St. Stephen's Church. The Reverend Roger Ard, interim rector; then the Reverend Dr. C. K. Robertson, rector; and Alice Fay, deacon, all of St. Stephen's Church provided clerical leadership and support to All Angels for the next year. Visiting clergy included Bishops Allan, Child, and Alexander; the Very Reverend Harriette Simmons, Christ Church Macon; the Reverend Paul

Queen Anne–style All Angels Church, Eatonton, built 1899 and restored 1999.

Norris, rector, Church of the Advent, Madison; and the Reverend John Via, vicar, Churches of the Redeemer, Greensboro, and Mediator, Washington.

In November 2000, Bishop Allan granted priest-in-charge status to the Reverend Robert B. Dendtler, formerly rector, Christ Church, Kennesaw, who led the congregation through a year of discernment. Worshiping Community status was granted in the spring of 2001 allowing regular church school and Holy Eucharist services. Shortly after his ordination as the ninth Bishop of the Diocese of Atlanta, the Right Reverend J. Neil Alexander initiated a final process of examination based on Canon Law. All Angels met the requirements, and he extended an invitation to petition the Diocese for admittance as a parish at the ninety-fifth Annual Council on November 9, 2001, at the Cathedral of St. Philip in Atlanta. All Angels' delegates were the Reverend Dendtler, Anna M. Haslbauer, and James P. Marshall Jr. joined by several other members as the group, proudly entered the Hall of Bishops to be formally recognized. On Sunday, November 11, 2001, the Steering Committee of All Angels met following morning worship and renamed itself the Vestry of All Angels and invited the Reverend Dendtler to become its first rector. He graciously accepted and continues to serve. Bishop Alexander dedicated and consecrated All Angels on Sunday, January 27, 2002, followed by a celebration supper.

Members of All Angels Church, Eatonton, exchange The Peace.

Antique stained-glass windows, originally installed in 1904 and 1905 in the sanctuary of the Second Street Methodist Church in Macon, Georgia, which was razed in 1999, were purchased by All Angels in 1999 and installed in the sanctuary. The large *Communion Chalice and Grapes* altar window and the *Cross and Crown* and *Ruby Cross* windows were installed in 1999 and 2000. Seven matching companion windows were restored and installed in 2004. The names of the 1904 donors as well as the donors to All Angels were placed on plaques with each window.

The congregation of All Angels, though small, is very active in outreach, supporting financially and in kind the Putnam Christian Outreach support services and food pantry; the Kids 4 Peace program; and other worthy causes. A large Education for Ministry class and Adult Bible Study group provide spiritual support. Fellowship events include Shrove Tuesday Pancake Supper, St. Patrick's Day Luncheon, the Annual Fourth of July Fireworks Party on Lake Oconee, Twelfth Night Seafood Dinner and White Elephant Gift Exchange, and the Blessing of the Animals service. Our Lord has truly watched over and guided us as we have worked together and moved steadily forward in our ministry. Thanks be to God.

Text and photos submitted by James P. Marshall Jr.

ALL SAINTS' EPISCOPAL CHURCH, ATLANTA

✠

In 1903 Mrs. Richard Peters gave land on the corner of West Peachtree and North Avenue to the Diocese to found a church and especially a Sunday school since St. Luke's was "too far downtown." A small wooden chapel was followed by a beautiful brown sandstone church built in 1906. Many furnishings provided by Mrs. Peters' daughter are still in the church: an ornate altar of white Caen stone from France, the carved oak Bishop's chair, communion set, and handsome brass cross. The stained-glass windows—six made by Tiffany and Company—depict stages in the life of Jesus Christ.

The first two rectors—Zebulon S. Farland (1903–1909) and W. W. Memminger (1910–1937)—organized the parish and started the traditions of beautiful music and fine preaching. One illustrious parishioner—Thomas Egleston—bequeathed $25,000 to build a Parish House, also constructed of brown sandstone and containing a Shakespearean stage! His many gifts to All Saints' included the pulpit and the magnificent east stained-glass window. Mr. Egleston founded Henrietta Egleston Hospital for Children in memory of his mother.

Deaconess Katherine S. Wood—always dressed in full clergy habit—organized a Mother's Club active for forty years and she was instrumental in starting Holy Innocents Mission. She joined All Saints' in 1905 and retired in 1946. Rector Dr. Theodore S. Will (1938–1944) guided the church out of the Great Depression and through World War II. The bank balance in 1933 was $4.61. From 1903 until 1980 All Saints' was considered a "low church" with a "substantial and dignified" congregation who enjoyed predictable and safe sermons. But changes were coming!

The Reverend Matthew M. Warren (1945–1952) steered All Saints' into uncharted waters. His progressive approach to Christian education encouraged married couples to teach Sunday school together. The emphasis was on loving and respecting the dignity of each child, not on memorized verses. Sympathetic towards people of color, his sermons reflected his liberal attitude. When Father Warren retired, the Reverend Milton L. Wood organized the Men of All Saints', which resulted in several missions: Hammer and Tongs, Counseling Group, Lay Readers, and Ushers.

Father Wood's tenure marked the heyday of the Women's Auxiliary, with fourteen different groups participating in worship, education, social interaction, mission work, and fundraising for many projects. The United Thank Offering was a vital part of their annual agenda. Wood instigated evening programs, gathering his congregation back downtown for spiritual enrichment. Every fall and spring featured a Monday "Church Night Series" with dinner at eighty-five cents a plate, followed by a choice of programs. The beloved tradition began of presenting unwrapped gifts for the sick children at Grady Hospital on the Sunday before Christmas.

In the 1950s, the college program was at its height. Students from Georgia Tech and Agnes Scott met as the Canterbury Club to worship, study, and socialize. To celebrate the church's fiftieth anniversary, Father Wood and the Vestry undertook the first capital campaign resulting in a Parish House. In 1957, amid great celebration, the building was finished, and the church was air-conditioned!

The Reverend Frank Mason Ross' ministry (1961–1980) reflected the many changes taking place in society. For the first time in the Diocese of Atlanta, a woman—Sue Brown Sterne—was elected to a Vestry. The Civil Rights movement brought many changes. Both Fathers Warren and Wood had prepared the congregation with their positive attitudes and blacks were welcomed. One group of parishioners met regularly with a group from a black church. After the U.S. Supreme Court's school desegregation decision, Fathers Wood and Ross both signed a "manifesto" to urge tolerance and obedience to law. Ross spoke from the pulpit in favor of desegregation, disturbing and alienating many. Despite efforts to achieve racial diversity, All Saints' has remained predominately white. Father Bill Swift—interim rector after Ross' retirement—shepherded All Saints' through a change in attitude toward homosexuality; acceptance of the gay and lesbian movement; and ministry to persons with AIDS. Volunteer dedication to this ministry was remarkably intense. In the early 1960s, All Saints' and St. Luke's formed Canterbury Court, a retirement home. In 1965, after many years of intense parish effort and dedication, St. Jude's home for recovering alcoholics was established.

In 1979 the Atlanta Hospital Hospitality House was founded, providing short-time temporary housing for patients' family members. Boy Scout Troop 42 served boys from a neighboring public housing complex and the parish. The Reverend Harry H.

Opposite Page: All Saints' Episcopal Church, Atlanta, West Peachtree Street facade.

Pritchett Jr. (1981–1997) came to All Saints' in a whirlwind of activity and continued the history of founding and serving many ministries. In the early 1980s, a homeless shelter was opened in the Parish House, serving fifty men each night. This became Covenant Community, a resident program to stabilize men recovering from alcohol and drug addiction.

One parishioner of All Saints' almost single-handedly started a tutoring program at C. W. Hill Elementary School, involving both the All Saints' congregation and Georgia Tech students. The parish collaborated with Exodus/Cities-in-Schools to target high school dropouts. An excellent Refugee Ministry focused on finding homes, food, clothing, and jobs for many families seeking refuge in the area. All Saints' has served within several agencies: Midtown Congregation Assistance Center, Episcopal Charities, Habitat for Humanity, and Meals on Wheels. Corporate donations enabled construction of the "Harry and Allison Pritchett Children's Center."

Renovations and additions have been ongoing since 1903, but perhaps the most outstanding undertaking was painting the apse red and gold in the early 1980s! The original church building has remained virtually the same since 1906. A spacious, beautiful Chapel replaced a small one in 1993. Music, always a top priority, engaged three organists/choirmasters for over twenty-five years each. Beth and Ray Chenault celebrated thirty years of excellent music in 2005. High choral standards now extend to several children's choirs. The recent installation of a John-Paul Buzzard organ provides beauty for the church and the community.

The Reverend Geoffrey M. St. John Hoare, becoming eighth rector in 1998, has carried on many traditional activities, such as the annual retreat at Kanuga near Hendersonville, North Carolina, informative communications, outstanding Christian education, and voluntarism especially in outreach and broadening the scope to include Global Missions. All Saints' has celebrated anniversaries in different ways: for the fiftieth—a new Parish Hall; for the seventy-fifth—an old-fashioned Jubilee; and for the one hundredth—a whole year of festivities! May all the Saints continue to celebrate, to seek and serve. Thanks be to God

Text submitted by Margaret Ellis Langford. Photos from the church archives.
Right: Chancel of All Saints' Episcopal Church, Atlanta.

✠   ✠   ✠   ✠

EPISCOPAL CHURCH OF THE GOOD SHEPHERD, AUSTELL

✢

Common wisdom holds that the Church of the Good Shepherd was established in 1905 in Austell. It was listed among those churches agreeing on May 16, 1907, to form the new Diocese of Atlanta. It was listed as one of twenty-three organized missions in 1910 and then as an "unorganized" mission in 1917. That congregation was dissolved some time in the 1930s or 1940s. Further history of that initial congregation remains lost.

In September 1961, a group of Episcopalians from Austell, Powder Springs, Lithia Springs, and Douglasville met to organize an Episcopal mission for the South Cobb—East Douglas County area. Services began in October of that year. In January 1962, the group petitioned the Diocese of Atlanta to become an organized mission. The Diocese granted its approval to become the Church of The Advent, Austell.

The church purchased six acres including a small house and a workshop, which was converted into the sanctuary. After several vicars served short tenures, the Reverend Robert Fisher became vicar in 1973 and served until his death in 1992. During his tenure, the church sanctuary was enlarged and the Diocese was petitioned to change the name to the Church of the Good Shepherd, Austell, thus reclaiming the earlier name.

Following the death of Father Fisher, the vestry petitioned the diocese for full-parish status. This was granted in 1993. Supply priests served until the Reverend Delmus Hare began his tenure (1993–1999). A modular building containing five classrooms, kitchen, and large meeting hall was built. Next Father Ronald Chrisner and Father Mark Moline served for two years each and in November 2003 the Reverend Canon Newell Anderson became the rector.

Good Shepherd is a small parish which conducts traditional services, and features music provided by the organist-led choir. A chapter of the Daughters of the King and an active Altar Guild contribute much to the life of the church. A major focus of the church is outreach. Along with other churches, organizations, and area businesses, Good Shepherd, Austell, supports Community Action Mission Program (CAMP) which assists the needy with food, clothing, and household goods. Donations of food and money are made every Sunday. In addition, a grant from the Diocese, supplemented by parish contributions, allows Good Shepherd to help people with utility bills and prescription medicines in emergency situations. On Mondays the church hosts a "come one—come all" community supper provided by Mission on the Move, a good-hearted group from Douglasville.

On Sunday and Monday nights a chapter of Alcoholics Anonymous meets at the church. Twice a year, Good Shepherd provides the food for the monthly Muscular Dystrophy dayroom hosted by St. Jude's in Smyrna.

Good Shepherd's sister congregation, New Commandment Ministries—"A new commandment I give unto you, that you love one another"—which is led by Pastor Jerry Brooks, holds services on Sunday afternoons and Bible study on Thursday evenings in the facility. The brothers and sisters of New Commandment are a blessing by their very presence and by their gracious willingness to take care of housekeeping and grounds maintenance. That congregation takes its name to heart.

An intrinsic mission is an ongoing residential alcohol-drug rehabilitation program, appropriately called Soul Changers, with a house for twenty-two men and another for eight women. Lost souls are welcomed, directed, and inspired through that ministry. The people of Good Shepherd meet critical needs in the community and with God's help will continue to serve its members and the community around it.

Text submitted by Frank Meadows. Photo from the Collins Collection, Diocese of Atlanta Archives.

✢ ✢ ✢

Church of the Good Shepherd, Austell.

ST. JOHN'S EPISCOPAL CHURCH, COLLEGE PARK

✚

On October 22, 1905, Bishop C. K. Nelson (then Bishop of the Diocese of Georgia) wrote: "College Park (St. John's): Held a meeting of Church people here and organized a Mission including 30 souls." That first meeting and service was on the second floor of the post office, still standing at the corner of John Wesley Avenue and Main Street. On October 14, 1906, Bishop Nelson returned to lay the cornerstone for a small stone church on the southeast corner of Hardin and Main. The parish did not first employ a priest, but Mr. C. K. Weller, a lay reader who eventually was ordained, officiated at most services.

As College Park, Hapeville, and East Point (the "Tri-Cities") grew, membership at St. John's increased until, in 1956, the current facility was built on the northeast corner of Hardin and Main. The donated land had been a pecan grove, and the church continues to enjoy many majestic pecan trees (and pecans!). The brick church is "English Gothic" with beautiful oak pews and glorious stained-glass windows from England.

St John's Episcopal Church, College Park.

In 1964, an Educational Building was attached to the church, and provides two floors of classrooms and offices. After that addition, St. John's School was built and operated until 1996, changing the lives of many students and families.

St. John's was vibrant and active in the community, famous for its festivals, dances, fellowship, and many outreach endeavors. The most notable outreach was founding the St. John's Bargain Shop in 1952, which still operates today (on Main Street in East Point) and which has raised over $1.1 million for good causes. The parish also reached out to the poor, and has sponsored refugee families.

The Tri-Cities area and the parish were prosperous. By 1969, St. John's had eleven hundred members. The 1970s became difficult for the area and the parish. Hartsfield International Airport expanded, condemning half the homes in College Park. MARTA (Metropolitan Atlanta Rapid Transit Authority) laid rapid transit lines along the railroad in the middle of town, reducing the number of at-grade crossings and cutting down the

The chancel in St. John's Episcopal Church, College Park.

As St. John's celebrates its centennial, it is also undergoing a renaissance: a renewed sense of mission, a reaching out to the community while nourishing its members. St. John's is very diverse racially, ethnically, and in terms of sexual orientation. In addition to operating the Bargain Shop, the parish runs "Begin Again," a supervised visitation center with the Fulton County Juvenile Court. Begin Again is a ministry of hospitality and reconciliation for distressed families. St. John's also takes dinner to Holy Comforter and worships with our friends there; supports Emmaus House in our budget and with special gifts at Christmas; supports work in Haiti; and provides strong support for Family Life Ministries (a ministry to the poor in the area). St. John's is proud to have hosted an AA group for over fifty years; and provided space to Odyssey Family Counseling Center (providing mental health services on a sliding fee scale) and Child and Adolescent Center. In recent years, we have resettled refugee families from Bosnia and Liberia, helped a family move from shelter to self-sufficiency, and continue to support the Interfaith Airport Chaplaincy.

The mission of St. John's Episcopal Church is to be a loving and diverse community celebrating the Good News of Jesus Christ by word, example, and service to others. Rectors have included: the Reverend C. K. Weller (1905–1913); the Reverend H. R. Chase (1921–1932); the Reverend W. E. Couch (1932–1943); the Reverend S. M. Hopson (1946–1953); the Reverend M. J. Ellis (1954–1955); the Reverend B. W. Lafebre (1955–1957); the Reverend J. R. Davidson (1957–1958); the Reverend E. C. Coleman (1958–1965); the Reverend Harold R. Bott (1965–1990); the Reverend Frank Larisy (1992–1994); the Reverend Stanley E. McGraw (1995–1997); and the Reverend James H. Pritchett Jr. (1998–Present).

Text and photos submitted by the Reverend James H. Pritchett Jr.

many dogwood trees along the tracks. As the population reduced and the demographics changed, the parish began to decline.

Today, College Park is referred to by *Atlanta Magazine* as "The Best Kept Secret in the Metro Area," but increasingly, the secret is out. The Historic District (including the church) is full of architecturally significant homes, and is listed on the National Register of Historic Places. There are new housing developments, and many older homes and the downtown area are being renovated. Developments at the airport will send much business toward College Park, a town of seventeen thousand.

✠   ✠   ✠   ✠

ST. JAMES' EPISCOPAL CHURCH, MACON

✠

At the birth of the twentieth century, Cherokee Heights was an exclusive subdivision on the north side of Macon. The professional and business people who lived there would ride the streetcar to and from Macon each business day. After a while, about seventy-five Episcopalians in the neighborhood became tired of either riding the streetcar into Christ Church or walking two miles to St. Paul's. The other alternative, to hitch up the team, was another inconvenience since it was the servants' day off and they were in their Sunday best. So they decided to form their own church.

On October 27, 1911, seven men met with the Reverend John S. Bunting, rector of Christ Church, in the home of Alexander Blair Sr. After other meetings, the first Sunday school met in the home of the L. P Hillyers on January 21, 1912, with thirty-five children and adults attending. The $1.40 collection was donated to the building fund.

St. James' was admitted to the Diocese as a mission at Council in 1912, and accepted as a parish the following year. The first church building was completed either in 1912 or 1915, "a little box of a building containing a most cantankerous and temperamental stove and a funny little pipe organ."

The story of the naming of St. James' is unclear. Legend has it that the parishioners wanted to name the church after St. James, the Greater, but there was already a church so named within the Diocese. The Bishop required that it be named in honor of St. James, the Lesser. The congregation yielded, but quickly dropped it from their title and their memory. Current practice is to give equal honor to all three James in the Bible.

By the 1950s, the church building, which had been expanded and modernized several times, was again operating at capacity, with chairs in the aisles. Macon had grown to surround Cherokee Heights and these were the years of the flight to the suburbs. Plans were made to follow the trend—and many of the membership—and move the church North. However, several of the old families objected and prevailed upon Bishop Claiborne, who had been their rector, to let St. James' stay. As a compromise, St. Francis' was established as a mission, and a number of the St. James' families left to be a part of that new church.

Today, St. James' is a small but active congregation, largely made up of white folks in a neighborhood that has become largely African American. It is a diverse group in other ways, including people from all walks of life. In fact, the only thing most of the members have in common is the church. Repeated efforts to bring in members from the neighborhood have not been successful, but continue.

In addition, the church supports and houses in its Parish Hall the Appleton Youth Ministry, a free after-school program for neighborhood kids which meets in the Parish Hall and involves help with homework, including the use of computers for research projects, Bible study, and activities. According to Diocesan canons, this Youth Ministry project is primarily financed by the Diocese of Atlanta's Appleton Family Ministries Trust and Thanksgiving offerings from the churches of the Diocese. This ministry takes no government funds.

Members are active in such ministries as Loaves and Fishes, an ecumenical ministry to the poor and homeless, and the weekend lunch program sponsored by Christ Church. One member serves as advisor to the Episcopal student group at Mercer University. The church sponsors one of the girls at the Little Roses Home for Girls in Honduras. Other members are active in Cursillo. There is a group of knitters who knit shawls as gifts to persons who are ill or otherwise under stress.

In 1997, a bequest from the estates of Gladys and Marvin Waters enabled St. James' to establish the Living Waters Trust, the income from which is used to support causes outside the parish. Grants are usually divided equally between local, Diocesan, and national church projects.

In summary, St. James' is a small but dynamic congregation, which fills a unique role in Macon and the Diocese.

Text submitted by the Reverend Carl Buice. Photo by Dale and Susan Myers.

Opposite Page: St. James' Episcopal Church, Macon, achieved parish status in 1913.

✠   ✠   ✠   ✠

CHAPTER THREE

THE ROARING TWENTIES, GREAT DEPRESSION, AND WORLD WARS

THE SECOND DECADE OF THE NEW DIOCESE OPENED WITH COUNCIL MEETING AT ST. PAUL'S CHURCH, MACON, ON APRIL 18, 1917. AFTER A TRIBUTE TO THE MEMORY OF BISHOP Nelson by the Right Reverend Theodore Bratton, the delegates began the work of electing a new bishop. After seventeen ballots, the exhausted Council elected the Reverend R. S. Coupland, rector of Trinity Church, New Orleans, who then declined the nomination! On June 26, 1917, a special meeting of the tenth Council, met at St. Philip's Cathedral and elected the Reverend Henry Judah Mikell of Christ Church, Nashville, Tennessee, and he became the second Bishop of the new Diocese on November 1, 1917.

The Bishop acknowledged Nelson's legacy and outlined his goals for the coming years in his first address, April 17, 1918, at St. Philip's. He mentioned the need for winning the war and calling for the dedication of the people, adding, "Now that we are facing realities let us make our service to the Church more real. The world needs the Church, and the things of Christ for which the Church stands as never before. Let us help the Church to meet this need, let us enable it to meet the demands of a trying time by giving it the strength of our individual work and contribution."

Strong feelings still prevailed among many towards the integration of the black community into the mainstream of Southern life. The Diocese of Atlanta had established a number of African American congregations during its first decade. Bishop Mikell emphasized the importance of fairness with regard to race and economic status. At Council at St. George's, Griffin, May 5, 1920, he claimed: "Our church is the only church doing any considerable work among our colored people which is not divided according to color into two organizations. This ought to give us a unique opportunity to make our influence felt towards a right relationship between the two races."

The Cathedral's location became the object of a resolution at the Council in St. James, Cedartown, May 11, 1927. Presented by the Reverend S. Alston Wragg, rector of Trinity Church, Columbus, the document noted that the urban growth around the present site required a location "more appropriate and more inspiring." Here began the effort to locate and secure property, which resulted in the acquisition of a lot at the corner of Peachtree Road and Andrews Drive, where the seat of the Bishop is located today.

At the twenty-first Council at St. Peter's, Rome, January 25–26, 1928, Bishop Mikell reviewed the past ten years of his episcopate. Communicants had grown from 5,644 to 7,203, representing a 23 percent increase. Mikell decried the closing of many mission stations due to membership drops and lack of enthusiasm. The twenties marked a happy time in United States history relative to the looming days of the Depression. Like the rest of the nation, the Diocese of Atlanta had danced through the Roaring Twenties!

✛   ✛   ✛   ✛

THE SUN SETS ON THE MIKELL YEARS

✠

In October 1929, the country's economy crashed like a house of cards. There is no mention of this financial crisis in Bishop Mikell's diary, however in his address to Council, January 22, 1930, in All Saints, Atlanta, he referred to "bad business conditions" and challenged the delegates not to use this as an "excuse for reduced benevolence." But the Depression years fell hard upon Georgia and the nation and giving to the churches suffered. The Diocesan newspaper during the early 1930s presented many articles on stewardship.

One Diocesan project that commanded attention during these years was the Appleton Church Home in Macon. This institution, established shortly after the Civil War by New York publisher William H. Appleton, initially provided a home for orphaned girls of Confederate soldiers. A community of deaconesses provided the care and nurture to the girls. In the mid-twenties, the home sold its original buildings to St. Paul's, Macon, and moved to twenty-five acres near the city. This home presented annual regular reports to the Diocesan Council and almost every congregation made regular contributions to its mission and ministry.

Bishop Mikell enjoyed camping and as early as 1922, he gathered a group of boys on farmland near LaGrange for the very first "Camp Mikell." By 1937, a camp at Toccoa Falls had a staff of twelve people for one hundred children under the direction of the Reverend Randolph Claiborne. By 1940, 262 acres of mountain and valley land had been purchased near Toccoa to form Camp Mikell. Opened in June of 1941, the Diocese continues to enjoy this resource for camps and conferences.

Another important emphasis during the thirties and forties involved work with the colleges, especially the University of Georgia. Largely under the supervision of Emmanuel Church, Athens, the National Church, in 1937, assigned Louise Starr, the daughter of an Episcopal priest, as "Student Secretary." That year, out of 2,500 students at the University, 195 were Episcopalians.

Bishop Mikell died February 20, 1942, a few months short of a twenty-five-year episcopate. The United States had entered the World War and the Bishop's last issue of *The Diocesan Record* was dedicated to the church's ministry to the armed forces. The Bishop began his term in financial hardship and ended it praying for peace in a world torn by war.

✠   ✠   ✠   ✠

THE WAR YEARS

✠

It took two days and twelve ballots to elect the Reverend John Moore Walker, rector of St. Luke's, Atlanta, as the new Bishop. A native of Macon, Walker had been rector of St. Luke's eleven years and received Holy Orders in 1913. His election took place April 29–30, 1942, in St. Peter's, Rome.

In his first address to the next Council, May 12, 1943, at Emmanuel Church, Athens, Bishop Walker mentioned three issues which he felt challenged the Diocese: (1) support for the men and women of the Armed Forces; (2) race relations; and (3) Christian unity. Walker said, "White Churchmen must cultivate an open-mindedness, must school themselves to the possibility of revising some of their points of view, and must never permit themselves to become creatures of prejudice."

The war in Europe and the Pacific and its resolution consumed much energy of the people of the Diocese during the early years of Walker's episcopate. Walker, himself, spoke out on the importance of institutions—both secular and religious—to insure a lasting peace. In the February 1945 *Diocesan Record*, the Bishop wrote, "We are rapidly approaching one of the most decisive of moments of crisis. Either a time of Just and Durable Peace, or times of ever more progressive destruction and terror face us and our children." He urged his readers to write the president and other national leaders to support the formation of "A World Religious Advisory Commission" to give a moral and spiritual basis to the peace efforts.

The postwar years brought radical changes for the Episcopal Church and the Diocese of Atlanta: massive cultural changes caused by the nation's effort to supply personnel and materials for battle; women working in factories producing arms and other military needs; and families moving as their members traveled to various duty or work stations. Seven current congregations were added during Walker's tenure: All Saints, Warner Robins (1944); St. Andrew's, Hartwell (1946); Mediator, Washing-ton (1948); Calvary, Cornelia (1950); St. Michael and All Angels, Stone Mountain (1950); St. Martin's-in-the-Fields, Atlanta (1951); and Good Shepherd, Covington (1951).

On July 16, 1951, Bishop Walker died at his home at the age of sixty-two. A memorial essay in the September 1951 *Diocesan Record* described him as "a benedic-tion to all who came under his influence. He lived from day to day according to the profession that he made. His was a full ministry, crowded with honors and responsibilities; but his kindly pastoral administrations will live on in the hearts of those he served, as a memorial to a truly great man."

Walker's episcopate opened with war in Europe and closed with war in Korea. Yet, the years included notable strides in race relations and Christian unity. Several all-black congregations had been closed and encouraged to worship with former white congregations. The Bishop noted with pride in a letter to the diocese, "The United Nations represents the civilized and reasonable method of meeting international frictions."

For a brief time, the leadership of the Diocese of Atlanta passed on to the Right Reverend John Buckman Walthour, dean of St. Philip's Cathedral since 1947. He was elected on the sixteenth ballot in Trinity Church, Columbus, October 9, 1951, and died October 29, 1952, at the age of forty-eight, ten months after his consecration. His death began in the pulpit of St. James Church, Cedartown, with a changed expression noted by his wife, Margaret. He completed the homily hastily saying, "Death is like going through an open door. We shed one garment and put on another. It is not hard to die. . . ." He died fifteen minutes later in a local hospital. Once again, the Diocese of Atlanta faced the task of finding a new bishop.

Text submitted by the Reverend William McLemore.

✠   ✠   ✠   ✠

ST. LUKE'S EPISCOPAL CHURCH, FORT VALLEY
✠

St. Luke's Episcopal Church, Fort Valley.

St. Luke's Parish had its origins in the Episcopal Church support of Fort Valley High and Industrial School in 1913, which it operated from 1919 until 1939. This was done in partnership with the American Church Institute for Negroes in New York, the Diocese of Atlanta, and the Diocese of Georgia.

Previously, the school, which began in 1895, was served by visiting clergy who officiated irregularly in a classroom or outside under a tree with a desk or table as the altar. In 1939 the school became Fort Valley State College and part of the University System of Georgia, Fort Valley College Center and Chapel officially became St. Luke's Episcopal Church in 1958.

Through a gift from New York philanthropist Ethel Mary Cheney Thorne, the current building was designed by Stanislaw Makieski and constructed in 1939–1940. The church continues as a vibrant and active congregation and mission of the Diocese of Atlanta. Its primary ministry is to the now Fort Valley State University and the surrounding community.

Text submitted by the Reverend Dr. Robert Robinson. Photo provided courtesy Absolom Jones Center archives.

✠   ✠   ✠   ✠

THE CHURCH OF OUR SAVIOUR, ATLANTA

✛

In 1924, forty-three people, mostly communicants of the Church of the Epiphany, met with Bishop Henry Judah Mikell and petitioned him to organize them as a parish. They desired a church which would provide more fully the Catholic worship and traditions of the Episcopal Church than the other parishes at that time. After several names were proposed, Bishop Mikell chose "The Church of Our Saviour," insisting that *Saviour* be spelled with a "u."

After meeting in homes and other churches for a period, the parish built a church at the corner of North Highland and Los Angeles Avenues in 1925. Over time, brick has been added to the old wooden structure, vestibule, Lady Chapel, and Rectory; but the church has continued in the same spot. Around 1960, apparently part of the congregation wanted to move the church out to suburbia; but after a divisive vote, the church stayed. Many parishioners did leave and contributed to the development of St. Bartholomew's and St. Bede's Churches.

The first two rectors, Father George Gasque (1924–1926) and Father Joseph Gubbins (1927–1928), had Anglo-Catholic origins. They introduced Eucharistic vestments, incense, and Stations of the Cross. For a period of ten years thereafter, the rectors were not Anglo-Catholic. Woolsey Couch (1930–1932) who came as a deacon, was ordained priest in 1930 as the third rector. In these Depression years when the cathedral could not afford a canon and dean, the Reverend William S. Turner was simultaneously canon of the Cathedral, vicar of the Church of the Ascension in Cartersville, and the fourth rector (1932–1935). In 1936, the Reverend Charles F. Schilling became both canon of the Cathedral and the fifth rector (1936–1940).

When Father Samuel C. W. Fleming (1941–1945) became rector, he restored the mass as the principal Sunday service. The Church of Our Saviour has continued as an intentionally Anglo-Catholic parish ever since. The church was consecrated by the Right Reverend John Moore Walker, Bishop of Atlanta, on November 30, 1944.

The long tenure of Father Roy Pettway (1945–1984) saw the development of the church's own liturgy with plainchant, an order of subdeacons, and reservation of the sacrament. Beginning in 1953, the church supported a parish missionary in Japan. The rector held services that led to the formation later of St. Martin's in the Fields. In 1950, the rector organized the Church of the Good Shepherd in Covington. A crucifix carved by a parishioner, Kendall Dane, was installed over the altar in 1962. Father Pettway was baptized in the Holy Spirit in 1970 and opened the church to the charismatic renewal. Small prayer groups were formed, healing masses, and lay prayer leaders were active.

Church of Our Saviour, Atlanta, built in 1925.

Father Thad Rudd (1984–1989) made Our Saviour's presence known in the neighborhood, incorporating many into the life of the church. He resigned in 1989 and was received into the Roman Catholic Church, which formed an "Anglican Use" congregation with some of our former members.

The ninth rector, Father Warren Tanghe (1990–2005), brought an emphasis on scholarship, teaching church history, liturgics, Christian formation, quiet days, and retreats. As a small congregation (about 125 communicants) widely dispersed, members of the church have sought out other groups to help in doing outreach: Nicholas House at St. Bartholomew's, Intown Community Ministries, and Gift of Grace House (Mother Teresa's Missionaries of Charity). A parish missionary was aided in Zimbabwe until the political climate forced him to leave. The church has also been host to several AA groups, a Serbian Orthodox congregation, and two Ethiopian Orthodox churches.

Church controversies have affected the congregation's numbers and morale. Many members consider the ordination of women a departure from the tradition of the undivided church, and so in 1992, the parish affiliated with the Episcopal Synod of America—which became Forward in Faith/North America (FIF/NA). For ten years Father Tanghe was the national secretary of this organization, which witnesses to Catholic, apostolic, and Biblical faith. After General Convention of 2003, along with other orthodox parishes and dioceses, Our Saviour joined the Anglican Communion Network. The question continues to be asked, can one be Catholic in the Episcopal Church? For eighty-one years, our answer has been "yes."

Now the parish is in the search process for a new rector with Father Keithly Warner the interim rector. But the church is trying to be a witness to the Catholic faith within this communion, sometimes in tension, sometimes in celebration, but always, hopefully, in love.

Text submitted by Dowman Wilson, with materials by Fathers Roy Pettway and Samuel Fleming. Photos by Mary Carolyn Pindar.

Right: View of altar crucifix carved by Kendall Dane in 1962 at the Church of Our Saviour, Atlanta.

THE EPISCOPAL CHURCH OF ST. ALBAN, ELBERTON

✠

The first known Episcopal service in Elberton, the Granite Capital of the World, was held on September 10, 1894, in the Methodist Church. The service was conducted by the Reverend O. T. Percher of Greenwood, South Carolina. The first organized Episcopal community was the Church of the Apostles in 1898, a ministry in the Diocese of Georgia. It was a mission church, which faltered and was disbanded in 1906. Services began anew in 1909—as part of the new Diocese of Atlanta—under the leadership of the Reverend Thomas Duck of Toccoa.

By the 1930s the mission was meeting in the home of Dr. and Mrs. Albert S. Hawes with services conducted by the Reverend David Cady of Athens. The name of the church was changed in 1941 to the Church of St. Alban, after the young first martyr of Britain, and an exquisite new church was constructed of native Elbert County granite. Bishop Henry Judah Mikell formally consecrated the structure that year. The building is solid granite, welcoming the worshiper in a warm environment of granite, exposed wooden beams, and a panorama of custom-designed stained-glass windows depicting the life of Christ.

Granite for constructing the new church building was donated by B. Frank Coggins Sr. His sons, Frank and John Coggins, are currently active communicants. The Reverend James Know Yeary, who recently served as canon for worship and administration at the Cathedral of St. Philip in Atlanta, had been the first infant baptized at the new font in the new church on April 26, 1942, by the Reverend J. B. Ellington. His mother, Mrs. Katherine Yeary, is still a member and has served as St. Alban's treasurer for over thirty years.

St. Alban's was granted full parish status in 1960. St. Alban's and St. Andrew's, Hartwell, were yoked partners in ministry from the 1940s until 2001, when St. Andrew's became an independent parish. The longest serving rector of the period was the Reverend Herschel Atkinson, from 1970 until October 31, 1997. On the occasion of his retirement he was given the title "rector emeritus." The Reverend James Shumard served the yoked parishes from 1997 through June 2001. St. Alban's alone was then served on a part-time basis by an interim rector, the Reverend Gene Britton, until August 2004. At that time, after a year of careful discussion and negotiation, St. Alban's formally yoked its ministry with the Church of the Mediator, Washington, thirty miles away, with the Very Reverend Dr. John Via serving as rector of the two parishes until mid-2006.

A small but vibrant group of parishioners live and teach by example the Good News in Christ. The parish is highly visible in the community. Vigorous parish groups include the Altar Guild, the Episcopal Church Women, and the Friday Bible Class, which draws members from that larger community and the mainline downtown churches of Elberton. Civic groups use the undercroft of the Parish Hall as their meeting place. The parish is a principal supporter of the SafeHouse Ministry, a local agency, which addresses the needs of battered women, of families in trouble, and of individuals who have trouble in their families. SafeHouse support has also come from the Episcopal Charities Foundation. St. Alban's provides the largest number of volunteers at the Elbert Memorial Hospital of any religious denomination. Other parishioners volunteer for the local Humane Society, Habitat for Humanity, various civic clubs and organizations, and tutor in several disciplines at various locations throughout the area.

Submitted by Mary Randall and the Reverend John Via. Photo by the Reverend John Via.

✠　　✠　　✠　　✠

St. Alban Episcopal Church, Elberton

CAMP MIKELL, TOCCOA

✛

Camp Mikell began its existence soon after Bishop Mikell became Bishop in 1917. In 1922 he experimented with a camp near LaGrange. During the first part of 1934, Bishop Mikell asked Scottie Eppes, a missionary stationed in the North Georgia field, to explore the possibility of having a two-week camp at the Toccoa Falls Institute. The result was the holding of our first of six camps for young people, ages fourteen to eighteen.

This was a fine arrangement with a swimming pool, tennis courts, ball field, and hills for hiking, but other groups in the church wanted to camp. Younger boys and girls, adults, and church groups of the Diocese needed a place for retreats, conferences, and camps. At the Diocesan Council in Macon, January 26, 1939, a camp committee meeting was held at which various campsites were discussed.

After the inspection of several sites, on June 12, 1939, Yearwood Valley in Toccoa was visited. It was decided on a rainy day in March 1940, after a visit by Bishop Mikell, that this would be the place for the Diocesan Camp. On June 9, 1941, carpenters completed their work on the buildings and camp opened that day.

During the 1950s, the dorms that are still presently used were built, as was the swimming pool that lasted through the summer of 2002. The Episcopal Church Women (ECW) of the Diocese were vital in supporting this construction. During these years, a multitude of seminarians and Diocesan staff directed the summer programs.

In the late 1970s, Bishop Sims had a vision about Mikell becoming a year-round conference center. The Reverend Charles and Wilmarose Davis were hired to make this dream a reality. The first order of business was to winterize and prepare the old cabins and chapel for winter conferences. There were no curtains, no lamps, no rugs, and no linens in the rooms. Many of the mattresses needed replacing. Much of the wiring and plumbing needed replacing.

The Board of Governors allotted about $20,000 for the initial face lift. The Board also began working on plans for a

Camp Mikell Chapel, built in 1941.

new dining hall. The chapel was also a main focus for refurbishing. It was dark and cold in appearance with a gray cement floor, a dark brown ceiling, a distant altar, and the heating system was inadequate. The chapel was improved to be bright, warm, and inviting. In 1981, the new Nelson Dining Hall was completed. Also in the early 1980s, a ropes course was built under the supervision of Bob Carr and from support of Holy Innocents.

During Bishop Child's tenure, there was new energy put into Mikell becoming a first-rate conference center as well as an outstanding summer camp. In the late 1980s, the Board completed plans for building a new dormitory as well as the retreat village, which was later named for Bishop Child. Carmen Jordan took over Mikell's directorship in the late 1980s and served until the mid-1990s. The Blue Ridge Outdoor Education Center began during his time at Mikell. In 1997, the Reverend John Hall became the director and served Mikell and the Diocese well through 2001. The Reverend Ken Struble became director in August 2002 and remains in that position. In 2002, the pool became unusable due to aging, and the Board decided to build a fine and safe pool complex. It was put into operation for the summer of 2003.

Mikell continues to serve the Diocese of Atlanta as a year-round facility accredited through the American Camp Association; to operate the acclaimed Blue Ridge Outdoor Education Center; and to host various Diocesan and non-Diocesan groups. Mikell has remained a central ministry of the Diocese of Atlanta for over sixty years, and many people's lives, both lay and ordained, have been affected by the life and ministry of Mikell.

Text and photos submitted by the Reverend Ken Struble.

Right: Youth enjoy the pool at Camp Mikell.

St. Andrew's Episcopal Church, Hartwell

✠

St. Andrew's story is one of faith beginning in May 1946 when Charles and Mary Eleanor Kidd moved to Hartwell from Alabama. There was no Episcopal church in Hartwell and no rector at St. Alban's, Elberton, so they attended Grace Episcopal Church in Anderson, South Carolina.

While visiting the Kidd's in their Hartwell home, the Reverend Roddie Reid wrote Bishop John Moore Walker suggesting the Hartwell Episcopalians start a mission and offering to assist this process. The Bishop soon assigned the Reverend Britt Ellington to St. Alban's in Elberton with instructions to minister to the Hartwell Episcopalians also.

The small Hartwell congregation chose the name St. Andrew's and held services in their homes. The Presbyterian Church soon offered St. Andrew's use of its facilities for one Saturday night service a month. The congregation accepted the offer with much appreciation and held their first evening service there in 1948, continuing for about five years.

Because of health problems Father Ellington soon left. The Reverend Victor Nicholson, already sworn into service as a Navy chaplain, took Father Ellington's place for a few months until he reported to active duty. Four priests served St. Andrew's while it held worship services in the Presbyterian Church: the Reverends Harrison Black, Toccoa; John Paul Jones, Washington; Roberts Bailey, Gainesville; and Martin Tilson, Anderson, South Carolina.

In 1956 the Reverend Bill Yon became rector for both Hartwell and Elberton. Young, energetic, and dedicated, he sought a place to hold weekly Sunday school classes and Sunday morning services. Use of the Hartwell Community Club House was secured.

Meanwhile, the U.S. Corps of Engineers' Lake Hartwell Dam plans were approved and a number of Episcopalians involved in that project moved to Hartwell. With the influx of new members, Father Yon and the members felt it was time to build their own church and had faith that they could reach this goal. There were many others in the community who supported St. Andrew's in many ways.

Right: St. Andrew's Episcopal Church, Hartwell.

Before construction began in 1960, Father Yon was called to the Diocese of Alabama as youth director. Father Frank Fortune became rector for both St. Andrew's and St. Alban's for five years. On Easter Sunday, 1961, Father Fortune and St. Andrew's members held the first service in their new chapel. Bishop Claiborne consecrated the new debt-free church on June 19, 1961.

In 1966, Father Milton Coward replaced Father Fortune, followed by Herschel Atkinson, who had retired from a career in the military when he began his second career as rector of the yoked parishes of St. Andrew's and St. Alban's. He served with grace and dedication for twenty-seven years with his last service on October 26, 1997.

By the mid-1980s the chapel was outgrown. The number of communicants had increased and had faith that they could build a new church. On St. Andrew's Day, November 30, 1987, Bishop Child consecrated the new church. All expenses had been completely paid before it was dedicated. When the Hartwell Lutherans organized in 1993, they were invited to use the Episcopal sanctuary for their services at 11:00 a.m. In 1999, Father Jim Shumard became the rector of St. Andrew's and in 2001 Father Cass Daly became rector. Under Daly's leadership, the church has become an "un-yoked," independent parish with its first full-time rector. The operating and outreach budgets have grown substantially and the altar and choir loft renovations have been completed, and a Memorial Garden built. St. Andrew's is a community leader in both spiritual and civic matters, ecumenical partners with the Presbyterians and Lutherans and continues as a strong Episcopal presence in Northeast Georgia. The journey in faith continues.

Text submitted by Mary Jackson. Photos from the church archives.

St. Andrew's Episcopal Church, Hartwell, Fellowship Hour.

Episcopal Campus Ministries, Georgia Tech and Georgia State University

✠

In 1949, after some discussion on how All Saints' Episcopal Church could be more involved in outreach in the growing Atlanta community, the first Canterbury Club was established at the church. Serving men from Georgia Tech and women from Agnes Scott, the Club served both social and spiritual needs of the students to whom it ministered.

In its early years, the success of the ministry was due largely to the involvement of generous parishioners. Frank and Mimi Player were among the leaders of the Canterbury support team. They arranged for volunteers to bring women back and forth to church from Agnes Scott, encouraged parishioners to take students home for Sunday dinner, planned and chaperoned dances in the Parish Hall, and offered up their Lake Burton

Episcopal Church Ministries—Georgia Tech and Georgia State.

lodge for many a college retreat weekend. The first chaplain was the Reverend Robert Mill, who arrived in 1954 and grew Canterbury Club to over two hundred students. Many romances blossomed from that group and from groups in the years to come and many Canterbury Club marriages were made between Scott women and Tech men.

In the last twenty years, as the Tech student body now includes women and Agnes Scott is now served by its local parish, Holy Trinity, Decatur, All Saints' has shifted its focus to include Georgia Tech and Georgia State University. The ministry is now called Episcopal Campus Ministries (ECM).

The motto of ECM is "the piece you've been missing." We support students through the difficult and exciting years of college and help them maintain ties to their church communities, while also making new ties to the All Saints' community. Programs include contemporary worship and more traditional Rite II Eucharist, Sunday brunch, cultural trips around the city, as well as frequent service opportunities around the Diocese.

In 1967, the Constitution of "The Canterbury Association of All Saints' Church" on file at Georgia Tech read: "The purpose of the Association is to serve the mission of Christianity in higher education by fostering among students a better understanding of the faith and practice of the Episcopal Church and the Christian Church Universal."

The students look a little different and the programs have a different flavor, but the purpose remains true the same. With a focus on worship, service, and fellowship, ECM brings together undergraduate and graduate students, professors, parishioners, and clergy to understand the work of God in the individual, the city, and the larger world.

Episcopal chaplains who have served include the Reverends Robert Mill, James Coleman, Harwood Bartlett, Phillip Cato, Paul Thim, Michael Milligan, Jon Bonell, Benno Pattison, Ellen Gallow, Thomas Morris, Denni Moss, and Noelle York-Simmons.

Text and photos submitted by the Reverend Noelle York-Simmons.

✠   ✠   ✠   ✠

ST. MICHAEL AND ALL ANGELS EPISCOPAL CHURCH, STONE MOUNTAIN

✠

St. Michael and All Angels started as a mission fifty-five years ago. The Reverend Harry Tisdale, rector of Holy Trinity Parish, Decatur, encouraged several parishioners to establish a church in the Stone Mountain/Clarkston area. On September 24, 1950, fifteen men, women, and children met in the William and Kathryn Beene home to begin this work. The following Sunday evening, Reverend Tisdale celebrated Holy Eucharist at the Stone Mountain Women's Club House. Twenty-four people attended this first service, celebrated on the Feast of St. Michael and All Angels, which was the source of the church's name.

The community welcomed the mission church. The commander of the VFW post offered the use of the VFW Hall's upper room chapel for Sunday services. Mayor Julian T. Harris and his wife, Margaret, were also very supportive of the mission. He served as senior warden during the parish's early years and Margaret served as the church's first choir director. The congregation erected a permanent church building after a donation of land in Stone Mountain Village and dedicated it on February 14, 1954.

The first community ministry was a thrift shop founded by the Episcopal Church Women (ECW). Its dual purpose was to serve the community and to help support the young church. A thriving outreach ministry throughout the years, the shop nets about $30,000 a year, with half used for community outreach and half for the church's needs.

St. Michael and All Angels, Stone Mountain, artist's sketch.

Another community ministry, the After School Program (ASP), was established in the early 1990s. The ASP was founded in response to a parish desire to help the church's surrounding neighborhood. It provides a safe, educational, and enjoyable environment for neighborhood children who otherwise would be "latchkey kids." Fees charged are about one-quarter of comparable commercial rates, and scholarships are available. The ASP is overseen by a paid director and loyal volunteers. The parish also supports the community through the Stone Mountain Cooperative Ministries program, with volunteers and donations of food.

Ministry, spiritual growth, and educational opportunities include Education for Ministry, Wednesday Morning Women's Bible Study, Christian Yoga and Meditation, ECW, a Seniors Ministry Group, and Daughters of the King. Sunday morning education classes are offered for all ages. The preschool and elementary children participate in Catechesis of the Good Shepherd, a Montessori-based program of spiritual formation. Youth take part in the Journey to Adulthood spiritual formation program. Adult education classes, intergenerational education programs and confirmation classes are also offered.

As Stone Mountain and Clarkston have become international communities, the church's five hundred baptized members reflect this international diversity. All parts of the worldwide Anglican Communion are represented. Some parishioners were born in Atlanta, and some have come from Europe, the Caribbean, the Americas, and Africa. The staff also represents various parts of the Anglican world. The Reverend Dr. Paul A. Elliott, rector, is from Queensland, Australia; the assisting priest, Ahamefula Echecka, is from Nigeria; and the assisting deacon, Cora Saunders, hails from the Virgin Islands.

Worship and music style reflect the international makeup. On any Sunday, besides standard hymns, the music may include traditional folk songs of the American South and from the Caribbean. Parish potlucks are feasts, featuring dishes from around the world sitting side-by-side with traditional Southern favorites. Throughout its fifty-five years, St. Michael and All Angels has been a friendly and welcoming church, seeking to serve and be part of the communities of Stone Mountain and Clarkston. The congregants strive to support each other and to reach out to the larger community.

Text submitted by Victoria H. Schwartz. Sketch from the church archives.

✠   ✠   ✠   ✠

ST. MARTIN IN THE FIELDS, ATLANTA

✠

In unlikely fashion, St. Martin in the Fields formed partly because of a death in the family. In 1948, the rector of St. Luke's Church, the Reverend Milton Richardson, had to drive all the way to Dunwoody to perform last rites. While Father Richardson and the decedent's family awaited the hearse, they discussed the need for a church in northeast Atlanta.

There was no Episcopal church between the Cathedral of St. Philip in Buckhead and Grace Church in Gainesville. A survey in 1950 found that many Episcopalians lived in Brookhaven, Oglethorpe, Chamblee, Dunwoody, and Doraville. The Very Reverend John B. Walthour of the Cathedral of St. Philip called three of those Episcopalians to join him for lunch. Two of those three were women. St. Martin's was organized as the Oglethorpe Mission and admitted to the Diocese on May 9, 1951, with services held in the chapel at Oglethorpe University.

In 1951, a parcel of land on Ashford Dunwoody Road was purchased from Oglethorpe and other purchases have provided a total of more than seven acres. Oglethorpe University was named for General James Edward Oglethorpe, founder of the Colony of Georgia. Because he was a member of St. Martin in the Fields, London, England, the mission was named after that church.

There were seventy-four communicants in June of 1952 when the Reverend A. L. Burgreen became the first vicar. The mission grew rapidly, and on Christmas Eve, 1954, the first service was held in the new chapel, which is the present church. In January 1956, Saint Martin's became a full parish.

From 1959 to mid-1965, the Reverend Samuel T. Cobb, a canon from the Cathedral of St. Philip, served as rector. Cobb, a strong education advocate, founded the Day School—a kindergarten of two classes with forty-three children. An Educational Building, Pierce Hall, was completed in 1961 and has evolved into St. Martin's Episcopal School, with nearly six hundred pre-kindergarten through eighth grade students.

Right: St. Martin in the Fields Episcopal Church.

Chapel remodeling in 1963 began with the addition of side aisles, a balcony, and other improvements and was completed April 5, 1965, almost doubling the size of the church. The church building has not been added to since, which explains St. Martin's five services every Saturday and Sunday for its two thousand members.

The Reverend Martin Dewey Gable was called in the fall of 1965 and served as rector for nearly twenty-four years. The current Parish Hall, named in his honor, was dedicated on December 11, 1977. It provided a large room to accommodate four hundred people, a kitchen, office space, parlor, choir room, and additional classrooms. The bell tower, with three bells, was dedicated on April 29, 1984, and is a source of great joy.

An Education Building, including a library, school office, and classrooms, was dedicated on January 10, 1988, and named Claiborne Hall, in memory of the Right Reverend Randolph R. Claiborne, D.D., the fifth Bishop of the Diocese of Atlanta and fellow parishioner. The robust growth of St. Martin's Episcopal School necessitated a further enlargement of Claiborne Hall. A new wing with eight classrooms was dedicated on September 6, 1991, and was named Young Hall after a former school headmaster. The current headmaster of St. Martin's is the Reverend Dr. James E. Hamner.

Following Father Gable's death, St. Martin's called the parish's fourth rector, the Reverend Douglas E. Remer, in January 1991. Under his leadership, St. Martin's continued its growth and service. In 1998 and 1999, the parish and school completed an expansion program including a Family Life Center with gymnasium and a classroom building, and extensively renovated almost all of the existing facilities.

St. Martin's has played a role in seeding other churches in the fast-growing northeast Atlanta region. Parishes it has helped inaugurate over the years include St. Patrick's and St. Columba's. The latter was the recipient of more than $55,000 raised as part of St. Martin's fiftieth anniversary celebration in 2001.

When Father Remer departed, St. Martin's Vestry called in 2004 the parish's fifth rector, the Reverend John F. McCard. Under his leadership, the parish has resumed its historic growth cycle and is a significant part of the community of faith in the northeast Atlanta area, "sharing its cloak" in St. Martin's style with the community. Now there are nearly a dozen Episcopal churches between Buckhead and Gainesville, and the many baptisms, confirmations, weddings, and funerals that take place in them are reflective of good long-range planning and a desire to live up to the parish mission statement: "To follow Christ and to lead others to him."

Text submitted by Tom Smith. Photos submitted by Tom Smith and Christopher Jost.

✛   ✛   ✛   ✛

Participants from St. Martin's in the "McCard Leap" sky diving fundraiser, pictured left to right: Charles Mixson, Dennis Matthews, Steve Short, Steve Hurlburt, Father John McCard, and Christopher Jost.

CHURCH OF THE GOOD SHEPHERD, COVINGTON

✠

With the theme "Celebrating Our Past: Building Our Future," Good Shepherd broke ground for a new church building and new era on August 28, 2005. The rector wrote, "Fifty-five years ago a small group of faithful Episcopalians worked and sacrificed to build a church to the glory of God in this community. . . . We celebrate the founders' work. . . . "

In 1950, Bea Tribble, an Episcopalian devoted to establishing a parish in Newton County, convened local Episcopalians. Regular services followed. A gift of land and substantial financial support from a few individuals, some of them local non-Episcopalians, allowed the construction of a church building, dedicated on September 17, 1951. The first Vestry was W. Ross Chambers (senior warden), James Rogers (junior warden), L. J. Moore, R. A. Tribble, and Ned Freeman. Mrs. M. L. Bolton and Mr. John G. Bolton were chosen secretary and treasurer, respectively. Two inspiring memorial stained-glass windows were dedicated in 1952. Because of its apparently strong financial condition, Good Shepherd became a parish without first having mission status.

Following the first rector, the Reverend J. F. G. Hopper, who served through 1952, are Henry A. Zinser (1953–57); Peyton Splane (1957–60); Gordon Mann (1960–64); George E. Home (1965–69); George Hampshire (1969–71); John L. Womack (1972–78); Robert F. Kirkpatrick (1979–90); Edward B. Hanson (1991–99); and Timothy H. Graham (2000–present).

Until 1954, there were no active Episcopal parishes or missions in any adjacent counties. Missions, established under Good Shepherd's sponsorship, subsequently drew from its membership. In 1954, St. Albans was established in Monroe, and then Advent in Madison. In 1964, six families from Good Shepherd helped to establish a mission, now St. Simons, in Conyers.

Sunday worship has always been the primary focus of Good Shepherd. Non-Episcopalians in the local community have long appreciated our form of worship

Church of the Good Shepherd, Covington

and have attended our services, especially on special occasions. Lay groups associated with worship, lay ministers, altar guild, and acolytes, have consistently drawn participants highly committed to their duties. In the 1950s lay readers played important roles in conducting services here and at our missions in Monroe and Madison.

Parish events have long been important to life at Good Shepherd: Shrove Tuesday pancake supper (continuously held since the 1960s), Lenten soup suppers (since the 1980s), fall picnic (since the 1970s), the fall spaghetti supper (since the 1980s), and Christmas parties. These events draw the parish together and boost morale.

Outreach began in the 1950s with programs involving students of Emory-at-Oxford. Individual students have found a spiritual home at Good Shepherd and have contributed to parish life. Community service began in 1965 with counseling programs. In the 1980s community outreach programs originated at Good Shepherd when they opened the Parish Hall to meetings of rehabilitation groups and began

Interior view of Church of the Good Shepherd, Covington.

funding outreach programs with proceeds from Shrove Tuesday pancake and fall spaghetti suppers. Literacy programs have used our facilities since the late 1990s.

Good Shepherd's involvement in the training of seminarians and those in the process of discernment has been a rewarding commitment. We hosted three seminarians in the 1980s and since 2000 three seminarians and four individuals in discernment programs. The church is currently sponsoring two of its own members in seminary, both candidates for ordination.

Good Shepherd's stated mission is "to share the Good News of God's love by welcoming others to our traditional Anglican worship, providing opportunities for spiritual growth, and reaching out to others in need. As the rector has written, "With God's grace, we will create a beautiful and efficient house, a place where we may be nurtured and strengthened and where we may offer help and comfort to others in the name of our Savior, Jesus Christ."

Text and photos submitted by Bill McKibben.

ALL SAINTS' EPISCOPAL CHURCH, WARNER ROBINS

✠

All Saints' Episcopal Church is a parish of 485 members representing 210 households. Warner Robins began as the village of Wellston. During World War II Robins Air Force Base was developed in rural flatland, and the city grew up around the base. The few Episcopalians in the area joined the communicants transferred to the area by the base. In the late 1940s twenty members began meeting in the First Presbyterian Church on Sunday evenings for Holy Communion led by the priest from nearby Fort Valley.

In 1949, the Bishop of Atlanta made his first visit to the people at this mission station in Warner Robins. During his visit these people convinced the Bishop that they could support a mission in a town of five thousand people. Property had been given by Thomas Walker, and $100 had been raised to build a church. All Saints' mission came into existence with a church built at a cost of $7,000 by the members themselves. The Diocese loaned the mission money to build a Parish Hall, which was completed in 1955 and expanded in 1960. In 1956 the first vicar of All Saints was appointed by the Bishop. Until that time the priest had been shared with St. Andrew's, Fort Valley.

All Saints' became a parish in 1965 under the leadership of the Reverend Hal Daniell. The Reverend Russell Daniel became rector in 1965 and for the next nine years until his retirement, the parish grew under his leadership and a Rectory was purchased in 1966.

In 1976 the Reverend Chester Grey III was called to become rector. Under his seven-year leadership the parish had a most significant period of growth in both communicants and activities. In 1977 the Rectory was sold with the proceeds starting a building fund. The Education Building was completely renovated and enlarged in 1979 at a cost of approximately $133,000 and is debt free. In 1982 the church building was completely renovated at a cost of approximately $120,000 and is debt free. All Saints' was consecrated on November 1, 1982, with the Right Reverend Charles Judson Child, Bishop Suffragan of Atlanta, presiding.

In 1984 a beautiful Zimmer pipe organ was added in the church to assist in the music

All Saints, Warner Robins—front and side views.

Newly confirmed youth at All Saints, Warner Robins, visit with Bishop Alexander.

ministry. Funds for the purchase and installation of the organ were raised through generous donations of parishioners and friends without adding any debt to the parish. In 1985, the Reverend J. Dennis Smart was called to become rector. Again the parish continued to grow and a Parish Hall with kitchen, a large meeting room, an Episcopal Church Women (ECW) workroom and choir room was added to the facilities. All of the facilities serve well in meeting parish needs and all are debt free.

The Reverend Paul F. Gerlock was called to become rector in 1991. Since that time, the parish has experienced significant growth and has 485 confirmed members. During the period 1991–2004 several new programs including Daughters of the King, Education for Ministry, and Disciples were started. Most significant to the spiritual life of the parish was the calling and ordination of two men to the priesthood: the Reverend Todd Dill and the Reverend Jeffrey Neuberger.

All Saints' Outreach efforts also increased during this period. A Food Pantry was established in 1992 and now serves over thirteen hundred families each year. A supportive relationship was begun with Westside Elementary School in Warner Robins. The school's student population is mostly low-income, minority children. All Saints' has pledged to support these children through providing school supplies, clothing, Thanksgiving dinners, Christmas gifts and Easter baskets, and support to parents through rent and utility assistance. Westside recently awarded All Saints' with an appreciation plaque. It was the first time in the school's history a church was so recognized.

Text and photos submitted by the Reverend Paul Gerlock.

ABSALOM JONES STUDENT CENTER AND CHAPEL

✠

The Absalom Jones Student Center and Chapel is the Episcopal/Anglican campus ministry at the historic Atlanta University Center in Southwest Atlanta. The Center, originally named Canterbury House, was renamed Absalom Jones after the first deacon and priest of African descent in the Episcopal Church.

Since the 1950s, the Absalom Jones Chapel has represented the love of God in Jesus Christ to the students, staff, and faculty of the six institutions of higher learning that comprise the Atlanta University Center, namely: Morehouse College, Spelman College, Clark Atlanta University, Morris Brown, The Interdenominational

Theological Center, and the Morehouse School of Medicine. The alumni communities of these six institutions still remain active in the life of the Absalom Jones Center and Chapel.

The Diocese of Atlanta, through its campus ministry at the Absalom Jones Student Center and Chapel, serves the members of these institutions by providing opportunities for worship in the Episcopal faith, access to a high-tech computer lab, forums for study and discussions, space for group meetings, counseling for personal and spiritual concerns, spiritual direction, food, and fellowship after the Eucharist services.

Since the Episcopal Church has come into a co-operative ecumenical relationship with the Lutheran Church, the Lutheran Campus Ministry shares office space in the Absalom Jones Center. Additionally, the Absalom Jones Center has become a home away from home for Anglican international students.

The Absalom Jones Student Center and Chapel's mission is to teach values and build leaders for the Episcopal Church. St. Paul's Episcopal Church, Atlanta, supports this campus ministry program, both financially and spiritually, through its mission and ministry. The Absalom Jones chaplain is priest associate at St. Paul's Episcopal Church in Atlanta.

Text submitted by the Reverend Harold J. Lockett, D.Min., Chaplain/Director. Photos from the Student Center archives.

Opposite page: Absalom Jones Center and Chapel, Atlanta.

✠   ✠   ✠   ✠

Students gather at Absalom Jones Center for fellowship.

CHAPTER FOUR
THE GOLDEN YEARS
1953–1971

O N NOVEMBER 7, 1906, THE VICAR OF JOHN'S MEMORIAL EPISCOPAL CHURCH, FARMVILLE, VIRGINIA, THE REVEREND RANDOLPH CLAIBORNE AND HIS WIFE, MARY, WELCOMED a baby they named Randolph Royall Claiborne Jr. Forty-seven years later, he was elected Bishop of Atlanta on the fifth ballot, January 13, 1953, at Emmanuel Church, Athens. Bishop Claiborne in his first address to Council, May 6, 1953, St. Peter's, Rome, paid tribute to his father, "I think of my debt to my father, who blazed the ecclesiastical trail for me in this state. Known to many of you, he was for eleven years rector of St. James Church, Marietta. From him I learned to love the Church. From him I learned to love Georgia."

He also challenged the Diocese to a revived faith: "Regardless of what our devotion has been, there is not one of us present who does not need a revival of the in-dwelling spirit of Jesus Christ in daily living. Our Church cannot go forward without that. If we are truly concerned with Christianity, if we are interested in the Church's mission, if we are committed to the salvation and redemption of the world, we must look into the face of Jesus Christ, fall on our knees and ask forgiveness for the things that we have left undone that we ought to have done, and pray that He will give us grace and strength to conduct ourselves as a member of His family, to be faithful stewards of all that He has give us in time, talents, and money, and set our footsteps in His way. Repentance and faith are the condition. Stewardship is the result."

At Claiborne's ordination, the Diocese had forty-eight parishes and missions with over thirteen thousand communicants. Rapid changes in the episcopate required careful guidance and determined leadership. The new Bishop provided all of this and more. In 1957, the Diocese celebrated its fiftieth anniversary in grand style. Dr. Henry Thompson Malone, associate professor of history at Georgia State College, received a commission to write the story of the Episcopal Church in Georgia. It was published as a part of this celebration. In the closing chapter, Malone wrote, "Hundreds of Churchmen crowded into the Hall of Bishops at the Cathedral of St. Philip on a December evening in 1957 to celebrate the Golden Anniversary of the Diocese of Atlanta. Speakers and printed programs commented on the achievements of fifty years of Diocesan history and the glories of more than two centuries of the Church in Georgia. Thousands of television listeners heard the vast throng pronounce a grateful Prayer of Thanksgiving for the blessings which had come to the people of the Diocese." Malone added that these were the "Golden years" of Atlanta.

Thirty-two congregations began during the Claiborne years. Among those which added members rapidly were: St. Anne's, Atlanta (1955); St. David's, Roswell (1956); St. Thomas, Columbus (1958); St. Catherine's, Marietta (1961); and St. Patrick's, Atlanta (1967). Perhaps the most successful was St. Anne's. Founded with a few Episcopalians who met with Bishop Claiborne to form a mission in North Atlanta, in two years it became a parish with over three hundred members. By the time of Bishop Claiborne's retirement, St. Anne's had over eleven hundred communicants.

Bishop Claiborne would be the first of our bishops to retire instead of die in office. At a meeting of the Standing Committee, August 31, 1971, just months before his sixty-fifth birthday, he announced his retirement to take effect February 28, 1972. The Reverend Harry Tisdale, editor of *Diocese*, offered a tribute to the Bishop in the August issue. He cited the bishop for great strides in mission and parish development, courage during the civil rights movement years, fiscal responsibility, and healthy administration both outwardly and inwardly in a godly manner. At his retirement, the Diocese of Atlanta numbered seventy-five parishes and missions with 35,292 baptized persons—certainly a progress worth the title of "Golden."

Text submitted by the Reverend William P. McLemore.

✠   ✠   ✠   ✠

ST. JOHN'S EPISCOPAL CHURCH, WEST POINT

The original Episcopal Church in this area was Christ Church, which dated from the nineteenth century. Christ Church was washed away in the "great flood" of 1920 and there was no Episcopal Church presence in this community for over thirty years. On March 8, 1953, a small group of Episcopalians met with the Reverend Jack Hopper, rector of St. Mark's, LaGrange. The enthusiasm generated from this small beginning resulted in the birth of St. John's which was admitted into the Diocese of Atlanta four months later. On August 7, 1955, ground was broken for the present church building and on June 17, 1956, the new church was dedicated.

The first vicar of St. John's was the Reverend Charles Roper who was followed by the Reverend Brevard Williams, the Reverend Howard Giere, the Reverend Lee Adams, and the Reverend J. Larrie Smith who came to St. John's in August of 1975. In 1978 St. John's applied for parish status and was accepted into the Diocese as a full parish. The Reverend Paul Cosby, a retired priest, was priest associate for a period of time until his untimely death in April 2004. Father Paul is buried at St. John's.

St. John's is an "Equal Opportunity Christian Community" situated on the Georgia-Alabama state line. As a people of God, the congregation is strongly committed to outreach and the membership is very diverse socially, theologically, and politically. This faith-centered community is deeply committed to making a difference in its community and the world.

The Reverend Smith notes that "As a community of faith we realize that disagreement within the Body is acceptable but animosity is not. Therefore, we agree to disagree knowing that we presently see through a glass dimly but one day we will see clearly.

Our diversity is one of the many things that help us to find unity as we gather around the Holy Table, Break Bread together, and celebrate our 'oneness' in the Lord. We are a people of God who know that we do not clearly discern the will of God at all times and in all places but we struggle to seek God's guidance in all that we undertake knowing that God calls the Church to lead and not to follow."

Text and photo submitted by the Reverend J. Larrie Smith.

St. John's Episcopal Church, West Point.

St. Bartholomew's Episcopal Church, Atlanta

✠

On December 12, 1953, thirteen Toco Hills area Episcopalians met with Rector Harry Tisdale of Holy Trinity Parish, Decatur, to explore establishing a mission, and held their first service in January. After Bishop Claiborne recognized St. Bartholomew's as a mission parish in February, the church purchased property and a World War II surplus barracks building—delivered on flatbed trucks. After parishioners' extensive work, the church held services on St. Bartholomew's Day, August 29. Bishop Claiborne celebrated, blessed the new church, and confirmed eleven adults. The Reverend Austin Ford was called as vicar and by 1957 St. Bartholomew's three hundred communicants were granted parish status.

Outreach, always a major element of St. Bartholomew's identity relied heavily on early efforts of women and addressed senior citizens' and teenagers' needs, and support for Camp Mikell. In the 1960s the Service Guild worked extensively with special needs and underprivileged children in various schools and organizations. St. Bartholomew's established in 1960 a new mission in the Northlake area, now St. Bede's parish.

St. Bartholomew's in 1976 joined other churches in an Ecumenical Community Ministry to public housing residents. The parish helped form Life Enrichment, an ecumenical senior citizen's organization, worked with Villa International, and supported the Meals on Wheels program. A women's bazaar to fund a new organ developed into a tradition—the "Olde English Festival." In 1976, the festival became a three-day annual event fostering a rich sense of community and raising money to fund nonbudgeted programs. By the 1980s, proceeds funded programs outside the parish, raising in ten years more than $250,000 until the twenty-fifth and last Festival 2000.

In 1982, to prevent homeless family members being separated to receive emergency shelter, the parish opened shelter for five families the first winter, joining with four additional churches the next year. In the 1980s, as the HIV/AIDS epidemic began, Project Open Hand prepared meals for its victims. The Parish Hall was used twenty hours a day by the programs.

The congregation of St. Bartholomew's Episcopal Church, Atlanta.

The parish next assisted homeless people with AIDS. After difficulties and opposition—but with ecumenical support—Jerusalem House opened in 1989. That same year, St. Bartholomew's converted St. Nicholas Hall into Nicholas House family shelter. Serving twelve families year-round, Nicholas House developed from an emergency shelter into one of Georgia's first agencies assisting families towards housing self-sufficiency. In 1993 the parish received the Thomas A. Donnellan Award for Exemplary Community Outreach by the Christian Council of Metropolitan Atlanta. In 1997 St. Bartholomew's joined churches in the Toco Hills Community Ministry, providing emergency assistance to prevent homelessness and groceries to needy applicants.

The church building started in June 1957, with worship and education wings joined by a glass narthex, was ready for Christmas services. Preschool, nursery, and offices remained in the original building—St. Nicholas Hall. During 1961–62 expansion was started on a contemporary twelve-sided Parish Hall named Warden's Hall joined in 1978 to the church by a two-story preschool and office wing.

In 1990, the church was converted into Parish Hall and Chapel and a new church was begun, with first worship in it on Good Shepherd Sunday, 1996. A new Rosales organ, designed for the new church, was first heard on Palm Sunday 2003.

Under Father Ford in the 1960s, the parish was strongly committed to civil rights. In 1970 St. Bartholomew's elected Petie Cason its first woman Vestry member, one of the first parishes to do so. During the 1970s and 1980s music ministries expanded. The choir membership grew and performed works such as the Fauré *Requiem*, a hand-bell choir was added; and the parish experimented with new musical forms, including jazz and folk masses composed for the parish. Liturgy was enriched, and the parish strengthened its own community through Foyers Groups, a men's group, and a Flower Guild.

In the 1980s the parish began its long and profitable experience with women priests and accepted the first openly gay priests in the Diocese. The current and sixth rector, the Reverend William McCord Thigpen, came to the parish in 2002. St. Bartholomew's Jubilee Year, the fiftieth anniversary in 2004, included dedication of the Rosales organ on St. Bartholomew's Day.

After fifty years, the parish continues to stress both a rich musical and liturgical heritage plus an expansive tradition of outreach and community engagement. As Father Mac put it: "This is a church that is not playing church—not simply holding services because people expect them—but a church that truly wants to be the church, people who truly want to be engaged by the gospel, the good news, and to live it out in their daily lives."

Text submitted by Robert E. Van Keuren Jr. Photos from the church archives and by John Whitt.

✣   ✣   ✣   ✣

The Holy Eucharist at St. Bartholomew's Episcopal Church, Atlanta.

ST. PAUL'S EPISCOPAL CHURCH, NEWNAN

✠

Established in Newnan in 1882, St. Paul's services were discontinued and the property sold in 1914. By 1954 the need for an Episcopal church was felt strongly enough to dictate action and Jim Hardin and Charlie Mottola decided to make it happen. It was not long until the first service was held in the Swinton Hotel Dining Room, later moving to the old WCOH Radio Station on Jefferson Street.

To link to the original church, the Bishop permitted it to be named St. Paul's. Steady growth led to a decision to build and on Easter Day, 1961, the first service was held in the new Roscoe Road church. St. Paul's achieved parish status in 1983 and on Easter 1984 the building that served for the next nineteen years was consecrated. By 1998, the leadership recognized the need for new and larger worship, education, and fellowship space. In 1999 the Vestry approved planning for new space and continued the heritage of stepping forward in faith.

The Reverend J. Russell Kendrick came to St. Paul's as rector in 1998, and had these comments about that early decision: "It was both a matter of necessity and vision. The congregation began to realize that we were running out of space to adequately house our programs. We also spent time discussing how our facility represents our identity as well as our understanding of God."

With joy and high hopes for the future, the congregation gathered for groundbreaking on Sunday, September 9, 2001. On Wednesday, September 12, many of these same people gathered again, stunned and grieving, believing that the place of celebration was also a place of refuge, comfort, and hope. St. Paul's new building was dedicated in July 2003.

St. Paul's Episcopal Church, Newnan, at evening.

Interior of St. Paul's Episcopal Church, Newnan.

The new church follows the traditional church layout but features an open and arching interior. Old and new pews are in place side by side. The 1961 church's altar is the west transept chapel altar. The window high above the chancel is a sunburst design featuring the "chi rho." Around the outer edge are the words "Let there be light" in eight languages. St. Paul's has a close relationship with the Bethlehem Ministries in Haiti and the new Bishop's chair and president's chair were hand carved by Haitian craftsmen. They are reminders that St. Paul's mission and ministry extend beyond Coweta County. Members and friends recognized loved ones by providing many of the

furnishings. These gifts are reminders that the St. Paul's family reaches geographically and historically beyond the immediate congregation.

Members represent a broad cross section including some of the earliest members still regular in attendance and active in parish work. The most active and energetic parish group is the young people. From preschool to senior high, the youth are engaged in Bible study, Christian formation, music, community outreach, and Diocesan youth programs.

In August 2005 the first parish associate rector, the Reverend Hunt Priest, was ordained at St. Paul's. This additional leadership for parish programs and pastoral care enables a continuous welcome as well as reach outward to people in need.

The words appearing on weekly service bulletins best captures the mind and spirit of St. Paul's. "To all who are weary and need rest; to all who are lonely and want friendship; to all who mourn and need comfort; to all who pray and all who don't, but ought; to all who sin and need a Savior; to all who rejoice and would offer praise; to all who are blessed and would serve their neighbor; to whosoever will come; this Church opens wide the door and says in the name of the Lord Jesus, WELCOME."

Text submitted by Joseph C. Daniel. Photos from the church archives.

St. Alban's Episcopal Church, Monroe

⁜

On January 4, 1954, eighteen Episcopalians, including the Reverend A. H. Zinser, met at the Monroe High School Auditorium to organize a church in Monroe. Some of them had been attending the Church of the Good Shepherd, Covington, located approximately twenty-one miles from Monroe. They had discussed plans to organize a new parish with Bishop Claiborne who gave his blessings.

Sally Launius, wife of prominent Monroe businessman Harry Launius, was one of the organizers. Mr. Launius was engaged in buying some land on Monroe's Main Street at the time of the meeting. Though not an Episcopalian, he stood and asked, "If I buy this lot, and build you a building, will you continue to organize this Episcopal Church?" The group gulped hard and said with enthusiasm, "Yes, sir and thank you." He did this in honor of his beloved wife. The group then worshiped temporarily on Sundays in the Rural Electric Association (REA) building boardroom.

A group of churchmen built a simple wooden altar which remains today in the small chapel. A neighbor to the "church lot" allowed the congregation to store that altar in an outbuilding behind her house. Every Sunday morning the men had to "tote" the altar across Main Street to the REA building where the ladies dressed the altar with linens for service. Mrs. Sue Henson is the only charter member still attending St. Alban's and remains very active.

Mr. Launius built the church as promised and the first service was held on June 20, 1954, with thirty-six attending. St. Alban's initially shared a priest with services held at 8:00 a.m. Because of the early hour, breakfast was prepared for the visiting priest. The building was small but adequate and was filled with the aroma of eggs, bacon or sausage, and coffee.

One visiting priest—over six feet tall and always late—came running in one memorable Sunday needing help with his vestments. The Altar Guild ladies helped him dress

St. Alban's, Monroe, with Celtic cross.

The congregation of St. Alban's, Monroe.

St. Alban's slowly grew under the guidance of Father Zinser. Also having served are the Reverends Payton Splane, Clyde Watson, Robert Fisher, Dawson Teague, Edmund Berkeley, Dale Harmon, J. E. James, and Al Scoggins.

In 1958, Mr. Launius gave a large donation to build a large sanctuary connecting to the original church. The new church was adorned with a huge limestone Celtic cross and is an outstanding and beautiful addition to Monroe's Main Street.

In 1992, the Reverend Foley Beach came to St. Alban's. Membership continued to grow and an addition including an Education Building and spacious Parish Hall was built.

On December 20, 2004, the Reverend Beach announced his resignation so that he might establish an independent Anglican Church in the area. A large number of communicants responded to the invitation to follow their former rector.

The remaining members took heart and with encouragement from Bishop Alexander and with the arrival of a new priest-in-charge, the Reverend Frank Wilson, who became rector in November 2005, the membership is once again growing. The church is alive with activity and on Sunday mornings there is much joy.

Text submitted by Mrs. Edna Pannell. Photos from church archives.

while he ran down the hall and through the sacristy from which a door opened into the chancel. The seated congregation watched as the wind slammed shut the sacristy door catching the priest's robes. He struggled to release himself, when suddenly, the doorknob turned, releasing his robes. He flew across the floor as if sliding into home plate. The homemade altar shook, spilling the candles; and the old pump organ gave out of air and groaned. Finally, he caught his balance, straightened up and faced the congregation, which burst into peals of laughter.

HOLY CROSS EPISCOPAL CHURCH, DECATUR

✠

June 20, 2004, marked Holy Cross' fiftieth anniversary as a congregation. Holy Cross began when fifteen families from Holy Trinity Church in Decatur held their first service as a mission congregation. Rapid growth of south DeKalb County drove the need for a new congregation, which initially met at the old Southwest DeKalb High School. Incorporated on September 1, 1954, the congregation moved just months later to a refurbished World War II Army hospital barracks on six acres in Decatur and celebrated its first service on Christmas Eve 1954.

The "Barracks Building" served until Royall Hall was built in 1961. Royall Hall served as the original church house, was consecrated in 1961 and named after John M. Royall Jr., a charter member. It became the Parish Hall when the new church was built and dedicated in 1971. The new cruciform-shaped church features a "sanctuary in the round" that seats 350. Royall Hall's 1997 renovations included a new kitchen and bathroom facilities suitable for church functions and meeting space for a several community organizations. The "Barracks" offices and classrooms were demolished in 2000 to make room for a two-story Education Building. The Education Building, which opened in 2001, houses the church offices and Christian education classrooms and activities. The upper floor will be completed later.

Holy Cross has been served by four priests. The venerable John Lee Womack served as vicar of the mission until 1962 when he became the full-time Archdeacon of the Diocese of Atlanta. He was succeeded by the Reverend Charles M. Roper who guided us to full parish status in 1967, became the first rector, and continued to serve Holy Cross until 1978, when called to another parish.

In 1979, Jamaican-born Father E. Don Taylor came to Holy Cross. Recently arrived from a church in Buffalo, New York, he had served as vicar of Holy Comforter, a parish located six miles away. Under his leadership Holy Cross doubled its membership, due in part to the large influx of Caribbean natives attracted by Father Taylor. He left Holy Cross in January 1987 to become the Bishop of the Virgin Islands.

Church of the Holy Cross' new building, Decatur.

Father Kent Belmore became the fourth vicar of Holy Cross in 1988. He came to Holy Cross from Charleston, South Carolina. Holy Cross experienced unprecedented growth during the early years of his leadership. Father Belmore left Holy Cross in May 2004 for a parish in Mobile, Alabama, and an active search process began.

Holy Cross Parish is one of the most culturally diverse congregations in the Diocese and has enjoyed a reasonably steady growth. The people are welcoming and family-oriented, and generally worship using multicultural liturgies. With nationalities from countries across the globe, the congregation maintains unique Anglican liturgical practices reflecting members' backgrounds.

Membership has evolved from an all-white congregation in 1954 to a majority-black congregation. The diversity of Holy Cross is unmatched in the Diocese. Members, either by birth or their parents' birth, hail from four continents, twenty-one countries, and twenty-six states. The diversity in service and outreach activities is a major strength of the parish. Deeply rooted in the Sacraments, it uses the strength of its diversity to build a more vibrant and functioning Christian community. The needs of all who rely on the parish for spiritual, moral, social, or economic support are met. Holy Cross offers a unique community for those seeking a somewhat quiet, moderately sized setting to worship, with traditional Anglican musical chants, and traditional Gospel hymns.

Outreach ministries have played an important part of parish life and have included: a Senior Day Care Center; reading to students at the neighborhood elementary school; and loan of the church property for a DeKalb County Summer Program for neighborhood youth. The facilities also serve as home to many Caribbean and African civic organizations that hold regular meetings and events there. Parishioners have participated in the Decatur Cooperative Ministry Programs.

Generous, compassionate members traditionally raise more money for the annual Atlanta Hunger Walk—a fundraiser for the Atlanta Community Food Bank—than any other Episcopal church in Atlanta. Funds enable Holy Cross to buy food for a monthly distribution to DeKalb County residents in need. In 2004, almost six thousand family members were fed. Several newly added "in-reach" activities enable

Decatur's Church of the Holy Cross choir.

broader programmatic impact. In 2005, a Family and Game Night became part of its programs to bring together all elements of the congregation and involve youth and young people in church activities.

The first annual International Fair on Saturday, October 16, 2004, organized by a number of members, was a success socially, financially, and spiritually. Fostering positive group relationships among the congregations of both the early and late services resulted in greatly improved fellowship. Encouraged by its success, and by God's grace, the congregation anticipates making it an annual fundraising endeavor.

The Young at Heart group consists of seniors and many retirees who enjoy trips to local and regional attractions, and cruises. Their annual banquet that raises funds is well attended by parishioners and others.

Text submitted by Jennifer C. Friday. Photos from the church archives.

St. Barnabas' Episcopal Church, Trion

✢

St. Barnabas', founded in 1955, grew slowly during the period from 1960 to 1990. In 1989, the Reverend Dr. King Oehmig of Chattanooga became the permanent part-time priest-in-charge. The church was an aided mission until 1990 when parish status was granted. Growth continued through the 1990s and in 2002 a Fellowship Hall was added. The church has an active Hispanic ministry and the Reverend Isaias Rodriguez of the Diocese comes and celebrates the Eucharist one or two Saturdays a month.

Episcopal services were first held for a group of communicants in the Summerville-Trion-LaFayette area in the LaFayette Presbyterian Church on Sunday afternoon, August 22, 1954. The two major Sacraments were administered, Baptism for Claire Elizabeth Davis of LaFayette, and Holy Communion by the Reverend W. Russell Daniel, rector of St. Peter's Church, Rome, officiant.

On Thursday, January 13, 1955, a dinner meeting was held at the Riegeldale Tavern in Trion to discuss organizing a congregation and petitioning Bishop Claiborne for admission to the Diocese as the organized mission of St. Barnabas. At January 1955 Council held at St. Luke's, Atlanta, the mission was admitted to the Diocese. Congregational representatives present at Council were Mr. and Mrs. Mark Cooper Jr., Mr. and Mrs. W. J. Welborn, and Mrs. R. D. Love.

Services alternated between LaFayette and Trion. It was soon deemed wise to establish the location of the church in Trion and services were held on Sundays in the foyer of Trion School. Lay readers from St. Mark's, Dalton, and St. Peter's,

St. Barnabas' Episcopal Church, Trion.

Rome, alternated reading in LaFayette and Trion. Holy Communion was celebrated monthly with the Reverend Donald G. Mitchell of St. Mark's, and the Reverend W. Russell Daniel alternating.

Building the church began in 1957 and it was dedicated on June 15, 1958. Numerous difficulties delayed construction, and at dedication, the nave lacked two bays, with plans to add them when financially possible. The church stands today as a building of beauty and spiritual inspiration.

A list of those who made the building possible would be extensive. The congregation's first gratitude would be to the Riegel Corporation who gave the property and their usual share of the original building costs for churches. This was truly a generous action. Bishop Claiborne, who was attending the Lambeth Conference in London, gave the church a thousand dollars and there were numerous other very

generous individuals and groups. All members have shared in the responsibility of constructing the building and acquisition of the furnishings. Kenneth Harris, Mark A. Cooper Jr., and S. A. Dunson served as chairmen of the Building Committee. Messrs. Harris and Cooper moved to other communities and were not able to see the building completed. To all who contributed go the thanks and appreciation of the congregation.

Today, St. Barnabas' Church is a reminder to the surrounding community that the dedicated determination of only a few can accomplish with God's help what seems almost impossible. Truly this is so with the devoted members of St. Barnabas' Church. May God grant them guidance of the Holy Spirit as they accomplish God's work in our community.

Text submitted by Dr. W. Kirk Krueger. Photo from the Collins Collection, Diocese of Atlanta Archives.

St. Anne's Episcopal Church, Atlanta

✛

St. Anne's Church in Northwest Atlanta can measure only a half-century, but her pioneering spirit is still active. On May 15, 1955, a group of forty-nine Episcopalians petitioned Bishop Claiborne for the right to begin a mission. First meeting at the old Lovett School, within two years, the congregation had bought and remodeled a derelict schoolhouse into both sanctuary and Parish Hall.

By 1965, a permanent church, designed by two of the founders, Fred Branch and Lou Swayze, was built. Peggy Swayze's colored glass illustrates parts of scripture from Genesis to the Apocalypse and the ten large clerestory windows depict the life of Christ. The Flentrop organ, which was commissioned by the church and built in Zaandam, Holland, provides magnificent sound.

St. Anne's Episcopal Church, Atlanta.

From the beginning through much later building, the mandate of Christ to minister to the world has not been forgotten. The women organized Episcopal Church Woman ECW chapters in the beginning, the first two being St. Prisca's and St. Martha's. In 1964, "hands-on" assistance was given to Sister Henrietta Keel of Kelly Street. Women of St. Anne's took clothes and toys, started a Day Care Center, and generally supported the Fellowship Mission.

St. Anne's major mission focus in the eighties and nineties was Perry Homes, a public housing community. As a Cluster of Churches member, St. Anne's members carried food on holidays; sponsored and equipped youth baseball teams; drove students to Saturday School; and assisted with a Day Care Center. Founding "STEP"—Support to Employment Project—designed to train and find jobs for residents was a major accomplishment. Bernard Rosser, then a priest associate at St. Anne's, was project missioner. The Cluster continues to serve the needs of Perry Homes.

Other projects are the Red Cross Blood Drive, held yearly the last Sunday in Advent since 1984; Habitat for Humanity in cooperation with other churches and synagogues; and the recent Kids for Peace Initiative. Twelve children from Jerusalem—Muslim, Christian, and Jew—join twelve Atlanta youth for two weeks of cultural exchange at Camp Mikell. St. Anne's members devised the Career Transition Ministry from 1993 to 2002. Initiated by Hugh Gordon and Jim Vaughan, over sixty volunteers served fifteen hundred people to advise and encourage anyone having job search difficulties.

The Sunday school children have pursued their own missions including collecting paperbacks for Atlanta jail inmates; toys for children in Afghanistan; and funding five goats for Heifer International.

An important mission project was the founding of the St. Anne's Day School. First housed in the old schoolhouse and Sunday school rooms, it has now been enlarged with handsome new facilities. Preschool and kindergarten classes, and a day nursery for toddlers are offered. The Day School has a reputation for excellence and its enrichment programs have been accredited by the Association for the Education of Young Children. Janet Reinertsen has served as the director for twenty-five years. At present she is implementing the Reggio approach to early childhood education.

Another exemplary project is St. Anne's Terrace, an attractive building with one hundred apartments for seniors. Each apartment is fully equipped, and the residents, who furnish as they wish, are supplied with dinners, linen, and cleaning services. The amenities include an exercise room, salon, library, chapel, and "Apple Annie's" convenience store. Burl Gault is the administrator and Mary Lou Duffy is in charge of activities, which include meetings, classes, devotionals, as well as field trips to plays and concerts.

The international director of the Cross of Nails, Eloise Lester, St. Anne's beloved priest associate, was the first woman ordained to the priesthood in Atlanta. Recently the congregation has been joined by Dr. John Westerhoff, noted teacher and theologian. Christian education has been important since the Sunday school started with twenty-seven members. The Youth Programs have been exceptional and pastoral care includes many services for newcomers. Parish Life is flourishing, with an annual retreat at Kanuga.

St. Anne's has had five Rectors: Dudley Colhoun (1956–1961); John Ball (1961–1976); Frank Allan (1977–1987); and John L. Rabb (1988–1998) later Bishop of Maryland. The present rector is Father Eddie Ard, assisted by Ellen Purdum, Lang Lowrey, and Deacon Bob Eckardt. With their guidance and the Grace of God, St. Anne's will continue to serve in Northwest Atlanta.

Text submitted by Marguerite Murphey. Photo from the Collins Collection, Diocese of Atlanta Archives.

St. David's Episcopal Church, Roswell

✠

The St. David's story began in 1956 when the Reverend Joseph T. Walker of St. James', Marietta, met with nineteen parishioners to sign an application for the establishment of a mission. At that time, Roswell was "way out in the country," but had a rich history. Many of its early families were coastal Georgia planters who arrived on the North Georgia frontier in the 1830s, establishing prosperous cotton and woolen mills. Their antebellum homes and landmarks are proudly on display in the historic district. Located along the Georgia Highway 400 corridor, St. David's bisects a densely populated northern arc of communities.

The first service at St. David's was held on September 16, 1956. The first building that became St. David's was constructed in 1958, and is still in use as the Parish Hall. St. David's attained full parish status in 1971. Its congregation was well served until 1981 by Fathers Herbert Smith, Lamar Speier, William McClelland, and Charles Kendrick.

On the Feast of Pentecost, 1981, the Reverend Hendree Harrison came to St. David's, and filled the nave on his first day with hundreds of bright red helium balloons! St. David's grew up rapidly under his leadership, including several building campaigns, and additional clergy including the Reverends Sandy Horton, Kenneth Struble (now at Camp Mikell), Kevin Kelly, and Ron Baskin. In 1994, St. David's founded St. Aidan's Mission, which grew to full parish status one year later. Father Harrison retired in March 2000 and was named rector emeritus. He remains very active in the Diocese of Atlanta.

In the fall of 2001, St. David's called the Reverend Paul S. Winton, from Charleston, South Carolina, as rector of St. David's. He inherited an active, thriving parish of seven hundred families, eighteen hundred baptized members, average Sunday attendance of 570 at two services, and a budget of $800,000. His first sermon was the Sunday following 9-11-2001, delivering a powerful message that is still being circulated today.

St. David's soon began a long-term strategic planning effort, to discern "what God has called it to do." Meetings and focus group interviews continued with parishioners over a period of several months, to develop a formal strategic plan. "Six Vision

New Celtic cross adorns St. David's, Roswell.

Elements" grew from the Strategic Plan: "our first instinct is to seek God's grace; we welcome, know, and care for one another; we are a church without walls; St. David's is where you want to be; young people are equipped to serve; and we give abundantly."

The Master Planning Committee took the strategic plan, and the "Six Vision Elements," and converted it into a "to-do list" of how to respond to what God has called us to do. One result of this is that an architectural firm is now engaged to develop plans for renovation and construction over the next few years.

St. David's is full of growing families, active in community participation, and full of volunteer spirit. While Roswell and Alpharetta are growing and changing communities, St. David's will remain a steadfast home for Christian worship and fellowship. It is a bustling parish of over eight hundred families, twenty-five hundred members, average Sunday attendance of over six hundred at six services (including one Hispanic service), a church school attendance of six hundred, and a budget that has grown by 40 percent since 2001. A strong family integration program is in place that results in adding about one new family a week, to the membership. Eighty thriving ministries continuously do the work of the Lord, including Honduras missions and a "Katrina House." There are often so many gatherings at St. David's that parishioners frequently meet in each other's homes. Truly, to find a parishioner, if not at home, at work, or school, look at St. David's Episcopal Church in Roswell.

Text and photos submitted by Patrick McBurnette.

Left: View of the altar of St. David's Episcopal Church, Roswell.

ST. JUDE'S EPISCOPAL CHURCH, MARIETTA

✝

In 1956, thirty-eight local Episcopalians petitioned Bishop Claiborne for a new church home in Cobb County. Several were communicants of St. James' and perhaps the name, "St. Jude's" was chosen because James was a brother of Jude.

St. Jude's Mission held its first service in the Mary Willis Scout Hut on Pine Street on February 5, 1956, officiated by Father Carl Nelson, assistant to Archdeacon John Womack. During the next few months, St. Jude's initiated a church school program, the Bargain Corner (later to become St. Jude's Thrift Shop), an Alter Guild, and a Woman's Auxiliary.

Over the next two years, St. Jude's met in Campbell High School and Belmont Hills Theater and other locations. The tenacious founding members held together and on July 19, 1956, the Vestry approved a resolution requesting the purchase of property. On September 14, 1956, C. C. Jones conveyed 110 Jones Shaw Road to the Diocese (later conveyed to St. Jude's in April 1958). In May 1957, a master building plan was approved. Archdeacon Womack, his assistants, and various lay readers from other churches officiated the first year until Father Herbert H. Smith, who, after graduating from seminary, became the first vicar, serving from July 1957 until December 1959. Father Smith also watched over a mission in Roswell and in time, the demands placed upon him with two missions, forced him to tender his resignation and he accepted a call in Virginia. Archdeacon Womack then appointed the Reverend Lamar P. Speier who served from January 1960 until September of that year.

The next five years were overseen by Father Nathaniel E. Parker who began in June of 1961. The number of active communicants nearly doubled, growing from 226 to 440 and total yearly attendance rose by almost 300 percent. In 1963, St. Jude's moved from mission status to that of aided parish and Father Parker had the distinction of being both the last vicar and the first rector.

The administration wing was added to the Parish Center in 1964 and the following year, under the guidance of Father Parker, the main church building was completed.

Left: St. Jude's Groundbreaking 1964. Left to right are R. Harold Richards, the Reverend Nathaniel Parker, and Benjamin Beig.

Father Parker resigned in February 1966. Almost one year later, in February 1967, St. Jude's achieved full parish status.

St. Jude's began its kindergarten in 1966 and in May 1966, Peter W. Calhoun became rector of St. Jude's. He remained until October of 1969 and his successor was Father W. Robert Abstein who heeded the call to St. Jude's in March of 1970. During his leadership the church saw significant positive changes financially and physically. In 1973, an education wing was constructed off the Parish Hall. The need for an assistant rector was apparent by this time and in July 1977 Robert Bruce Birdsey entered his deacon internship, being ordained in August 1978. He remained in this position until November 1981. During this time a part-time position of director of Christian education was also authorized.

The Reverend Sam G. Candler, now dean of the Cathedral of St. Philip, joined the staff at St. Jude's in June 1982 and at Father Abstein's resignation in August 1984, Father Candler served as interim until the arrival of the current rector, Father Frank Baltz, in November 1985.

During Father Baltz's leadership, Father Peter Steube served as assistant from June 1986 until June 1990 and Father David St. Clair served as assistant from January 1994 until July 2003. Due to demographic changes in St. Jude's neighborhood, a Hispanic congregation began in 1997, with its own service. Eighty communicants attended its first Sunday. Associate priests ministering to the Hispanic congregation were first, Father Ismael Sanchez; next Father Bill de Orteaga; and currently Father Ramone Betances. Recent years have also seen an influx of communicants of African and Caribbean origin. Currently there are twenty-seven countries represented in the membership of St. Jude's. To further the neighborhood outreach, a day school was begun in June of 2002.

Adjunct clergy includes Father David Collins, former dean of the Cathedral of St. Philip, and Father Charles Fulton, director of Acts 29 Ministries, formerly Episcopal Renewal Ministries (ERM). Traditional hymns are augmented with contemporary praise music at Rite II services.

At one point during Father Baltz's leadership, a slogan was adopted which reads: "St. Jude's, a little bit of heaven." When one witnesses the diversity of the parish and the dedication of its members, one does indeed experience a little bit of heaven.

Text submitted by Jim Glover. Photos from the church archives.

Members of St. Jude's, Marietta, strike a pose for the Centennial Book.

St. Augustine of Canterbury, Morrow

✛

Miss Ida E. Baumgartner of Forest Park wrote in 1957 to Bishop Claiborne requesting a mission be established in the Clayton County area. An organizational meeting was held on January 15, 1958, at St. Timothy's Lutheran Church in Forest Park, and Council approved the formation of a mission.

St. Augustine of Canterbury Episcopal Mission's first service was held February 2, 1958, at the home of Mr. Guy Chunn in Forest Park. The Reverend H. Augustus Sheppard Jr., first deacon and vicar, served from July through December 1958. The first church was a chapel prepared in 1958 in the home of Miss Baumgartner. Members of the congregation cleaned, painted, and furnished the chapel. Other churches and the Diocesan Department of Missions gave furniture and fixtures. Music was provided on an Army field service organ. Lillie Brown became the first organist and choirmaster in May 1958.

On January 11, 1959, the Vestry petitioned Bishop Claiborne to purchase the present church property for construction of a permanent facility which began on St. Martin's Founders House on June 12, 1960. The first service was conducted there on September 11, 1960.

The Reverends James L. Johnson and Norman Siefferman were the second and third vicars, with the Reverend Peter Calhoun becoming vicar in 1962. The membership continued to grow, and a building fund campaign began and a second building—the present Nave, Canterbury Hall—was started in March 1963 and dedicated on August 11, 1963.

St. Augustine of Canterbury in Morrow.

The Reverend Harry Tisdale served as assistant vicar until the installation of the Reverend Robert Bailey as the fifth vicar from September 18, 1966 through April 1971. A third building—the Hall of St. Peter and St. Paul, now known as the Parish Hall—was completed in 1967. The Reverend Ronald Gibson became the sixth vicar in 1971. In 1974, Mrs. Grace Caudle became the first full-time organist and choirmaster.

The Reverend Thomas M. Stubbs served as the first rector from 1974 until 1982 and parish status was achieved in January 1977. A Consecration and Confirmation Service was held November 21, 1982, with the Right Reverend Judson Child officiating, and Father Jerry Zeller as celebrant.

Father John R. Stanton was rector from 1983 until his retirement in the fall of 1993. A chapter of the Brotherhood of St. Andrew was formed on November 30, 1984. During the period of time from 1974 to 1993 many other ministries were initiated, including the Episcopal Church Women, Trinity Towers, and the Airport Chapel. Extensive renovation of all property was completed in 1992, following repairs of damage by an electrical fire to the Parish Hall. The three buildings were connected by a breezeway, and the driveway and parking lots were rebuilt.

Father Barry Griffin arrived in August of 1994 to serve as the parish's third rector. Experiencing continued growth, in 2000 the first parish administrator was hired, the nave was renovated, the parking lot expanded, and a garage building added to accommodate grounds equipment. In 2001, St. Augustine's first seminarian, Terri Tilley, entered General Theological Seminary. A Natural Spirituality/Dream Group was formed in 2002, and a local chapter of Daughters of the King and

The Guild of St. Francis were commissioned in 2003. The year 2004 saw the formation of a Verger Guild and two milestones were celebrated: Father Barry Griffin's tenth anniversary as rector, and Grace Caudle's thirtieth anniversary as organist and choirmaster.

Today St. Augustine's remains the only Episcopal Church in Clayton County. Its membership reflects the diverse community it seeks to serve.

Text submitted by Robert A. Harrell. Photos from the church archives.

✛   ✛   ✛   ✛

St. Augustine's first building September 11, 1960.

St. Mary's Episcopal Church, East Point

✠

In January 1958, nineteen people met at Bill and Mable New's home and pledged themselves to the establishment of an Episcopal church in East Point. The church was organized under the direction of Archdeacon John L. Womack. Thirty people were present at the first meeting and Vestry and committees were elected. At that meeting the name St. Mary's was chosen because there had been another St. Mary's, which was started in East Point around 1929 that had been abandoned due to the Depression.

The first service was held February 9, 1958, with the Reverend Womack officiating with fifty-one present. Services were held in Harris Street Elementary School.

In April 1959, the Reverend James L. Johnson became its first priest. Earlier that year, the church purchased 6.75 acres for $15,000 for the proposed church buildings. In February 1961, phase one construction of St. Mary's building program began. The first building served as an all-purpose building. In June of 1961, Father Johnson officiated in the new building. That same year, Father Norman Siefferman's tenure started and he left in 1964 with attendance at one hundred.

The new Church of the Resurrection built in 1961 within East Point attracted many St. Mary's communicants. The enthusiasm of the Reverend John D. Noble, assigned as vicar in September 1964, helped keep the church attendance at St. Mary's at a high level, where it remained until September 1968, when Noble departed to serve a large church in New Haven, Connecticut. The new priest, Father Thomas Moody, was assigned to St. Mary's and was highly instrumental in the planning and completion of Trinity Towers, a retirement apartment facility, in July 1975. Trinity Towers was sponsored by four churches: St. Mary's; Church of the Resurrection; St. John's, College Park; and St. Augustine's, Morrow. Church attendance, however, dropped during that same period.

Exterior of St. Mary's Episcopal Church, East Point.

Interior of St. Mary's Episcopal Church, East Point.

tough times. We're awfully small. We're close knit and get along well." This tiny community remained small for several years. Some members testify that they had been praying "for a miracle to happen." They had to wait until 1998, when Bishop Allan asked if they would accept a Hispanic community in their midst with the Reverend Isaias A. Rodriguez as leader of the Latino group. St. Mary's members were happy at the news and both congregations started to worship at different times.

In December 1999, upon Father Clarke's retirement from active ministry, the small group of Anglo-speaking members made the decision to leave the church and its savings to the new Hispanic congregation. It was a very generous decision.

The Hispanic congregation is very young and has potential for a great future. Regularly on Sundays there are more children than adults. A group from the Episcopal Church Women of the Diocese—led by Ginger Mulherin—faithfully provides Bible classes for St. Mary's children every Sunday during the school year. Because the actual sanctuary of the church is small, plans are being made for a Parish Hall to accommodate the growth of this congregation.

Text submitted by the Reverend Isaias Rodriguez. Photos from the church archives.

In 1976 St. Mary's was served by visiting clergy, and then by Father Frank Thomas who served from August 1976 to January 1, 1978. In September 1977 there was talk of closing St. Mary's Church, but the faithful group remaining with an average Sunday attendance between twenty-five and thirty persons pledged to follow through in efforts to meet the crisis and to maintain the bonding of God's Love.

In April 1983, Father Jim Clarke became the priest at St. Mary's. Although he managed all the duties of full-time priest, Father Clarke was considered part-time because he was also general manager of Trinity Towers. That year, Ned Nichols, member of the church and president of Trinity's Board of Directors said: "We've been through some

✠　　✠　　✠　　✠

St. Thomas' Episcopal Church, Columbus

⁜

St. Thomas' Church was founded in 1958 in the outer edge—now "Historic Midtown"—of Columbus. Tradition says "Thomas" was chosen as patron and name because "they doubted we would make it." "We" did, and have been a witness to the Risen Lord for nearly fifty years. Outreach, reconciliation, mission, a culture of caring, and a celebration of arts and worship have characterized the church's history.

St. Thomas' has been blessed with resources. An early gift was a large piece of property and a pioneer member left a large bequest to the parish. These resources were immediately made available for outreach and service. An example of this generosity was the creation of St. Thomas Day School, a preschool created shortly after the founding. Year after year community children have been welcomed, their lives and characters formed in this household of faith. St. Thomas' stands as the longest active church preschool in the city.

The school is but one example of community welcome. The St. Thomas' property has been home to Boy Scout troops, Young Life youth program, various twelve-step programs, an interfaith food pantry, the Columbus Boy Choir and Cantus Columbus—a professional choral ensemble. The parish helped create Columbus Hospice and the Pastoral Institute and has always been known as a gathering place for good things

Outreach to the poor has been a central ministry and was given a formal focus in 1980 with the formation of Chattahoochee Valley Episcopal Ministry (CVEM). Initially this ministry was the direct assistance arm of the several area churches. Under leadership of longtime director Vicky Partin, CVEM has reached a wider arena of service and transformation. Some services include the Thompson-Pound Arts Project, a multicultural, interfaith summer arts program that helps teens and children cross religious and cultural divides and celebrate reconciliation and diversity; and Beallwood Area Neighborhood Development, Inc., is a grassroots revitalization of a neighborhood blighted by drugs, crime, and commercial zoning. The Chattahoochee Credit Union provides an opportunity for secure savings and credit opportunities; and Conversation Café—a regular gathering of women mentoring women on economic challenges.

Front of St. Thomas' Episcopal Church, Columbus.

The chancel and altar, St. Thomas', Columbus, at Christmas.

After September 11, 2001, St. Thomas' again facilitated reconciliation at the same time the parish ministered to military families awaiting outbreak of war, with a series of community dialogues with the city's Jewish and Muslim communities. These conversations led to building an Interfaith Habitat House, a first in the Southeast.

Mission is an important dimension of St. Thomas' identity and was deeply involved, with the convocation, in the founding of two other Columbus parishes, sending members and financial support to St. Mary Magdalene and St. Nicholas Churches. Recently the church has given much support to the McCann African Mission, a medical and educational partnership with the Diocese of Central Tanganyika (Tanzania). Also several priests have been supported in the Diocesan Discernment Program.

Music and art hold an important role in the church's identity. The St. Thomas Olde English Festival was a highlight for years. Recent offerings include Jazz Worship, Cabaret Supper Clubs, and Blue Grass concerts. The outstanding choir was recognized for excellence by a 2005 invitation to perform at Washington National Cathedral.

The inner life of St. Thomas' has been nurtured by commitment to all-age education, parish life, music programs, and rich worship, including a focus on Bible study and issues of faith, as well as programs that address contemporary church and cultural issues. Members are moved to a faith journey calling for inner growth, community involvement, and a life of service. They have sought to be God's people in this part of God's world and pray for wisdom and courage to continue.

The reconciliation ministry has resulted in various partnerships for ministry. Wynnton Neighborhood Network joined several neighborhood churches and synagogues together for mutual ministry and celebration. The parish has long been involved in programs of racial reconciliation, interfaith dialogue, creation of an Integrity chapter, and a Peace and Justice group.

A reconciliation symbol is the "Peace Garden," begun during the first Gulf War, which gave space and resources to provide pastoral support to active duty soldiers' families. Participants and community leaders funded the garden on the parish grounds. A central contemporary obelisk carries the word *Peace* in many languages. An outdoor labyrinth was created adjacent to the garden.

St. Thomas' rectors have included the Reverends Dewey Gable (1958–66); Hal Daniel (1966–77); Charles Roper (1978–94); John Boucher (1995–1997); and Douglas Hahn (1999–present).

Text submitted by the Reverend Doug Hahn, Ann Burr, Ann Johnston, Amy Nerone, Vicky Partin, and Sherry Wade, with stories from others. Photos from the church archives.

St. James' Episcopal Church, Clayton

✠

On May 23, 1958, Shirley Cheatham of Clayton and the Reverend Robert Wright, rector of St. Mathias', Toccoa, organized a meeting in Clayton to determine interest in forming an Episcopal mission. The new mission's first service was June 1, 1958, in the Clayton Community Center with about twelve people attending Morning Prayer led by John Dillon, lay reader from St. Matthias'. Bishop Claiborne named Father Robert Wright vicar and the mission St. John the Baptist.

In January 1959, the Reverend Milton Murra Jr. of Grace-Calvary, Clarkesville, was named vicar. In September the Diocese was petitioned to move St. James', Tallulah Falls (fourteen miles away) to Clayton and dissolve St. John the Baptist, thus creating St. James' Church. The chalice and paten presently used at St. James', Clayton, were originally used at St. James', Tallulah Falls. In January 1960, the Reverend Charles Taylor Jr., rector of St. Matthias', Toccoa, became vicar. In mid-1960, St. James' moved services from the Community Center to office space on Savannah Street. St. James' became known as the "downtown storefront church."

In 1962, a "summer visiting clergy" program began—facilitated by the large number of Episcopal clergy vacationing in the mountains coupled with the desire of the members for more frequent Eucharists. By 1966, the parish numbered about twenty and had outgrown the storefront space. By 1966, three more priests had served part time at St. James'—the Reverends Wilson Snead, J. Powell Eaton, and James Henry. In 1967, two acres were purchased but were sold in 1973 before any construction started. The present church site on Warwoman Road was bought in 1976.

In 1977, a consultant from the Episcopal Church Building Fund Foundation in New York City designed the church. A local contractor began construction in 1978. The first service in the new building was Christmas Day, 1978, with dedication on July 8, 1979, by Suffragan Bishop Judson Child. In 1979 members numbered fifty-six, and the following priests had served part time: Gordon Shumard, Dawson Teague, Edward Jordan, Luther Williams, and Lyon Williams.

The Reverend Homer Carrier, of Franklin, North Carolina, became supply clergy in 1980 and served in

Evening falls on St. James' Episcopal Church in Clayton.

essentially a full-time basis until 1982. By 1983, the mortgage was paid and a "note burning" service was held. On February 15, 1984, twenty-six years after its humble beginnings, St. James', with eighty-four communicants, had its first full-time vicar—the Reverend Arthur J. Lockhart—appointed by Bishop Judson Child.

Father Lockhart's tenure was marked by change: an 8 o'clock service and a Wednesday healing service, a choir and Foyer groups, and a paid organist were added. Needlepoint altar-rail kneelers and other cushions were made and the Memorial Garden was created. Father Lockhart retired in December 1987 and the Reverend Arthur Cody, served as the supply priest on a regular basis until the Reverend Allen T. Peyton III was named vicar on July 16, 1989, by Bishop Allan. Father Peyton left in March 1992 and in June, Bishop Allan appointed the Reverend Donn Brown as vicar until his retirement in 1996.

The Reverend Mollie Douglas became vicar in October 1996. During her tenure, St. James' took on a more dynamic parish and community ministry. The Daughters of the King were reactivated, adult Christian Formation and Bible studies and the mid-week healing service with laying-on of hands were initiated. Members helped form the Community Pantry and Community Partnership. Attendance and pledge and plate contributions at both services have continued to increase. A Liturgical Arts Committee was formed to create new seasonal paraments and vestments. She was called to Bruton Parish in Williamsburg, Virginia, in early 2000.

In May 2001 the Reverend Brenda Monroe became vicar. The church became self-supporting and Bishop Alexander installed Reverend Monroe as the first rector of St. James' on November 28, 2001. Christian education adult studies continued to be offered, but the families with small children gradually left or moved away. Currently congregational members staff the nursery weekly for visiting children. A very skilled professional choir director was hired, additional vestments and paraments were created, and an outdoor labyrinth was built before she left in March 2005.

The Reverend James Clarke from Clarkesville is serving as a part-time supply priest until a new part-time rector is called. The congregation continues a vibrant ministry and attendance and giving have increased.

Text submitted by the 2005 Search Committee. Photos from the church archives.

The congregation at worship at St. James' Episcopal Church in Clayton.

St. Mary's Episcopal Church, Montezuma

✛

When early settlers came to Marshallville in the 1840s from Orange County, South Carolina, they brought with them the Episcopal Church. They formed St. Mary's and built a church in Marshallville. The membership dwindled and the church building was moved or torn down.

It was more than a century later in 1956 when Episcopalians in Montezuma began meeting, along with their friends in the Women's Clubhouse. As founding members, Mrs. Reuben (Evelon) Black, Mrs. William (Mae) Elrod, Mrs. James (Elizabeth Ann) Geeslin, and Mr. and Mrs. Robert C. Wooten voted to name the new parish St. Mary's. An upstairs room in the Robert C. Wooten home on North Dooly Street was fitted out and used as a chapel from 1958 to 1961.

Father Robert D. Battin, the rector of Calvary Church in Americus, became vicar of the church on January 17, 1960, and led the congregation to make plans for a church building. J. B. Easterlin, William Easterlin, Mary Ann Easterlin, Judge Jule Felton, and Tom Marshall gave several lots of land for the church building. The first service in the new building was on February 12, 1961, and the dedication was held on March 5, 1961. Over the years St. Mary's has been served by clergy from both the Diocese of Atlanta and the Diocese of Georgia.

Many gifts of historical significance were donated by friends. The close is paved with bricks made in Macon County and were originally used in the old Bank of Oglethorpe. Bricks in the wall around the close were made in Macon County in the 1800s and were once part of the Macon County Jail. The iron gates in the close wall came from the home built by Elijah Lewis, congressman from this district. The church bell was brought to Macon County in 1837 by James Madison Wicker from the Cut Off Community in South Carolina, where it had been used as a farm bell. In 1971, a Parish Hall was added to the church building and a small but loyal group has continued to make up the parish of St. Mary's Episcopal Church.

Text submitted by Christy Armstrong McKenzie from the Macon County Life, 1933–1983. *Photo from the church archives.*

St. Mary's Episcopal Church, Montezuma.

EPISCOPAL CENTER AT THE UNIVERSITY OF GEORGIA

✠

Since before the turn of the twentieth century, Episcopal students attending the University of Georgia (UGA) gathered under the care of Emmanuel Parish in Athens. The Episcopal Center at UGA was established in 1959 as an outreach arm of the parish when the Reverend J. Earle Gilbreath was rector. Two contributing factors to this historic move were the success of the parish-based ministry accomplished for several years by Mr. and Mrs. E. R. Hodgson Jr. and the arrival to Emmanuel of a new curate, the Reverend Nathaniel Parker. It was the Reverend Parker who led in the development of the Lumpkin Street properties by first securing the donation of the house at 980 South Lumpkin Street. The two-story boarding house was named the Hodgson House in honor of E. R. and his wife Mary and immediately became the center for Episcopal Student Activity at UGA. After renovations a portion of the house was dedicated as the Chapel of St. Mary the Virgin, a name customary to collegiate chapels and reminiscent of the historic St. Mary's mission (whose steeple still stands near the river bottom on Oconee Street just east of downtown).

The Reverend Parker saw the ministry through a successful start and was followed by the Reverend Dawson Teague in 1961. In the early years members of Emmanuel Parish provided many volunteer hours cooking and hosting events at the house. The greatest portion of the center's history was accomplished under the creative and generous leadership of the Reverend Ralph Marsh. Installed in 1965, he began fundraising for much needed property development. Bishop Bennett Sims deemed the center a freestanding Diocesan institution and the chaplain's role as curate of Emmanuel was greatly reduced.

A cafe and a small boarding house adjacent to the Hodgson House were purchased with funds from around the Diocese and in particular from members of Emmanuel, including Mildred V. Rhodes. By 1983 donations allowed razing the two structures and ground was broken for the construction of a new St. Mary's Chapel. Included in this work were renovations of the Hodgson House, replacing the kitchen, adding a rest room, and enlarging the living room and parlor into a single space. The Chapel was dedicated in 1984 with the stained-glass altar window in memory of Mildred

UGA Center. Watercolor courtesy of Jill Leite.

University of Georgia Episcopal Center Chapel in Athens.

After Ms. Sarah Fisher had very ably served the center as its lay director for nearly a year the Reverend Sean Ferrell came to the center and served as curate for Emmanuel in 1999. Sean renewed the development work begun under the Reverend Graham and instituted two major fundraising programs: game-day parking and the construction and leasing of a cell-telephone tower. Sharing responsibilities with an outreach committee of St. Gregory's Parish, the center's parking lot quickly became the major revenue source for program expenses. Income from the cell-tower was directed into the Diocesan general fund and offset some of the funding support provided by the Diocese. In January of 2003 Chaplain Ferrell answered the call to become campus minister of Michigan State University and left directing of the center to UGA grad Joseph Green.

With the help of the Reverend Tripp Norris and the Reverend Dann Brown the center continued to flourish under Mr. Green's direction. In June of 2003 the Reverend Brown began full-time service to the center and on the Feast of St. Agnes of Rome, January 21, 2004, his new ministry as the sixth "Chaplain to the Episcopal students of the University, Vicar of St. Mary's Chapel and Director of the Episcopal Center" was celebrated by Bishop J. Neil Alexander. The occasion was highlighted by the visit and preaching of the Right Reverend Henry J. Louttit, Bishop of the Diocese of Georgia. The center is an autonomous ministry of the Diocese of Atlanta and is served by a priest not on staff at either of Athens' parishes.

Text and photos submitted by the Reverend Daniel B. Brown.

✠   ✠   ✠   ✠

Rhodes. Throughout his years of service Father Marsh maintained a vibrant ministry not only for the students and faculty of the University but for many members of the community's congregations who needed a periodic rest away from their home churches. Father Marsh remains the person most remembered and still associated with Episcopal Student ministries at UGA.

In 1996 General Seminary graduate the Reverend Timothy Graham became chaplain and curate to the rector of Emmanuel with the balance of his time and focus still largely on the student ministry at UGA. During Father Tim's service tough decisions were made about the use of the heavily worn and aging Hodgson House. The upstairs apartments were closed and plans for upgrading the property were begun with the support of Emmanuel's rector, the Reverend Eddie Ard.

ST. FRANCIS' EPISCOPAL CHURCH, MACON

⚜

On a cold and sunny day, Sunday, November 18, 1959, St. Francis' Church celebrated its first communion. But it wasn't nearly as simple as that. Who knows what would have happened if, many years before that day, Macon's own heavyweight world boxing champion, Young Stribling, hadn't been killed in a motorcycle accident on his way to the hospital to see his newborn child. His young widow, a member at Macon's St. James' Episcopal Church, later fell in love with and married the rector, who became the Bishop of Atlanta.

Macon's 1950s Episcopal presence was limited to old settled neighborhoods. The Diocese planted a mission, Church of the Messiah, in the south, and encouraged St. James' to move from historic Cherokee Heights to north Macon. For some months, St. James' worshiped in two locations—in Cherokee Heights and the new one in Wimbish Woods. The plan to close down the old church was not to be. An appeal went to their bishop—their former rector and their kinsman in marriage. St. James' remained in Cherokee Heights, leaving the north Macon upstarts to seek a new identity. "St. Francis" was chosen and Bishop Claiborne celebrated their founding with Evensong on Thursday night before that cold and sunny day in November 1959.

St. Francis' struggled with "high/low" liturgy issues and formed a caring community. From 1967 to 1972 Father Woody Bartlett led St. Francis' into social action and advocacy and St. Francis' has continued to play a role in local social justice issues disproportionate to its size or wealth.

When the Appleton Home left its facilities in the early 1970s, St. Francis' gained education and fellowship space. The struggling Church of the Messiah eventually voted to merge with St. Francis'. On June 1, 1975, Bishop Sims wrote: "Your decision to merge . . . is conspicuous for its humility, generosity, and practicality." The small Appleton Chapel was expanded. With the Reverend Don Greenwood's leadership, the newly enlarged St. Francis' became the renewed church in Macon, where folk songs were sung. Faith Alive, Cursillo, and Daughters of the King shaped the ethos of the day.

For the first half of the 1980s, St. Francis' was introspective, taking the Myers-Briggs test and reading Jung. For the next half, St. Francis' was evangelical and

St. Francis' Episcopal Church, enlarged from the former Appleton Chapel, Macon.

inclined toward Episcopalians United. It was a confusing, conflicted decade. In 1990, the Reverend Sandy Horton came to St. Francis' as Macon's first woman rector. Her focus on AIDS ministry established a mission priority that is still alive.

For thirty years St. Francis' was blessed with the devoted service of able horticulturalist Eugene Basinski, who tended the grounds with love, sweat, and skill. Old school Episcopalian Dr. Hasell LaBorde "Anglicanized" St. Francis' by insisting on fidelity to traditions. In the sacristy, Nell Morgan softened one's disposition with a sweet smile and gentle soul. Father Luther Williams epitomized the spirit of the church's patron saint with an uncanny ability to find destitute people with specific needs and enlisted members of the congregation to meet them. He lived in self-chosen apostolic poverty himself. He just passed gifts of clothes on to those who needed them more. Dr. Dorothy Brown inspired action for ministry to the church's sister parish in Ecuador. Milla Wilson sat on the porch in his jumpsuit, smoking cigarettes and drinking coffee, in between chipping our fallen branches into mulch for Eugene's flower gardens. St. Francis' Episcopal Church was consecrated as a holy family and a holy place by these and many other saints now in the nearer presence of God.

With the congregation still are true heroes of the faith. Mary Coates, the beloved matriarch and a founding member of the local PFLAG Chapter kept the church open hearted. Today, Gail and Ranny Moulton inspire the parish to form a sister parish relationship with St. Marc's in Haiti. Marcia Aldridge sustains the ongoing Bible study. Others lead in housing rehab and race-relations work. The Woody Bartlett tradition of service beyond the church's walls continues.

St. Francis' has had its internal struggles—but those who have been the most ardent adversaries have held each other's hands in times of sorrow and loss. Personal relationships in Christ overcome personal opinions. Over the past ten years, rocking chairs placed on the porches turned them into welcoming gathering spaces. A new fellowship, education, and music wing has been added. The church' mission has grown through sister parish relationships with Macon's Holsey Temple CME Church and with churches in Ecuador and Haiti. Each year new Franciscans bring new gifts, talents, and vision. The members of St. Francis' Episcopal Church eagerly look forward to playing their part in the Diocese of Atlanta for the coming century.

Submitted by the Reverend Dan Edwards. Photos by Dan Edwards, and Dale and Susan Myers.

St. Francis' Episcopal Church Parish Hall, formerly part of Appleton Church Home, Macon.

✠   ✠   ✠   ✠

ST. BEDE'S EPISCOPAL CHURCH, ATLANTA

✝

St. Bede's Episcopal Church began in 1956, when the Diocese of Atlanta purchased 7.5 acres at the corner of Henderson Mill and Midvale Roads, between Tucker and Chamblee and near the historic Henderson Mill site. Legend says Mr. Henderson declined several purchase offers because he wanted a church built on his "Jesus Patch." The church was a mission from St. Bartholomew's, and though the first parishioners wanted the name St. Francis, Bishop Claiborne decreed that it should be called St. Bede's. He also reportedly authored the unfortunate label (or libel) of "St. Bede's in the weeds," perhaps in honor of our heavily wooded site!

St. Bede's was incorporated in 1960. The first regular service was held in June at Briarlake Elementary School. The first building was constructed in 1962, with parishioners doing much of the interior and finish work. A second building in 1968 holds the Parish Hall, classrooms, and choir room. A connecting commons area was added in 1982. St. Bede's Day School has existed since 1963.

During the 1960s and 1970s the congregation was largely young suburban families. The congregation stabilized in the 1980s: the 1984 *Parish Profile* stated that "[St. Bede's] remains a diverse congregation with different kinds of people who have different points of view and different ideas, but it is not the ever-changing, no-roots-or-traditions parish of the 60s and 70s." St. Bede's today has parishioners from many different backgrounds enjoying strong bonds of affection and mutual respect.

After much discussion and prayer (and some conflict!), the parish decided that a new nave would accommodate a new organ and also enable St. Bede's to develop a worship space that reflected an active, inclusive, serving vision of our faith community. The decision to build a new nave was originally disapproved by the Diocese, but they persisted, and an unexpected Pentecost donation from a visiting worshipper assisted in the capital campaign to build this new worship space. It is now, as it should be, the focal point of the church. The organ itself, the seventeen-rank Richards and Fowkes Opus

St. Bede's Episcopal Church, Atlanta, exterior view.

St. Bede's Episcopal Church, Atlanta, Youth Group.

IX, was dedicated with great joy on March 11, 2000, and has drawn praise from the congregation and the local music community.

St. Bede's has been blessed by the service of two long-term rectors: the Reverend Milton Murray (1970–1984), and the Reverend John Porter (1985–2002). The current rector, the Reverend Janice Chalaron, continues their tradition of empowering, compassionate, and inclusive leadership, along with the associate rector, Laura Bryant, and a dedicated staff. St. Bede's has also benefited from strong lay leadership.

St. Bede's has combined outreach and engagement with devout worship and continuing commitment to Christian education. The church's vision statement affirms the qualities of its patron saint and sets as its aim "to empower for service compassionate disciples who respect the dignity of every human being." Both the choir in 2001 and the Journey to Adulthood class in 2003 have made pilgrimages to Jarrow, England, the home of the church's patron saint. The congregation has supported parishioners who have become ordained clergy.

A warm, committed parish family, St. Bede's has taken a varied approach to worship—from medieval chanting to folk mass—yet remains devoted to the beautiful and moving liturgy that is the heritage of the Episcopal Church. Among our principles is a phrase deriving from St. Thomas Aquinas: "In essentials, unity; in nonessentials, diversity; in all things, charity." As St. Bede's approaches its fiftieth anniversary, its members look to the future with strong and active faith!

Text submitted by Stan Meiburg, with special thanks to Ray Callaway, Aileen Hiscutt, Paul Holbrook, George Shingler and Jan Swoope. Photos from the church archives.

ST. CHRISTOPHER'S EPISCOPAL CHURCH, PERRY

✣

Although Perry is one of middle Georgia's oldest cities, its Episcopal Church, St. Christopher's, is relatively new, only now approaching its fiftieth year. In January 1960, eighteen Perry residents who had met since the previous March received a charter from the Diocese to establish a mission. Named for St. Christopher, the patron saint of travelers, it reflected Perry's slogan as the "Crossroads of Georgia." Before St. Christopher's

had its own building, it met at various locations including the Perry Manufacturing Building, the American Legion Hall, and the Presbyterian Youth Center.

With Diocesan help in 1962, the new mission built the current church. When dedicated by Bishop Claiborne on December 20, 1962, the new building was relatively Spartan and served as the place of worship and Parish Hall, using screens to conceal the altar during meetings. As the mission grew, the building became inadequate and after the mortgage was paid and the mission became an aided parish in 1977, an addition was built including a true Parish Hall, office space, and classrooms. It was dedicated in May 1980, and is essentially the church as it stands today.

St. Christopher's was served during its first decade by several vicars, some shared with other nearby churches. They were the Reverend Hal S. Daniell Jr. (1960–64); the Reverend W. Russell Daniel (1964); the Reverend Louis Parker (1965); the Reverend James R. Borum (1965–67); and the Reverend Graham Glover (1967–70). Stability was finally achieved when the Reverend Thomas L. Arledge Jr. arrived in 1970 and remained for over twenty-five years.

For many years, particularly the early 1990s, church finances were strained, and the Vestry minutes record a need for a special Sunday collections

St. Christopher's Episcopal Church in Perry.

Dedication of the Children's Garden at St. Christopher's Episcopal Church in Perry, Georgia.

part of the local community. Major successes were the end of aided parish status during his tenure, increased attendance at services (including Holy Week), a much healthier financial condition, and the remodeling and renovation of the church's building and grounds. Upon his retirement from St. Christopher's and active ministry in 2004, the Parish Hall was renamed Buchanan Hall.

Canon Buchanan had planned for transition to a new rector upon his retirement and in 2003 planned with Diocesan help to hire the Reverend Bill Anderson, a deacon from South Carolina, as curate, with the intent of his being ordained and called as rector upon Buchanan's retirement.

Father Anderson, ordained in October 2003, became rector in June 2004. Weekly attendance at the primary Sunday service now averages one hundred. Father Anderson is president of the Perry Ministerial Association and in December 2004 St. Christopher's hosted an interfaith memorial service for parents who had lost children. This intensely emotional and well-attended service may become a tradition.

South Houston County is growing rapidly and St. Christopher's, a decade after being in danger of closing, is poised to meet that growth. The parish is determining the best way to expand its physical space, has added two new weekly Eucharist services, and is investigating adding space for Christian education and community outreach. St. Christopher's has truly replaced the problems of survival with the problems of growth!

Text submitted by Paul Davison and the Reverend William Anderson. Photos from the church archives.

to pay the power bill to prevent the lights from being shut off! Membership had steadily declined to the point that its continued survival was in doubt, with attendance at some services reported to have been in single digits.

In 1995, the Reverend Canon John Buchanan became vicar. An experienced priest with prior service in Texas, Georgia, and in Europe, he provided new energy to the parish and began reversing the decline. His often-stated goal was to build St. Christopher's to a point to replace him with a full-time resident priest who was truly a

ST. CATHERINE'S EPISCOPAL CHURCH, MARIETTA

✠

Bloom where you are planted," they heard, and that is just what happened on October 30, 1961, when thirty-five Episcopalians organized St. Catherine's Mission, initially meeting with the Reverend John Womack, archdeacon of the Diocese. For most of its first five years, it was served by the Reverend William McClelland Jr. Over four decades and several building programs with visionary rectors, the church has seats for over four hundred, an attached Education Building, more offices and staff, and a large commercial kitchen.

In 1962, the present ten acres was acquired for $12,500 for a four-phase building program. By 1967 the mission had grown to ninety-five communicants and the Reverend James Clarke was appointed part-time vicar. Construction of a larger facility was completed in 1968. The cost of the church with classrooms in the undercroft was $40,000. Much of the construction was done by volunteers. St. Catherine's is a visible expression of its members. The first service was held in March 1970 and Father Clarke became full-time vicar.

On February 15, 1973, Father Clarke accepted the post of institutional chaplain for the Diocese of Atlanta and the Reverend Michael B. Milligan, curate of St. Paul's, Macon, began May 22, 1973. With his leadership, a "Mothers' Morning Out" program was begun by two St. Catherine's moms who saw a need for this kind of childcare and ministry. Under Father Milligan, the church went from aided to unaided parish status. He left in 1976 to do consultation work and to further his education. The Reverend David F. Wayland from Covington, Kentucky, followed Father Milligan.

The spring of 1980 was a pivotal time for St. Catherine's when the Diocese had purchased land for a new church about five miles to the east of the church. Bishop Sims asked the people of St. Catherine's to consider relocating to the new location. The Vestry advised Bishop Sims that the church would stay on Holt Road, and its theme and slogan became "Bloom where you are planted."

And bloom, it did, with a new addition that connected the church building with parish offices, new classrooms, and a new kitchen. New ministries and programs were also added. The Mother's Morning Out grew to become the highly respected preschool, which now has about two hundred students. The church's connection with MUST Ministries grew and it became involved with building Habitat Houses. More staff was added and a new organ purchased. In 1986, the sanctuary was renovated by church members. In January 1988, Father Wayland celebrated his final service and groundbreaking for a new education and

office wing. The Reverend Doris Graf Smith, who had been ordained deacon and priest at St. Catherine's, became priest-in-charge during the vacancy.

Father Laurence Packard became rector on May 7, 1989, and began his ministry with a large hole in the ground—later the educational wing. He oversaw the completion of the building. As membership grew, a third Sunday morning service was added and a Memorial Garden was completed near the church. Packard resigned on July 7, 1996, to accept a new call and the Reverend Newell Anderson served as interim, until 1998, when the Reverend Jim Nixon came to St. Catherine's.

As Cobb County grew, so did the membership to nearly seven hundred members. In 2002, the Reverend Sherry Coulter of Memphis became assistant rector. Father Jim saw the need of a long-range planning group and began "The Emmaus Project" and this group indicated the need for a much larger facility.

Midway through the church expansion, remodeling and refurbishing, on January 10, 2004, St. Catherine's was devastated by an electrical fire, interrupting the building process. St. Catherine's Pre-School was so badly damaged that the church was forced to find a temporary home. Nearby congregations and schools opened hearts, hands, and doors. After ten months of rebuilding, the church was dedicated in the new and gloriously rebuilt worship space by Bishop Alexander. St. Catherine's continues to bloom and grow.

Text submitted by Eileen Motter. Photo from the church archives.

✠ ✠ ✠ ✠

Exterior view of St. Catherine's sanctuary, Marietta.

THE EPISCOPAL CHURCH OF THE ATONEMENT, ATLANTA

✛

The Episcopal Church of the Atonement began as a mission of Holy Innocents of Sandy Springs in January 1962, as the Reverend Hugh Saussy Jr. realized the need for the area from Roswell Road East to Fulton-DeKalb County line, and from Mount Vernon Highway to Buckhead. At the first meeting on January 7, 1962, eighteen couples stood, and signed a petition to Bishop Randolph R. Claiborne Jr. At another meeting, Mary Wood Bullock suggested "At-One-Ment with God," which was accepted by the Diocese.

The first service, with thirty communicants, under Father Saussy Jr., priest-in-charge, was held at McClatchy School on February 18, 1962. The Reverend Dr. E. Eager Wood Jr. became vicar in the summer of 1962. Services moved to Guy Webb School in March 1963. On December 13, 1963, eight acres were purchased, with groundbreaking October 1, 1967, where the church stands today. In January 1964, upon petition to, and acceptance by the fifty-seventh annual Council of the Diocese as a parish, he became the rector. On March 4, 1967, fellow parishioner, C. Bruce McCaskill, was ordained perpetual deacon, as assistant.

Members of Atlanta's Church of the Atonement receive communion.

The original mortgage was paid off and papers burned about three years after its initiation—a record until recently as being the "fastest retired mortgage for a parish in the Diocese of Atlanta." Outreach ranged from art and variety shows, Six Flags trips for children and adults to the Lynwood Exchange and Day Care Center that our members helped local churches renovate and staff, which established year-round programs for seven- to eighteen-year-olds.

After Dr. Wood, the Reverend Patrick H. Sanders' leadership and teaching qualities helped the church redefine their financial obligations to the structural facility and outreach by making it a line item in the budget of 10 percent. "Festival for Friends" bazaar ran for two years with food, games, and varied activities for all ages. Thanksgiving and Christmas dinners are taken to Hollywood Homes residents. Members helped with St. Luke's Soup kitchen and Community Action Center. A $5,000 Scholarship Fund was sent in Sanders' honor to Virginia Seminary upon his leaving.

The Reverend John P. Brewster encouraged the church to expand their facility with a new Parish Hall, kitchen, offices, and bathrooms to offer ministries to larger groups community wide.

In 1996, a longtime parishioner bequeathed $25,000 to the church, which began the Shepherd's Fund, an endowment administered by a committee. Grants were given to groups in the metro area to improve the lives of people in need.

The Reverend Dr. Trawin E. Malone adds a new and spirited ministry and outreach with his varied musical background. A coffee house—reflecting Father Malone's many years in New Orleans—was started as a semiregular event for local teens hosted by the church's teens. Music has always been a major part of worship and outreach at the church, combining offerings from opera to jazz to occasional liturgical dance all open to the entire neighborhood.

The church's greatest outreach has been presenting for ordination the Reverend J. Eloise Haley, the Reverend Lynnsay Buehler, and the Reverend Joan Pritcher. Their varied talents and personalities continue to enrich the state and world.

Faithfully submitted and with many thanks to all the Angels who helped present this report by Thelma Nunn English. Photos from the church archives.

Opposite page: Exterior view of Church of the Atonement, Atlanta.

✛ ✛ ✛ ✛

CHURCH OF THE TRANSFIGURATION, ROME

✠

The Episcopal Church of the Transfiguration—conceived by an adult church school class at St. Peter's Church, downtown—was a faithful aided mission of the Diocese for forty-one years. In 2003 the congregation finally reached full parish status. The parishes' first rector, the Reverend Canon Michael Owens, notified the Bishop that financial aid was no longer needed, and that the tithe to the Diocese would continue in thanksgiving and gratitude. A gala forty-fifth anniversary year in 2006 was planned to celebrate and give thanks for what has been, and for God creating in our midst a fruitful future, gathering many ministers in Christ's name.

Each Sunday the adult class at St. Peter's made an offering for the West Rome Mission Fund. In 1961 the Diocese purchased 3.6 acres of land at the corner of Coosawattee and Shorter Avenues, some five miles from downtown. Beginning the first Sunday in July, regular services and church school were held at West Rome High School. Bishop Claiborne assigned Blount Grant, a senior seminarian, to assist. The petition for mission status was signed by all adults present at a meeting on the eve of the Feast of the Transfiguration on August 5, 1961. The petition was approved at the January 1962 Council.

Father George Forzly, the first vicar, arrived in September, also serving St. Barnabas' in Trion. The late Ralph Ayers was first senior warden and George Joyner, still quite active, was junior warden. Connie and son, Donald, and Bonnie Joyner have also continuously served, as have Bill and Pat Rudolph and Jean Churchfield. Many others have remained active for twenty to thirty years.

Groundbreaking was March 31, 1963, with Bishop Claiborne present. Many at St. Peter's helped make this first building possible, especially Jack and Sissy Rogers. The beautiful wrought-iron work was done by local artisan Karl Dance, and the woodwork and the carving on the credence tables by parishioners Billy Kay and Billy Rudd. Even the children helped.

In late 1967, the Reverend John M. Flanigen was named vicar; also serving St. Barnabas'. In May 1972 Father Nathaniel Massey became vicar, serving part time with

Church of the Transfiguration, Rome.

Members of the Church of the Transfiguration, Rome.

Child dedicated the building on October 7, 1984, with worship space for 125 persons, classrooms, offices, Parish Hall, and kitchen. Members, including the children, helped in much of the construction.

Following Father Home's retirement, the Reverend Robin Smith became vicar on August 5, 1986. During her service the Twenty-fifth Anniversary was observed. The Reverend Dr. Jerry Zeller was appointed by Bishop Allan to serve as priest-in-charge in 1990. During this period the church became yoked with St. James', Cedartown, and a period of revitalization in ministry, membership, the youth group, Sunday school, and outreach ministry began.

The Reverend Hazel Glover became rector in 1993 but was called to St. James, Marietta, after a short tenure. In 1994 and 1995, the parish lost both members and momentum before calling in 1996 the Reverend David Kidd who faithfully and lovingly guided the church, and an active lay leadership corps led the members toward a more active and vibrant mission.

The Reverend Michael Owens accepted the appointment by Bishop Alexander on August 1, 2002, as a part-time priest-in-charge, then became the vicar and assembled a dynamic lay team which led the church into a third major renewal. Asked to be both minister and evangelist, the members responded, using their many gifts. In three years average worship attendance grew from 40 to 75, membership from 85 to 135, and giving by 100 percent. In January 2004 Father Owens became the first rector of the renewed parish.

Gathering for worship, prayer, study, and fellowship, and then going forth in service to others in Christ's name, both locally and beyond, continues to be the rule for the church's life in faith. Future plans include expanding gathering/worship space; a prayer garden; more welcoming grounds; a burial garden renovation; continuation of an African Tractor Project; and development of a local ministry to serve the faith community of Floyd County.

Text submitted by David Hicks, George Joyner, and Michael Owens. Photos by Walter Bunte.

St. James', Cedartown. During Father Massey's tenure, pews replaced chairs, beautiful old stained-glass windows were temporarily installed, and the community grew steadily. On October 15, 1978, Father Massey left to serve at St. John's Cathedral in Jacksonville, Florida.

The Reverend George E. Home, native Roman, became the fourth vicar in October 1979. Membership grew under his strong leadership. The existing building became inadequate and Bishop Sims urged a move into a neighborhood. The present site on Coker Drive was purchased. In November 1983 groundbreaking was held, construction began, and temporary space was found at Westminster Presbyterian Church. Bishop

St. Simon's Episcopal Church, Conyers

⁜

St. Simon's Mission held its first service of worship on June 7, 1964, in the community room of the DeKalb Federal Building, with the Reverend Gordon H. Mann, rector of Good Shepherd, Covington, officiating. It was under his guidance, along with Archdeacon John L. Womack, that the church took shape, beginning with six families who had been active at Good Shepherd.

Ground was broken for the new church facility in December 1966, after a gift of land from John and Demaris Humphries, and the estate of Clarence Vaughan. A portion of this land was to be used as a community park, but the fledgling church lacked the financial resources to construct it, and that portion was offered to Rockdale County, which then built Pine Log Park. With $17,000 worth of materials, some fifteen families worked in their spare time to construct the first building, which was consecrated in April 1967. The first part-time vicar of St. Simon's was the Reverend Robert Fisher. It was during the tenure of the Reverend John Womack (1972–1982) that the parish began to grow and expand, achieved the status of aided parish, and constructed several additions. After Father Womack's death, the Reverend Dean Johnson served the church for nearly three years, during which time St. Simon's achieved parish status. This also signaled a time of growth, requiring a third Sunday service, and eventually a larger worship space, which was built during the tenure of the Reverend Charles Davis Jr. (1989–1993). Membership peaked in the early 1990s, at 330 active members, during the tenure of the Reverend G. Lin Watts (1994–1999)

The new millennium, with issues of human sexuality in the Church at the fore, brought changes to St. Simon's. In 1999, Father Lin Watts retired from active ministry, signaling the loss of some membership. The parish suffered another setback in 2003, with the election and consecration of the Right Reverend V. Gene Robinson, after which attendance leveled off at approximately 150 active members. The Reverend Newell Anderson (1999–2003) served ably as interim during that period. In September 2003, the Reverend Daniel Crockett was called as the fourth rector of St. Simon's. During the two years since, the parish has slowly begun to grow again. With tremendous growth potential in Rockdale County, the church members are optimistic about the future.

Text submitted by church members. Photo from the Collins Collection, Diocese of Atlanta Archives.

⁜   ⁜   ⁜   ⁜

St. Simon's Episcopal Church, Conyers.

ST. DUNSTAN'S EPISCOPAL CHURCH, ATLANTA

✠

St. Dunstan's was founded as a mission of the Diocese of Atlanta in December 1964 by eight families, most of whom had been members of St. Anne's Parish. They wanted to develop a modest, family-oriented neighborhood parish with a strong commitment to local outreach, and a supportive Christian community stressing Christian education.

The mission began regular services at Tuxedo Elementary School in January 1965, and the Reverend Don Harrison became the first rector in April 1965. Under his leadership St. Dunstan's grew and gained a reputation for innovative programs for members and the surrounding community. Early in 1969 St. Dunstan's became a parish of the Diocese. That April Father Harrison left to pursue his long-held interest in affordable housing. The Reverend George Home accepted the call to St. Dunstan's in August 1969.

Having rented space for the first five years, the Vestry decided in 1970 to build a small facility at 4393 Garmon Road, Northwest, on five acres of land that had been purchased by the parish some years before. First services in the new building (which is now the Parish Hall) were held on Christmas Eve, 1971. Father Home resigned in August 1979 to become vicar of the Church of the Transfiguration in Rome. The Reverend Camille Littleton served as interim rector until April 1980.

She was followed by St. Dunstan's third rector, the Reverend Richard Pocalyko. Using his strong administrative and organizational skills, he led the congregation through construction of the current sanctuary, a simple wooden structure like the Parish Hall, with much clear glass giving views into the surrounding woods. He resigned in 1990, and the Reverend Maggie Harney became interim rector. She returned to St. Dunstan's in 1994 as a nonstipendiary priest associate and founding director of "Mary and Martha's Place," a center for spiritual enrichment and development.

In December 1992 the Reverend Margaret Rose accepted the call to become St. Dunstan's fourth rector. She ushered in a period of membership growth, particularly families with children.

The median age decreased, facilities were expanded, the music program enhanced, a variety of other programs were enriched and developed, and a full-time youth director was hired. The Reverend Margaret Rose connected the church to the environment, to the city around it, and to the national church.

In the winter of 2003, she accepted the call of the national Episcopal Church to lead its worldwide program of Ministries for Women. The Reverend P. J. Woodall served as interim rector until the summer of 2004, when the Reverend Patricia Templeton was called as the fifth rector. She, her husband Joe Monti—a professor at the Episcopal Seminary at Sewanee—and their small son, Joseph Henry, immediately became a vibrant part of this community.

St. Dunstan's has a reputation for being a warm, outgoing congregation. They are caring of their spiritual and physical environment and cherish their five beautifully wooded acres, especially a circle of beech trees around a large lawn, which is the site of many parish events.

Text and photos submitted by members of the church.

✠ ✠ ✠ ✠

Exterior of St. Dunstan's, Atlanta.

St. Mary Magdalene, Columbus

✣

Just as biblical scholars have struggled to identify the real Saint Mary Magdalene; so has the congregation bearing her name, now in its fourth decade, failed to come up with a definite self-image. In 1963, Trinity Church and St. Thomas encouraged the development of a mission near Fort Benning. Three years later, the Diocesan Department of Missions borrowed $14,000 to purchase property for the development of St. Mary's. At this same time, the Reverend Thomas M. Stubbs became vicar of the new congregation. Under his leadership, land was acquired on St. Mary's Road and a 100-by-26-foot Army surplus building was moved to the site to become the hub for the congregation's worship and education.

Bishop Claiborne, concerned for the deteriorating condition of St. Christopher's Episcopal School and Church for African Americans in downtown Columbus, persuaded this congregation to sell their building and become members of St. Mary Magdalene. Many of these persons and their descendants remain active and faithful members of the present parish. A "Welcome to St. Christopher" sign graces the wall of the current fellowship hall.

The Reverend Tom Stubbs served St. Mary's from 1965 to 1974 and was succeeded by the Reverend Ron Gibson. Both of these priests also provided services for the Episcopal Church of the Resurrection in Phenix City, just across the Chattahoochee River. Father Gibson left St. Mary's in 1985 and the Reverend Ramona Rose Crossley spent two years as the vicar. The Reverend Crossley was succeeded by the Reverend Steve Lipscomb who also gave leadership for two years. During the tenure of Father Gibson, the congregation, with the aid of the Diocese, constructed a handsome modern church building with a fellowship hall in the basement. The worship space, in the round, offered a dignified but intimate setting for their services.

In 1994, the congregation called the Reverend Benjamin E. K. Speare-Hardy, a native of Liberia, and chaplain at Christ School, Virginia, as their vicar. Ben brought exceptional leadership to the people. The congregation grew rapidly and he led them through the process of developing housing for the elderly and handicapped through the U.S. Department of Housing and Urban Development. The project, named "St. Mary's Woods," is located on the acres directly behind the church. "Father Ben" left in 1999 to accept a call to the Diocese of Southern Ohio and St. Mary's has had a succession of interim clergy since then. In spite of their setbacks, the people of St. Mary's remain strong and a vital core continues faithful service and witness to Christ in their southeast Columbus location.

Text submitted by the Reverend William P. McLemore. Photo from the Collins Collection, Diocese of Atlanta Archives.

✣   ✣   ✣   ✣

St. Mary Magdalene Episcopal Church, Columbus.

ST. PATRICK'S EPISCOPAL CHURCH, DUNWOODY

✠

On December 6, 1966, the Church of St. Martin in the Fields hosted an organizational meeting for a new mission to serve Dunwoody, Doraville, and Chamblee. It was, for reasons no one presently living can recall, named for Patrick of Ireland, the great missionary who, in contrast to his contemporaries managed to spread the Gospel without actually killing anybody.

The Archdeacon John Womack held the first services, as he did for so many parishes. For several years, under several part-time clergy, service took place in neighborhood school cafeterias. Following the abrupt departure of the first full-time priest, Bishop Sims assigned the Reverend P. Roberts Bailey as vicar. Bob's wife Jane brought emotional healing to a damaged little congregation. Together with Jane, he introduced St. Patrick's to the power of the Holy Spirit through work with the Order of St. Luke. By the end of Bob's tenure, the parish was vitally involved in Bible study and "exploration into God."

When Bob left to join the Bishop's staff in 1974, the congregation called the Reverend Gray Temple as its first rector. Gray has served St. Patrick's ever since.

St. Patrick's has pioneered liturgical renewal (not so much by refinement as by release), a rare combination of personal piety and social outreach, and mission. For example, St. Patrick's led the way for Holy Comforter to be adopted by other parishes as a mission center, and a challenge grant spurred the formation of Saints Mary and Martha of Bethany in Buford.

St. Patrick's has been distinguished for its stewardship for most of its life. The parish has also produced an average of one priest every three years. In the summer and fall of 1993 owing to an adult study of the sacramental status of homosexual Episcopalians, roughly half of the congregation left the parish and the Episcopal Church in response to the rector's admitting his favorable view of gay marriage and ordination. Though reduced in numbers, the parish's budget did not suffer fatally.

Over the years, in addition to stimulating a large number of men and women to seek holy orders, St. Patrick's has enjoyed the ministries of a distinguished list of priest-associates, deacons, and seminary interns, a disproportionate number of whom have gone on to staffs of cathedrals and dioceses.

For three decades St. Patrick's has daily demonstrated what its purpose openly states: that "Spirit-led worship generates a caring fellowship of men and women who undertake ministry in the Church and in the World."

Text submitted by the Reverend Canon Gray Temple. Photo from the Collins Collection, Diocese of Atlanta Archives.

✠ ✠ ✠ ✠

St. Patrick's Episcopal Church, Atlanta.

EMMAUS HOUSE, ATLANTA

✝

A little more than halfway through its first century, the Diocese of Atlanta considered what the church could do to address the everyday problems of black, inner-city poor people in Atlanta. The Reverend Austin Ford, deeply affected and moved to action by the injustices of the segregated South, had already as rector of St. Bartholomew's inspired his parish and others in the community to take part in the civil rights and antiwar movements. In 1967, when the Bishop of Atlanta challenged Father Ford and the Diocese to do something concrete, he purchased a $2-a-night flophouse in the Peoplestown/Summerhill community, moved in, and created a Diocesan ministry to apply the love of Christ incarnate in Atlanta. During four decades Emmaus House has acted as a good neighbor, helping area residents with legal, social, and economic problems.

Emmaus House offers summer and after school programs for community children. The Poverty Rights Office helps people in need to apply for assistance, obtain ID cards, and receive mail. The Community Art Project helps children, teens, adults and senior citizens to learn woodturning and woodworking, pottery, jewelry-making, stained-glass, and painting. The Community Supper every month includes all generations for fellowship and a hot meal. The Senior Strollers enjoy lunch, classes and crafts, transportation to stores and field trips. The Reidsville Trip takes family members to visit loved ones at the state prison. The Christmas Program provides gender-appropriate wrapped gifts to hundreds of children on Christmas Eve, gift baskets for seniors and families, and an evening of fun and refreshments.

An outgrowth of the social ministries at Emmaus House is the Emmaus House Chapel, a congregation of neighborhood residents and visitors from all walks of life and diverse backgrounds and experiences. The Chapel began with simple Eucharist gatherings in the living room of the main house, mainly for the staff that lived at Emmaus House. Later, children began to attend and a Sunday school was established. As more people began to attend, the Chapel became a "worshiping community" of the Diocese and finally a parish in 1992. Services are held at 10:30 a.m. on Sundays.

The Emmaus House campus consists of five Victorian houses on the corner of Hank Aaron Drive (a continuation of Capitol Avenue) along the east side of Turner Field. Included are the Emmaus House Chapel, Ford Hall, Ezzard Hall, and Emmaus House itself, as well as a potting shed and the Poverty Rights Office and Study Hall buildings. Parking is permitted on Hank Aaron Drive. Recent improvements have included replacement of porches and electrical wiring, fresh paint, a newly acquired school bus, and expanded restrooms. Upcoming projects will include additional wiring, replacement of obsolete furnaces, repairs to the drainage system and kitchen, and fire safety improvements. The Poverty Rights Office is in need of improved facilities.

Emmaus House is supported by the Diocese of Atlanta, by contributions from individuals, parishes and other organizations, and by the volunteer help of numerous people from within and outside the Diocese. Visitors are always welcome as are program volunteers who tutor, cook, drive, advise, guide, play, and organize; administrative volunteers who serve on the Advisory Board, answer phones, help with mailings, and do general office work. Facilities volunteers paint, weed, make repairs, improve property safety, beauty, and usefulness. Financial volunteers contribute to make everything else possible.

Text submitted by Robert E. Van Keuren Jr. Photo from the Collins Collection, Diocese of Atlanta Archives.

Opposite page: Emmaus House, Atlanta.

✝   ✝   ✝   ✝

Episcopal Church of St. Edward the Confessor, Lawrenceville

✠

Like the earliest Christians, this congregation is a people of the Word. More, they are a people of stories: individual testimonies of how they came to the church and persevered as Episcopalians; chronicles of how and why they stay together as a community of believers.

St. Edward's began as a mission to Gwinnett County in the fall of 1968. The first service was held in a Duluth living room with fourteen souls in attendance. Within a month, they were invited to move into the offices of the *Gwinnett Daily News* by the owner/publisher and founding member. They were officially chartered at their first annual meeting on November 17, 1968, when they elected their first Vestry and claimed their name.

Needing space, St. Edward's moved into a strip shopping center in Lawrenceville, and began ministering to the wider community: Wheel Chair Club, AA, Al-Anon, and even a thirsty itinerant circus elephant! Barbecue was sold along the highway to pay for the first organ, starting two bedrock ministries within the congregation: the ambitious, outstanding and varied music ministry and the "Pit Crew," which produces not only the main course for St. Edward's feasts but also the church's favorite incense when the smoky barbecue cooks walk down the aisle to receive communion.

During its first four years, St. Edward's was faithfully served by vicars Doug Turley and Vic Nickelson, their vicar emeritus. The current campus, a former strawberry field, was begun on December 10, 1972. Construction was interrupted by a freak June windstorm that destroyed every roof truss the very night the last one was nailed into place. During a workday before the first services in our new church, a parishioner opened a stairwell doorway to find the floor covered with monarch butterflies. They took glorious flight into the sunshine, like King Edward's heraldic martlets, on October 6, 1973, seven days before the Feast of St. Edward.

Leaping from mission directly to parish status, St. Edward's called its first rector, Father Tom Kehayes, in 1976. He led the parish through transitions of the Prayer Book, Hymnal, and the ordination of women. The church undertook a campaign to build its current administration and Christian education building. The ministries housed and expanded in these facilities continue to be central to their parish life: food, fellowship, celebration, and Christian education.

Exterior view of St. Edward the Confessor, Lawrenceville.

Interior view of St. Edward the Confessor, Lawrenceville.

When Father Kent Branstetter arrived in October 1996, the pews and parking lot were full every Sunday. Within a year, a third service was added on Sunday morning and an assistant priest. A memorial garden was built in 1999. The new nave was dedicated and the parking lot enlarged in 2001. The house next door was donated to the church in 2001, and it has become the home of the youth ministries and the headquarters of the two newest outreach ministry partnerships: Counseling Center and Family Promise, a multichurch transitional housing ministry. Most recently, the outdoor classroom and chapel, constructed as Eagle Scout projects organized by two young parishioners, were completed in 2002–2003.

St. Edward's membership now includes individuals and families from Europe, Asia, Africa, South America, and the Caribbean, in addition to folks from Canada and Mexico and all over the United States—which makes for rich worship, pastoral challenges, and fabulous potluck meals! Members believe their communion will only continue to grow as they welcome all believers and seekers to the Lord's Table at the church.

The years 1987 to 1995 under their second rector, Father Bill Payton, brought out St. Edward's true character: serious about liturgy, stewardship, and education; light-hearted about pretty much everything else. St. Edward's fellowship style is now legendary. The party celebrating our newly paved parking lot boasted an Elvis impersonator and two visits from the local police asking us to quiet down. The Roasting of the Rector and *All Things Remembered*, an irreverent play commemorating St. Edward's Twenty-fifth Anniversary, were other highlights of a fun-loving approach to congregational life.

Several of the events begun during Father Payton's tenure have become cherished St. Edward's traditions: Boar's Head Feast, and Medieval-themed entertainment. Super Sundae Sunday, which kicks off the church school year, features a thirty-foot-long ice cream sundae.

Throughout their history, the character of the Episcopal Church of St. Edward the Confessor is perhaps best expressed in the way they live their mission: To celebrate the love of Christ through worship, service, fellowship, education, witness, and stewardship.

Text submitted by Rebecca Branstetter. Photos from the church archives.

✠   ✠   ✠   ✠

CHAPTER FIVE

THE TIME FOR CHANGE
1971–1983

AT A SPECIAL COUNCIL OF THE DIOCESE, CONVENED AT THE CATHEDRAL, NOVEMBER 3, 1971, AMONG THE DOZEN OR SO CLERGY NOMINATED AS BISHOP WAS THE REVEREND BENNETT Jones Sims, associate dean for continuing education at Virginia Theological Seminary. He was elected on the third ballot. The Right Reverend Milton LeGrand Wood, Suffragan Bishop of the Diocese, withdrew his candidacy before this ballot. Articles in the diocesan newspaper characterized the new Bishop as a great pastor with approachable warmth. In his opening address at the Cathedral, January 24, 1973, Bishop Sims praised the former bishops who had preceded him as having "carried, each in his own way, the colors of Christ as a Banner," and outlined four areas of focus: provide support for ministry, clear policies for mission development, stewardship, and discovery of the new liturgy with the development of a new prayer book.

The seeds of change had already been sown in the Episcopal Church. An earlier General Convention had extended Holy Communion to baptized children and women were taking their place as Vestry members, servers, and lay readers. Prayer Book revision affected local congregations with trial liturgy and renewal of the hymnal was under way. As with all change, Bishop Sims experienced resistance from many corners of the Diocese. The most significant crisis in Sim's early years surrounded the surprise ordination of eleven women in Philadelphia by four Bishops of the church. The Reverend Roy Pettway, rector of the Church of Our Saviour in Atlanta, wrote in *The Diocese* of September 1974: "The so-called ordination of eleven women in Philadelphia was not only invalid, in the sense of being illegal or not recognized by Church law, but it was also void and empty, since there is no such thing in the Holy Catholic Church as a female priest or priestess." In his address to Council, January 22, 1975, Bishop Sims likened the ordination of women to "a compelling moral urgency" that had in the past always forced the church to deal with human oppression like slavery and segregation. On June 12, 1976, at the Cathedral of St. Philip, the Bishop ordained the first woman, Eloise Eubanks Lester, as deacon.

In the late 1970s, final revisions to *The Book of Common Prayer* emerged to replace that of 1928. Even though the new book provided for the celebration of the Eucharist almost exactly as in the older book, many mourned the loss of the former. The Reverend Franklin Ferguson, rector of Emmanuel, Athens, in a letter to his congregation, said he would respect the use of the 1928 *Book of Common Prayer* for wedding, funerals, and private baptisms. However, many congregations welcomed the new Prayer Book and used its contemporary Rite II Eucharist as the norm for worship.

At a Clergy Conference at Camp Mikell in May 1977, the Bishop announced his plans to call for the election of a Suffragan (assistant) Bishop. On October 15, 1977, the Reverend Charles Judson Child, for ten years canon pastor at the Cathedral, received the Diocesan election for the office. As Suffragan Bishop, Child assisted with congregational visitations, parish development, mission property procurement, and staff supervision in the Diocesan office. Shortly after his consecration, Bishop Child, making a confirmation visit, directed an acolyte to the Bishop's chair, only to have the boy smile and whisper that only the Bishop was supposed to sit there.

In January 1983, just after General Convention approved the publication of a new hymnal, *The Hymnal 1982*, Bennett Sims announced his retirement effective in October. Church canons prohibit a Suffragan Bishop from becoming the Bishop, but in this instance, Judson Child allowed his name to be entered with four other candidates, won the election, and was formally installed later that year. The Reverend Bruce Birdsey, editor of *The Diocese*, interviewed Bishop Sims in the September 1983 issue and asked what he had liked best about his tenure. Sims replied, "I've developed a strong attachment to the churches, especially the smaller ones. . . . Those churches are like persons to me, with their distinct individuality, the fulfillment they are reaching for in different ways, their idiosyncrasies and failings and strengths. I will miss this most—the Sunday visitations."

Text submitted by the Reverend William P. McLemore.

✠   ✠   ✠   ✠

St. Anthony's Episcopal Church, Winder

✝

In the fall of 1964, a few interested persons gathered in the basement of the Barrow County Health Center for the first organizational meeting of what would become St. Anthony's Episcopal Church. A petition was submitted to the Diocese, and in December 1964 Bishop Claiborne granted permission to organize the Mission of St. Anthony. St. Alban's Episcopal Church, Monroe, was most helpful in aiding the new mission by inspiring Winder's small congregation and by supplying lay readers before and after St. Anthony's first lay readers were trained.

The first meeting place was in the Winder Woman's Club building. Members of St. Anthony's would set up and take down furnishings for each service. A metal cabinet accommodated the storage of prayer books, hymnals, kneelers, and other items. The Reverend Dawson Teague was the congregation's "God Send." He would arrive, inspire, and lift spirits with his presence or with some gift he had gotten for the mission. On some Sundays he was the pianist, the usher, and the priest.

Before the days of yard sales, the women of the church were diligent in running St. Anthony's Thrift Shop each Saturday—rain or shine. This shop served a real need for the community and was an important moneymaker for the church. Funds earned were instrumental in obtaining a loan for purchase of land as well as helping to build the church mortgage-free. The 3.5 acres of land were purchased and this land, the church's present location, became 174 St. Anthony's Drive in 1971.

In August 1970 the Reverend J. Victor Nickelson was assigned to St. Anthony's and St. Edward's Episcopal Church (Lawrenceville). The Winder congregation continued to grow and had plans for a church drawn up by church member S. W. Draper. The construction of St. Anthony's Episcopal Church began in 1971 and on January 30, 1972, the first service was held in the new building. Since then St. Anthony's has completed two additions and remodeled the Parish Hall. The original Parish Hall was partitioned providing more Christian education rooms. Also added were an outdoor chapel, a memory garden, landscaping, and a paved parking area.

Outreach has always been a big part of St. Anthony's mission. The church provides a meeting place for many local civic organizations along with volunteers and funding of many local agencies. The Fall Yard Sale, Christmas Bazaar, and the Spring Arts and Crafts Festival allow St. Anthony's to share these resources with the community. Two members of the congregation have been sponsored in seminary. "In Reach" programs are many, fun, and growing (St. Exuberance, Women's Weekend, a Book Club, Holy Rollers, Saintly Scrubbers, etc.). A monthly newsletter, *Tidings*, is available to members and visitors. E-mails and calls are shared more frequently. Christian education reaches a very large percentage of members from youngsters through the elderly.

There are currently two services each Sunday. At the second service members enjoy music and the choir. Sunday school runs from September through May. Vacation Bible School is held during the summer for children and adults. A Palm Sunday service and Blessing of the Animals service are held in the outdoor chapel (weather permitting); a Sunrise Service is held on Easter Sunday; an annual children's Christmas Pageant and a Candlelight Christmas Eve Service are Christmas highlights.

A lot of prayers, sweat, and tears have gone into the making of St. Anthony's Parish. The members give thanks to Almighty God for his love and for the continued life and growth of the church.

Text and photos submitted by Kathy Ash, Elaine Hearn, and Barbara Wallace.

Opposite page: St. Anthony's Church, Winder, built 1971–72.

✝ ✝ ✝ ✝

St. Anthony's, Winder, Fellowship Hall and Christmas Bazaar.

St. Gregory the Great Episcopal Church, Athens

✝

One Sunday in April 1971, the rector of Emmanuel Church, Athens, launched an idea to his congregation—to form a mission in Clarke County in five years.

Some enthusiastic parishioners immediately began meeting to discuss starting this mission: people in their thirties and forties who had moved to Athens during a University of Georgia growth spurt in the 1960s. They came from all over the country and had not yet put down roots in Athens' 128-year-old established Episcopal Church. By November, they were holding regular services in the Barnett Shoals Elementary School on the east side of the city.

In January 1972, thirty-six enthusiastic, idealistic Episcopalians petitioned and were accepted as an official mission by the Diocese of Atlanta. They were hands-on, building what they needed, baking Communion bread, setting up church each Sunday, and putting it away after the service. Members constructed a rolling storage/altar (fondly called "God-in-a-box"). They voted for the name St. Gregory the Great.

Peter Rice, the first senior warden, believes the character of the church was set in those early days. When something was needed, members of the church would do it. That was part of the culture of the church, along with beanbag pews, tee-shirts, and talking before the service. Members always liked The Peace; they didn't want to stop. It used to be said the measure of a priest at St. Gregory's is whether he can get the service going again after The Peace.

After eighteen months with visiting clergy, the Reverend Kenneth Kinnett officiated as vicar on June 18, 1973. Land was bought across the street from the school, and in 1978 an all-purpose worship, fellowship, education, and office building was completed. Continuing its hands-on tradition, the sanctuary was furnished with a carved wooden pew seat, altar, and lectern by a local artist; a screening memorial wall, the work of a local potter; a mural of the saints and wall hangings painted and created by artist members.

Exterior view of St. Gregory the Great Episcopal Church, Athens.

The Reverend Arthur Nick Johnson was vicar, then rector, from 1981 to 1985. The Reverend Gene Britton, the second rector, from 1986 to 1995. A separate building constructed in 1989 serves as the Parish Hall; parishioners completed the interior of the second story. An outdoor chapel in memory of Laurie Britton, Gene Britton's deceased wife, was dedicated in 1992.

The Reverend G. Porter Taylor served from 1996 to 2004, when he was elected Bishop of the Diocese of Western North Carolina. Some one hundred parishioners went to celebrate his consecration.

The current sanctuary, seating 325, was completed in 2002. Cathedral chairs replaced stacking chairs, but traditions of informal dress, enthusiastic exchange of The Peace and receiving Eucharist in a circle around the freestanding altar continued. The Reverend Gloria Bowden served as assistant rector for a year, then the parish continued under the care of one priest.

By 2003 membership totaled nearly five hundred communicants. St. Gregory's, a program church, has resolved to maintain the strong sense of community of the early years. The Center for Spiritual Formation, founded in 1997 in part with a Lilly Foundation grant, brought in speakers, a labyrinth, and sponsored men's and women's retreats, and small prayer and spiritual direction groups.

The Reverend P. J. Woodall currently serves as interim rector. As it searches for a new rector, St. Gregory's has approximately 580 members, largely made up of University of Georgia employees. There are more than 140 children and youth, and an active Christian education program. The church encourages community through lay participation, nametags, potluck suppers, coffee hours, Foyers groups, sports, and special events. There is hospital visitation, an active prayer list, neighborhood networks, and home-cooked Manna Meals delivered to members who need them. Outreach has always been valued. Local organizations and causes receive 10 percent of the budget and members work on building projects, sheltering homeless people, and cleaning paupers' graves at the cemetery.

Text submitted by Conoly Hester. Photos from the church archives.

Youth processional at St. Gregory the Great Church in Athens.

ST. CLEMENT'S EPISCOPAL CHURCH, CANTON

✠

After the Civil War, Cherokee County, created in 1831, prospered from cotton and marble mills established after the completion of the first railroad in 1882. An unsuccessful effort was made to establish an Episcopal mission by a priest from St. Mark's in Dalton in 1881. A lot purchased in Canton was sold by Bishop Nelson in 1902. The nearest Episcopal churches were located in Marietta and Cartersville where a handful of Cherokee County residents attended services prior to St. Clement's creation.

The seeds for St. Clement's were planted when a group of individuals eager to establish a local presence, met with the Right Reverend Milton L. Wood, Suffragan Bishop, on May 1, 1973, at Brown's Farm in Canton. Key organizing members were Walton and Mary Elizabeth Davis, Cranston and Nell Gray, Bobby Pate, Austin and Bea Flint, John and Pat Matthews, Bill and Nell Magruder, Shubael Beasley, Dave Griffin, and Luke Delong. A mission "To build an effective Christian family in the Episcopal way to meet the needs of individuals and of the community" was adopted.

That same year, Father Louis Tonsmeire from the Church of the Ascension in Cartersville, aided by Diocesan consultant Carolyn Westerhoff oversaw its formation and early organization. The name St. Clement's was selected and the church was officially established on December 16, 1973. St. Clement's (Bishop of Rome, circa A.D. 88–97) symbol, an anchor draped with a red cloth, was the inspiration for our award-winning newsletter, *The Anchor*.

St. Clement's met originally in several business locations and shared temporary quarters with the Catholic mission in the second-floor meeting space of Georgia Power in downtown Canton. St. Clement's later moved to Brown's Farm, historic residence of Judge James R.

St. Clement's Episcopal Church, Canton.

Brown, brother of Civil War governor Joseph E. Brown and then home of organizing members Cranston and Nell Gray. Two brick outbuildings served as the chapel, with an altar and room for twenty-six people, and a Parish House for refreshments and fellowship following the services.

On April 6, 1977, St. Clement's purchased a building and three acres for $25,000 from the Holly Springs Bible Chapel in South Canton. Adjacent structures and acreage were subsequently acquired and evolved into the present sanctuary and Sunday school and community center known as Davis Hall. St. Clement's experienced substantial growth in its congregation n the 1980s and 1990s. Jim Hamilton was critical to St. Clement's music agenda by volunteering as the first choirmaster. St. Clement's continues today to expand its outreach program to young suburban newcomer families, retirees, and local converts. The church has also participated in charitable and civic organizations such as MUST, Habitat for Humanity, and Riverfest. Father Bob Rickard became part-time rector until such time as finances permitted the church to elevate his employment to full-time status. Unfortunately, that was not financially feasible, resulting in his departure in 1995.

During this time of transition and challenge, Lucy and Ino Martinez arrived and their ministry carried St. Clement's to a new dimension. Deacon Lucy served in a clergy capacity, subsequently working with the next part-time rector, Jim Pace. St. Clement's vestry made a decision to expand and make significant improvements to the sanctuary and Davis Hall. They were catalysts for renewed faith, healing, theological expansion, and spiritual growth. In 2002, Father Jim resigned to teach full time at Vanderbilt University. The first full-time current rector, the Reverend Jamie Stutler, held his first service on January 11, 2004, and has brought a wide array of spiritual and secular strengths.

Father Jamie is enthusiastic for what lies ahead: "God has already begun a great work at St. Clement's and our obligation as disciples of Christ is to build on that work into the future. We will always strive to be what St. Clement's always has been: an inviting place to discover God in Christ in the midst of a loving and caring faith community."

St. Clement's has an expanding, diverse membership in excess of 150 families. St. Clement's warmth is uniquely that of a small town, reaching out to all and characterized by acceptance, good will, fellowship, and reverence in the tradition of Christ's teachings.

Text submitted by Judson Roberts. Photo from the church archives.

✜   ✜   ✜   ✜

Episcopal Church of the Holy Spirit, Cumming

✛

In February 1974, Holy Spirit's charter families met with the Reverend Dr. James Hopewell at the home of Jean and Emory Lipscomb in Cumming. Of their experience, Hopewell wrote:

Beginning in 1975, a new congregation grew up around me. A group of Episcopal laity and I as their priest set out to form a loose fellowship. . . . I avoided ecclesiastical trappings and tried to promote service to the neighborhood instead of the internal activities. . . .

To our first Eucharist, held in a bank, I brought the bare minimum: bread and wine, prayer books, and a card table. On the second Sunday, however, someone brought a cloth to cover the table. The following Sunday another person produced a cross and candlesticks. Our fellowship became a congregation . . . constructed its own building, grew to full parish status, called its own rector, and burned its mortgage . . . I learned to appreciate the capacity of an ordinary group of Christians to bring to maturity a unique and vibrant congregation.

Front view of the Church of the Holy Spirit, Cumming.

The Forsyth County Episcopal Fellowship was officially formed by covenant on the Day of Pentecost 1975, and was received as a mission named the Episcopal Church of the Holy Spirit by the Diocese in January 1976. Christmas Day 1977 saw the first service in the first building on the present site, purchased the previous May. Deacon Claiborne Jones was appointed July 1978 to assist. The Reverend Donald B. Clapp became vicar in May 1980, and was followed by Father R. Bruce Birdsey in December 1981. The congregation next achieved financial independence and celebrated Easter 1986 in a larger new building.

Early in 1987, a group of civil rights marchers met with violence in Forsyth County. When the marchers returned, the Reverend William R. Payton, interim rector, led Holy Spirit to join with area churches as witnesses for reconciliation. Beginning in December 1987, with visionary priest the Reverend Samuel G. Candler's direction, the church underwent programmatic and congregational growth. Mothers with young children organized a Mothers' Morning Out program, which developed into the Cumming Preschool by autumn 1990.

Deacon Lynda Moore arrived in 1992, became assistant rector, and served as interim. The congregation purchased adjoining property in March 1994, bringing the total property to 8.99 acres. Holy Spirit called as rector the Reverend Dwight E. Ogier Jr., who instituted a strong commitment to pastoral care in October 1994. With inspiration from interim priest Father Roger H. Ard, who arrived in July 1999, the congregation began a period of self-examination and discernment.

The church celebrated its twenty-fifth year debt-free on Pentecost 2000. In May, Holy Spirit dedicated the Hugo "Dutch" Jahnz Bell Tower, and in December adopted

"Vision of the Future," a plan for the new millennium. Spirit-filled interim rector William L. Evans arrived in December 2001, and in October 2002, the Reverend Melanie Mudge became rector. Father Donald Harrison became associate rector in July 2003.

Thirty years ago, the Church of the Holy Spirit began with emphasis on outreach. This vision of service has been a unifying factor for the congregation. The church has provided meeting space for Alcoholics/Narcotics Anonymous, Grief Share, and Family Haven, and furnished space and observers for supervised family visitations through the Child Advocacy Center. Holy Spirit has maintained the only nonfood pantry in Forsyth County and has helped build a Habitat for Humanity house.

The congregation has prepared meals for "The Place," provided refugee support, and knitted caps for Northside Hospital preemies, distributed book bags and school supplies through Forsyth County schools, and given Christmas gifts by way of "Hands Across Forsyth" and Emmaus House. Holy Spirit supports "Jessie's House" and "The Lodge," group homes for teenagers and international programs "Bethlehem Ministries," "Food for the Poor" and "The Heifer Project."

The dream of the Reverend Dr. Hopewell and the founding members continues to be realized in this "unique and vibrant congregation."

Text submitted by Ms. Beverly Clemmer. Photos submitted by Martha Wayt.

Members of Church of the Holy Spirit delight in one of God's gifts.

ST. TIMOTHY'S EPISCOPAL CHURCH, CALHOUN

St. Timothy's Episcopal Church was not Calhoun's first Episcopal church. The first, St. James', was organized in 1881. The one-story wooden chapel in downtown Calhoun seated two hundred people and had a sweet-tone reed organ. It stood on the site of what is now City Hall. St. James' Episcopal Church of Marietta had made a large donation to the church, which is probably why it took the name of St. James' Episcopal Church. Father James Craighill was the first priest and began services in 1883. The church was consecrated by Bishop Nelson in 1889. Father Frances Ambler was the last known priest of this early parish.

St. James' was dissolved in 1927 and today the building, which was moved out of town, is part of a summer home for a family in Calhoun. The end of St. James' was not the end of an Episcopal parish in Calhoun. In 1970, a small group of Episcopalians began meeting for worship in the old community room of Calhoun First National Bank on Sunday evenings. This group was supported by the ministry of St. Mark's, Dalton. The congregation had expanded by 1973 and was meeting monthly for socials as well as Sunday evening worship.

A petition for mission status was made at the Diocesan Council in November 1973. St. Timothy's Episcopal Church became a reality and employed Father George Sparks as its first vicar. The church rented the Seventh-day Adventist Church on South Wall Street and formed a congregation. The first Vestry was elected in 1974. Those serving were Dorothy Jordan (also organist), Bill Anderson, Billy Baxter, B. J. Bell, Ron Purdy, Mike Reich, Jim Tinsley, and Lyn Warmack. During the early

Entrance view of St. Timothy's Episcopal Church, Calhoun.

Members of St. Timothy's Church, Calhoun, enjoy Sunday fellowship hour.

In 1989, plans were made for St. Timothy's congregation to purchase the Presbyterian's Church building on Trammell Street. The church and the manse next door (which now serves as the church offices) are made of native rock and were built in 1925 by W. L. Hillhouse, a well-known architect at the time. After the purchase, renovations were made to better suit the Episcopal liturgy. Priests who served St. Timothy's have also included Father John Bolton, Father John McKee, Father Pegrum Johnson, Father Don Clapp, Father Milton Coward, and Father Bill Kennedy.

The Reverend Sam Buice became vicar in June 1991, and St. Timothy's saw growth and progress during his two-and-a-half-year tenure. In the spring of 1994, Father Louis Tonsmeire, though retired, became the priest. He continues to serve St. Timothy's today. Under his leadership and guidance the church has seen growth and expansion in church and community outreach activities. In 1998, the church purchased, at moderate cost, the house adjoining the church property. For almost five years, the house was rented to a refugee family from Kosovo, who were sponsored by St. Timothy's and other churches.

In the summer of 2005, the Reverend Dr. Denni Moss joined as an assistant to Father Tonsmeire. The church provides space and meals for several groups each week as part of its outreach to the community. Lay ministers are licensed by the Diocese to provide Holy Communion to those unable to attend regular services. The Mission Statement of the congregation reads: "To emulate Christ and to be a loving and caring family to the community and to ourselves."

Text submitted by Kay Baxter, Rita Collins, Jerry Lackey, and Phyllis Purdy. Photos from St. Timothy's Church Archives.

years at St. Timothy's, the congregation became a close-knit group through worship, social events such as camping, and through fundraising efforts that included bazaars, pig roasts, and running concession stands.

St. Timothy's Church was incorporated in 1975 and purchased the Adventist Church building. It was formally dedicated in 1978. Several priests served as part-time vicars at St. Timothy's during this time. In 1980, St. Timothy's had its first full-time priest who resided in Calhoun—the Reverend Bertie Pittman, who also was the first female parish priest in Georgia. In 1983, Father Paul Ross became a yoked priest, serving Jasper and St. Timothy's Churches. He remained with St. Timothy's for seven years.

CHRIST EPISCOPAL CHURCH, KENNESAW

✛

Christ Episcopal Church was founded in March 1975 when a group of thirty-one Episcopalians petitioned Bishop Bennett Sims to establish a worshipping community way out in the woodlands and farms of northern Cobb County. They first met in homes, then at the First Methodist Church in Kennesaw and the Pacemaker Inn. By October 1976, the name Christ Episcopal Church was chosen, and on March 22, 1977, Bishop Bennett Sims, awarded the new congregation mission status on a trial basis. On November 22, 1978, Christ Episcopal Church became an organized mission.

In April 1977, the property, 7.333 acres, with a house and tractor barn, was purchased for $95,000. During the first two years, interim and visiting clergy served the mission. In March 1977, Bishop Sims assigned the Reverend Gene Britton as the first regular clergy on a part-time basis. The Reverend Richard Williams became the first full-time vicar in May 1978.

The early years were marked by the conversion of the tractor barn into a chapel for worship, increasing church programs, acquiring furnishings, and achieving financial independence. In March 1985, the Reverend Scott Holcombe was named vicar. In January 1986 the worshiping community was admitted as a parish. The parish grew from 75 active members in 1985 to 266 in 1987. It was clear the house and tractor barn were no longer able to support the parish. In 1988, construction began on the church building. The new worship center was dedicated on June 4, 1989. The house became the Christian Education Center and the tractor barn/chapel became the Youth Center. In 1989, The School at Christ Church was founded as a preschool.

During the winters of 1990 and 1991, the unfinished basement of the worship center was hurriedly refurbished with a kitchen and bathrooms in order to house the Cobb-Marietta Winter Shelter for homeless people, which later became The Extension, Inc.

On July 26, 1992, Father Holcombe answered a call to another parish. A search committee called the Reverend Robert Dendtler, who began his ministry in March 1993. His first worship service, on March 17, 1993, was interrupted by the "snowstorm of the century." Again the Parish Hall was used to shelter stranded travelers.

In 1994, parking places were added to accommodate the church's growth. In 1999, because the sanctuary and parking were unable to support the growing worship community, a third service was added on Sunday. In 1999 the Vestry concluded that the highest priority was to build Christian education facilities. Construction began in 2002, and Bishop Alexander dedicated the new Christian Education Center, Dendtler Hall, on August 17, 2003.

In March 2000, the Reverend Dendtler retired and the search for a new rector began. The Reverend Doris Graf Smith was called to be rector and began her ministry at Christ Church in March 2002. In 2006, Christ Church, Kennesaw, celebrated its thirtieth anniversary.

Text submitted by Ron Owens. Photos from the church archives.

Opposite page: Christ Church, Kennesaw, sanctuary and Dendtler Hall.

Christ Church, Kennesaw, the Reverend Doris Graf Smith, Deacon Swiss Britt, and members of Boy Scout Troop 217.

✛   ✛   ✛   ✛

St. Andrew's-in-the-Pines, Peachtree City

✠

St. Andrew's-in-the-Pines is aptly named for its beautiful setting in the trees along Peachtree Parkway and for the patron saint of Scotland. The combination distinguishes the new church from other churches in the Diocese named for St. Andrew.

In 1974, the population of Peachtree City was under three thousand, with two established churches: Presbyterian and Baptist. An earlier attempt to establish an Episcopal church (St. Nicholas) in Fayetteville was unsuccessful and by 1974 that church no longer held services. Many Episcopalians from Fayette County attended St. Paul's, Newnan, the nearest at twelve miles distant.

Twenty-eight Fayette County Episcopalians organized a meeting on April 25, 1975, to explore starting a new mission church. Skip and Cynthia McMorries hosted the meeting at their Peachtree City home. The group asked the Bishop for guidance and for a meeting with a priest. At the next meeting the group welcomed the priest and celebrated its first communion service and discussed challenges in starting a mission. A Peachtree Elementary School classroom housed Sunday services during the summer of 1976. The Bishop sent a supply priest for each Sunday worship service. Following the first service at the school, the fellowship selected its name.

At the next Sunday service the priest offered a meaningful and insightful sermon on the chosen name: "Think about the pine tree—it provides shade with a soft bed of needles below and as a church it should be a place of comfort and rest for all—but always remember that the needles, while soft, should also stick us and prod us into action to help others in the world." This proved to be a prophetic statement.

The church met for the next two years in the Gazebo at the McIntosh Amphitheater complex—now known as the Fredrick Brown Amphitheater. The Bishop assigned Father Jack McKee as priest for the next year followed by Father William Bradbury who led the fellowship in the early years. During

Left: Front view of St. Andrew's-in-the-Pines Bell Tower, Peachtree City.

this time the first Vestry was elected, and the five acres where St. Andrew's-in-the-Pines Episcopal Church now stands were purchased.

The present Parish Hall stands on ground broken in 1980 with the present church being built in 1994. A new building and renovation program started in 2004 welcomed the opening of the new Parish Hall in October 2005. The Garden of Remembrance for internment of ashes was dedicated in 2001. Phase two of the building program includes expansion of the church building.

Father Dan Brigham has guided the church through spiritual growth and membership expansion since 1983. Father Frank Larisey became associate rector in 2000, leaving in 2005 for South Carolina.

St. Andrew's-in-the-Pines now welcomes over 380 families, having grown from twenty-eight devoted members. As it grew in numbers and diversity, so did its commitment to reach out to the community and its parishioners through stewardship and community outreach programs. Stewardship activities and groups include: Commission on Stewardship, art auction, Episcopal Church Women, lay readers, servers, Altar Guild, ushers, greeters, Flower Guild, nursery attendants, youth and Christian education programs. Other groups and committees include the Order of the Daughters of the King, finance committee, newsletter, choir, OPUS (*Old People up to Something*), and publicity.

Community outreach includes: Cub Scouts pack, Boy Scout Troop 209, Girl Scouts, Peachtree City Angel Network, Fayette Samaritans Food Bank, Emmaus House, supporting our soldiers, Thanksgiving food baskets, hurricane relief, "Family Connections," Habitat for Humanity, Compassion International, Operation Christmas Child, Baby Peachtree, Heifer Project International, African Team Ministries, donations to local charities, Southland Nursing Home, and Adopt a Family for Christmas.

St. Andrew's also provides without charge meeting facilities for Alateen, Alanon, Boy and Girl Scout troops, Overeaters Anonymous, AA and Women AA, and a complete facility for preschool. The congregation of St. Andrew's-in-the-Pines looks forward to continued growth and extends a welcome to all who wish to worship with them.

Text submitted and edited by Eleanor E. Corbin from Cynthia McMorries' original, with additional information from Father Dan Brigham and parishioners. Photos from the church archives.

✠   ✠   ✠   ✠

ST. JULIAN'S EPISCOPAL CHURCH, DOUGLASVILLE

✠

In August 1978, the announcement in the *Douglas County Sentinel* was simple: "The Episcopal Diocese of Atlanta plans to establish a new mission in Douglas County. For further details call one of these numbers." Fifty persons responded, taking the initial step of what was to become a decade-long, circuitous journey to the realization of a church in Douglasville.

Following three organizational meetings, the first headed by Bishop Judson Child, the group temporarily known as "The Episcopal Church of Douglasville" prepared for its first service in Whitley Memorial Funeral Home on Bankhead Highway (US 78), 10:00 a.m., Sunday, October 22, 1978. At a makeshift altar—a chest of drawers draped with a white sheet—the Reverend Scott F. Ackerman celebrated the church's first Eucharist. Vessels for the Eucharistic elements were a covered butter dish and salad dressing bottles, with a cereal dish as a lavabo. The chalice and paten were borrowed.

During 1979 the now St. Chrysostom's Episcopal Church, flourished. Every Sunday worship services, a church school, and nursery were held. There were an active senior choir, Altar Guild, and a men's and a women's organization. The group purchased an organ and by July 1, the Diocese had purchased land for the construction of a church. How bright the future looked!

St. Chrysostom's remained at Whitley Chapel until January 1982 at which time it moved to the Retardation Work Center on West Stewarts Mill Road until May 19, 1983, when an early morning fire raced through the Work Center. St. Chrysostom's lost its organ, choir music, and church school materials. Hymnals, prayer books, altar, and credence table were damaged. The communicants had no building and no organ, but they did have a beautiful wooded lot with an open picnic pavilion. Sunday morning found a band of determined worshipers singing hymns to the accompaniment of two guitars and a flute.

Word spread. Bright Star United Methodist Church responded and soon St. Chrysostom's was holding services there. Its members were unified by a common goal—to pay off the mortgage on the land and to construct their own church.

In 1991, the Reverend Richard H. Callaway came from the Diocese of North Carolina, a leader committed to the establishment of an Episcopal Church in Douglasville.

He understood the past struggles and knew these people were ready for the next step: a name change. On November 19, 1992, communicants of St. Julian's Episcopal Church, now an unaided parish, moved forward.

By November 1993 St. Julian's parishioners had celebrated their fifteenth birthday, dedicated a new organ, and broken ground for a new building. On a cold, wet day in January 1995, they again celebrated by writing their names in their unfinished building. On May 8, 1995, the feast of Julian of Norwich, St. Julian's Episcopal Church in Douglasville, was consecrated.

There is continuous commitment to the church's ministries, especially Meals-on-Wheels, supported for more than a decade; and Starting Over, a program in which parishioners supervise visitations each Thursday and Saturday for families who have been separated by a court order. Other programs are celebrated, particularly the Red Top Mountain Retreat, a fall family getaway, begun in 1986. And St. Julian's grew so much that an addition to the original structure was completed by 2001.

During that year St. Julian's began its search for a new rector. In August the Very Reverend Richard H. Callaway assumed his duties as canon to the ordinary for the Diocese of Atlanta. On October 19, 2003, St. Julian's Episcopal Church celebrated twenty-five years of labor and love as it welcomed its new rector, the Reverend Stewart Tabb. Today, under her leadership, St. Julian's ministries to each other and to members of the broader community continue, its communicants abiding always in the faith that all shall be well.

Text submitted by Lonnell McCall Clark. Photo by the Reverend Stewart Tabb.

✠   ✠   ✠   ✠

St. Julian's Episcopal Church, Douglasville.

CHRIST CHURCH, NORCROSS

✢

Christ Church mission was founded on August 13, 1978. The first service, however, was a fellowship meal and Eucharist on June 11 for a small group at the home of Gary and Ida Cobb led by the new vicar, the Reverend Joel Hudson. Services continued in homes and Norcross High School before purchasing on June 5, 1980, the West Peachtree Street property vacated by the Galilean Baptist Church for $142,000. After renovation, the first service was held December 7, 1980, with Bishop Sims as celebrant.

Attendance grew, a second service was added and a new Parish Hall was completed and occupied on March 26, 1989. Further improvements including an organ, pews, library, and a church office were made with a $200,000 bequest from the estate of faithful member Mary Webster, for whom the office was named.

By 1996 worship space, classrooms, and parking were outgrown. The Vestry voted to locate and move to a new church site, a decision finally embraced by the congregation in May 1996, with the hope of also starting a school. A capital campaign produced pledges of $1.55 million. After an extensive search, the present facilities on Holcomb Bridge Road were purchased, again from the Galilean Baptist Church. The cost of the fifteen acres including renovations and additional construction totaled $2.8 million. The move-in occurred in August 1998.

Christ Church, from its beginnings under the guiding hand of Father Hudson, his staff, and capable and committed lay leadership, has created and supported ministries to serve the congregation and the wider community. In recognition of its ministry, the church was designated as a "Jubilee Center," a rare national honor from the national church.

Among the more notable ministries created and continued during the short life of Christ Church include: Thrift Shop; Norcross Cooperative Ministry—food and support to those in need, now supported by many churches; Adopted Families; Resiliency House—assistance to former prisoners; Hispanic Ministry—worship space and pastoral care; Advancing Authentic Leadership, Inc.—a twenty-seven-week course emphasizing self-understanding and servanthood; Stephen Ministers—trained parishioners ministering one-on-one to individuals; and Boy, Girl, and Cub Scout groups.

Right: Christ Church, Norcross, entrance.

Processional at Christ Church, Norcross.

In addition to lay staff personnel, committed clergy who have assisted the rector and the congregation over the years include Lori Lowe, 1987–91; JoAnn Smith, 1991–93; Nancy Yancey, 1993—director, Rainbow Village, Inc.; Andrew Frearson, 1996–2004; and Joe Herring, beginning 2005.

Father Joel Hudson retired on March 1, 2003, after twenty-five years of service. Under his dedicated leadership the little mission grew from thirty members to over twelve hundred, thirteenth in size in the Diocese. Everyone he encountered grew in their relationship to Christ and worked to spread His kingdom.

Following Father Hudson's retirement, Father Andrew Frearson served as interim rector until September 2004. Following an extensive search, the Reverend Dr. Rock Schuler became second rector of Christ Church in December 2004. Christ Church is a strong vibrant community of believers dedicated to its mission to "communicate Christ's love through its ministries."

Text submitted by Karl Woltersdorf and the late Frank Anderson. Photos from the church archives.

✠   ✠   ✠   ✠

Rainbow Village, Inc.—a transitional housing ministry for families leaving homelessness grew from several houses, gifts from Georgia Power Company, and an "angel" donor to the current sixteen residences made possible by a $500,000 gift from developer Scott Hudgins. Now supported by many area churches, it serves those seeking a new beginning.

Another vital ministry is Christian Formation. Emphasis is placed on programs and instruction from dedicated teachers to help children, youth, and adults grow in the knowledge and love of Christ. Special programs at Advent and Lent, and youth pilgrimages further enrich the formation process. The Christ Church Episcopal School opened in 1999 to grand expectations. Declining enrollment and financial difficulties necessitated closing in 2003.

ST. MATTHEW'S EPISCOPAL CHURCH, SNELLVILLE

✝

On April 5, 1979, fifty-eight persons met with Bishop Child at the Snellville Civic Center concerning organizing an Episcopal Church in Snellville. Two weeks later thirty-five persons met at Ed Bowen's office and celebrated Holy Communion with the Bishop. The first directory (June 1979) listed twenty-six families. An organizational meeting was held July 23, 1979. St. Matthew's was named and became a mission station. Regular services started August 5, 1979, with Gene Ruyle as priest-in-charge, at Centerville Elementary. The first Parish Meeting was August 26, 1979.

Father Franklin Thomas was received as vicar on January 6, 1980, with 115 present for the service. On January 26, 1980, St. Matthew's received full-mission-church status. The first confirmation class of sixteen persons received confirmation from Bishop Child at the Cathedral of St. Philip on Easter Eve, April 5, 1980. On June 1, 1980, the congregation began holding Sunday services at the Snellville Civic Center. The Lord has blessed St. Matthew's with rapid growth, and in August 1980 seven acres on Oak Road were paid for in full. In December 1980 the second confirmation class presented twenty-seven candidates to Bishop Sims in Snellville. September 1981 found the membership gathered for groundbreaking, and on April 4, 1982 (Palm Sunday), 592 attended the first service in the new church building.

Strong feelings for orthodoxy, appreciation of tradition, and emphasis on children's education have been evident from the beginning. With limited fellowship space, home gatherings helped the members realize that their parish was truly a family. Father

St. Matthew's Episcopal Church, Snellville, new sanctuary completed in 1998.

Thomas—a professional musician before becoming a priest—made sure that the services included well-known hymns, and from its beginning St. Matthew's has been noted for its singing. Because of his outreach, the church soon found that it had more new Episcopalians than cradle Episcopalians.

In 1983 former Dominican Monk Father Paul Gerlock, became assistant priest. Father Thomas resigned that year for health reasons. Father Gerlock and other visiting priests filled in as the search began. In September 1984 Father Edward Hanson was named vicar. St. Mathew's soon became self-supporting and Father Hanson became rector. Sunday school rooms were overflowing and county codes prevented further building until the parking lot was paved. Funds were raised and the paving and education-office wing was completed in 1987.

St. Matthew's, Snellville, groundbreaking in September 1981.

The pulpit, large cross, altar railing, and other items were crafted by members of the parish. Sue Tomlinson found and obtained an antique altar to replace a temporary table altar. It came from an English country church and after being refinished and re-dedicated by Bishop Allan, it has been in use since 1998. The Building Committee had selected an English village church design.

The Reverend Maggie Harney was ordained at St. Matthew's on June 11, 1988, and became assistant priest. She assumed parish leadership when Father Hanson left in 1991. In August 1992, Father Douglas Coil came from Florida and in 1997 Father James Johnson became assisting priest.

More classrooms were needed and were completed in 1997 and named the Sandra Strickland Educational Wing and contains restrooms, children's class rooms, and a music room. The overflowing sanctuary and the burning of the mortgage for the existing building enabled a loan for a new sanctuary. Construction began in 1997 and was completed in 1998 with the first service there on Palm Sunday 1998.

In 1999 converting the old sanctuary into a Parish Hall with commercial kitchen was completed. The Coil Chapel was dedicated in 2000 in celebration of Father Doug's twenty-five years of priesthood. In 2003 a columbarium was installed in the Chapel. At the close of 2004, Father Johnson resigned and a Search Committee formed.

The burning of the new sanctuary mortgage made 2005 a historic year. St. Matthew's now has a red door—indicating a paid mortgage. St. Matthew's mission is to continue the Incarnation of our Lord Jesus Christ by serving the greater community by loving its children, caring for the unfortunate, and witnessing to the healing power of God's love.

Text and photos submitted by members of St. Matthew's church.

☩   ☩   ☩   ☩

CHATTAHOOCHEE VALLEY EPISCOPAL MINISTRY, INC.
✠

The Chattahoochee Valley Episcopal Ministry, Inc. (CVEM) is a Jubilee Ministry of the Episcopal Church and an outreach ministry of the Chattahoochee Valley Convocation with its primary office in Columbus and a satellite office in LaGrange. CVEM is managed by lay missioner Vicky Partin.

Celebrating its twenty-fifth anniversary in 2005, this convocational outreach ministry seeks to show God's love through direct assistance, advocacy, mentoring, peace and justice theology, and community development ventures. Churches supporting CVEM include St. John's, West Point; St. Mark's, LaGrange; St. Mary Magdalene's, Columbus; St. Nicholas, Hamilton; St. Thomas', Columbus; St. Thomas of Canterbury, Thomaston; Trinity, Columbus; and in nearby Alabama: St. Stephen's and St. Matthew's-in-the-Pines.

Direct service, where volunteers hear needs, offer gifts, and make referrals, is unceasing throughout the year. In 2005 CVEM assisted over seven hundred families and individuals through the offices in Columbus and LaGrange.

Beallwood Area Neighborhood Development, a grassroots organization, was established in 1994 to fight drugs, blight, commercial zoning, empower its residents, and provide youth development in a Columbus neighborhood. It now has a community center, board, staff, and programs. The Chattahoochee Federal Credit Union, a community-development credit union with low-income designation, originated in Beallwood and opened in 2001. In 2005 it merged with ECA, a larger credit union, providing more financial stability.

The Thompson-Pound Art Program (TAP) is a multicultural, interfaith arts program for children focusing on tolerance and diversity. TAP-Columbus is ten years old; TAP-LaGrange began in 2003. Conversation Café and Lunch Bunch are two programs addressing women's issues. In LaGrange, Lunch Bunch meets monthly and provides women with information, fellowship, and support. Café is a woman-to-woman ministry of mentoring, education, and life skills training. Participants and mentors meet weekly; all attend monthly forums as a group.

CVEM is involved with programs/organizations enhancing the safety and welfare of children and youth; promoting antiracism and interfaith work; embracing active nonviolence through study and action; and working to provide affordable housing, eliminating homelessness and sheltering families. Beginning in 2006, CVEM developed and implemented its new Youth Leadership Program with over $26,000 seed funds received from anniversary donations.

Text submitted by Amy Narone.

✠ ✠ ✠ ✠

THE EPISCOPAL CHURCH OF ST. PETER AND ST. PAUL, MARIETTA

✠

A gathering of a few people at the home of Father Louis Tonsmeire on the Feast Day of St. Peter and St. Paul, June 29, 1981, started the Episcopal Church of St. Peter and St. Paul in Marietta. A quarter century later, the church has grown to serve more than two thousand parishioners in East Cobb County.

The fledgling congregation initially held services in a shopping center and in November 1981 moved to Dickerson Middle School, which served as the church's home for eighteen months. Groundbreaking on a 7.5 acre property on Johnson Ferry Road occurred in August 1982, and the first service in a new building was on May 1, 1983. As a mission, the church received substantial financial support from the Diocese, the Cathedral of St. Philip and Holy Innocents' Parish. Aided-parish status ended in January 1985, when the church became self-supporting.

Front of St. Peter and St. Paul Episcopal Church, Marietta.

Over the next ten years, the church experienced much growth along with the surrounding community. Father Michael Owens became associate rector and took a special interest in growing the youth ministry. Father Owens accepted a 1988 call to serve as a missionary in South Africa, and Father Tonsmeire resigned in 1989. Father John Bolton helped navigate the congregation through a difficult transition period resulting in Father Jerry Hardy becoming rector in July 1990.

Father Hardy resigned after two years, and was succeeded by the current rector, Father Aaron Uitti, under whose leadership the church has thrived. Three full-time clergy—the Reverend Elizabeth Knowlton and the Reverend Cecilia Duke serve with Father Uitti. The church has grown into a larger sanctuary, completed in 1997 in time for a glorious Christmas worship celebration. The former sanctuary became the Parish Hall, equipped with a large kitchen. The lower floor supports a thriving preschool that provides quality early childhood education for children aged eighteen months through four years.

The motto of St. Peter and St. Paul (SPSP) is "Growing in Christ Together, Sharing His Love." Members live this mission by participating in a dazzling array of outreach ministries and "in-reach" programs designed to support one another on their faith journeys. Following are examples of how members work at being faithful stewards of the talents and treasures with which God has blessed us.

"Saturday Night Live" at Holy Comforter is held the second Saturday of each month and SMSP members travel to Holy Comforter, the Diocese's mission church in East Atlanta, to provide a worship-music sing-a-long and serve a hot meal. At Christmas members "adopt" Holy Comforter parishioners and take them presents of clothes during the annual SPSP and Holy Comforter Christmas Celebration. The church supports an Episcopal parish and school, which started in one classroom with 13 students, in Ambato, Ecuador. It is now a three-story building supporting 140 students! SPSP parishioner support aids in the student tuition as well as school supplies. The "Five & Two Hunger Ministry" focuses on fighting hunger in Jesus' name. Efforts include the Fall Harvest Food Drive, the Lenten Food Drive, and "Kroger Bucks" in which parishioners purchase Kroger Gift Cards every month through the church. Kroger donates 5 percent of the money donated to agencies such as the Atlanta Community Food Bank. Volunteers prepare meals at St. Elizabeth Inn in Marietta eighty times a year for MUST Meals. Every summer, parishioners assemble twenty-five hundred brown-bag lunches that are distributed by MUST to latchkey children.

SPSP hosts an annual "Cool Girls" back-to-school day, and approximately 175 young, inner-city girls "shop" for clothing donated by parishioners. Each girl receives a backpack with a new outfit and school supplies. "Sweet P's Arts Festival" is the annual spring arts and crafts fundraiser, which benefits community outreach. The event draws professional crafters from throughout the Southeast.

The activities designed to build church community and spiritual growth are equally impressive. SPSP was a pioneer in embracing Alpha, the popular evangelism program. Ten Alpha courses in the past five years have transformed the lives of many members who were previously on the fringes of church involvement. The annual Parish Family Retreat at Kanuga is a well-attended highlight of the church year. The music ministry provides two adult and four children's choirs. EFM, ECW, Daughters of the King, Brotherhood of St. Andrew, Cursillo, and Stephen Ministry all thrive at SPSP.

As East Cobb development has slowed, SPSP has recognized a greater need to evangelize among its existing neighbors. Now, more than ever, their faith calls them to support the Great Commission, to be more intentional about their invitation to worship, serve, learn, and grow in Christ, together, sharing His love.

Text submitted by Deelee Freeman. Photos from the church archives.

Right: St. Peter and St. Paul Episcopal Church, Marietta, view of the nave and chancel.

✝   ✝   ✝   ✝

EMORY CAMPUS MINISTRY, ATLANTA

✠

The Emory Campus Ministry (ECM) became a full-time campus ministry funded by the Diocese in the fall of 1982 when Bishop Bennett Sims appointed the Reverend Nancy Baxter as Episcopal chaplain. Students were previously served by nearby parishes, particularly Holy Trinity Parish in Decatur. During the 1950s and 1960s, Fathers Harry Tisdale and Jerry Zeller were particularly welcoming to Emory students and brought many into the Episcopal Church, including Frank Allan, Class of '57, and later Bishop of Atlanta. In the 1970s, Father John McKee was part-time chaplain and lecturer at the Candler School of Theology. Bobbi Patterson arrived during this period as assistant university chaplain, was ordained in 1984, and developed a wide-ranging ministry as a faculty member in Emory's Department of Religion.

After Nancy's first year as chaplain, Father Chet Grey offered a close-working association with St. Bartholomew's, the parish of many Emory staff and faculty. Its "Ministry to Others" budget began supporting ECM and she became a priest associate in that parish. The arrangement has proved beneficial to ECM and the parish. Since ECM has no Sunday services, students become very involved in parish worship. They teach Sunday school, preside over Children's Church, sing in the choir, and serve as lectors, vergers, and chalice bearers.

ECM originally shared space in the Religious Life staff suite. In 1989 space for an office, worship, and fellowship arranged with the Baptist Campus Minister resulted in upstairs rented space at the Atlanta Baptist Association house on Clifton Road. Unused for years and in severe disrepair, it was rehabilitated by many labor-intensive hours during 1989–90 of students and friends and opened its doors in the fall of 1990 to welcome students. St. Bartholomew's parishioners Bert and Georgia Carroll were particularly supportive during this transition. The Reverend Shelley Baer served her deacon year at ECM in 1990–91 before becoming assistant priest at St. Stephen's, Milledgeville, and chaplain to Georgia College.

Bishop Sims' 1982 charge to Chaplain Baxter was "go out to Emory and start something." He wanted a supervisor and lecturer in the Episcopal Studies Program. Candler School of Theology had only one woman on its faculty—a part-time lecturer in Christian education. The Diocese sent postulants to Candler, including the first women, in the early 1970s. These women

Emory students enroute to DYVE Retreat at Camp Mikell, 2003.

reported a lack of mentors and models for women in ministry. Since 1982, the chaplain has served in the Episcopal (now Anglican) Studies Program, working closely with the Reverend Dr. Charles Hackett and has supervised many seminarians, Episcopal and Methodist, in a middle-year experience of campus ministry. Every Methodist who has interned at Emory Episcopal Center has joined the Episcopal Church and several have been ordained in other dioceses.

Bishop Sims recognized the pastoral care need in the Emory hospitals. The Emory ministry to patients and families has expanded to include the gifts of retired clergy. The Reverend Kim Dreisbach has served faithfully for years as a regular priestly presence in Emory Hospital one day a week. Bishop Child expanded ECM to include Wesley Woods, care facilities for seniors associated with Emory Healthcare. Over the years, three separate congregations and hundreds of seniors have participated in weekly Eucharists. A faithful cadre of lay ministers has assisted, including the Cathedral's Dabney Hart and St. Bartholomew's Christina Dondero. These congregations provide a clinical setting for participants in the Diocesan program for discernment of vocations to the priesthood (VDP).

The ECM was the seedbed for the Diocesan discernment process for college students (DYVE) begun in the early 1990s. Bishop Allan asked the chaplain to design a program to address her concern at the loss of gifted seniors to other vocations, given the church's reluctance to ordain young adults. DYVE has helped identify and support many young vocations to the priesthood and is a model for other Dioceses. Fall 2006 marks the beginning of the twenty-fifth year as Episcopal chaplain to Emory University of Nancy Baxter.

Text and photos submitted by the Reverend Nancy Baxter.

✠　　✠　　✠　　✠

The Reverend Nancy Baxter talks with His Holiness the Dalai Lama in 1998.

THE EPISCOPAL CHARITIES FOUNDATION

✠

The Episcopal Charities Foundation (ECF) was the brainchild of Bishop Bennett Sims (1972 until 1983). In response to federal budget cuts by the Reagan administration, the church wanted to respond to the drastic cuts in assistance and concern that the poor would have no one to provide for them. A committee was convened, including, among others, the Reverend Austin Ford of Emmaus House, the Reverend Stan McGraw, and Gene Bowens. The Reverend Woody Bartlett proposed a strategic plan and Bishop Sims appointed him the first director of the Episcopal Charities Foundation.

The ECF was announced at Council in January 1982 and Bartlett was named executive director soon thereafter, and made some fundraising visits before leaving his post as rector of St. Bartholomew's Church in June. Most of the first million dollars came within the first year. The Board set up the guidelines for funding and the first grants were awarded in November 1982. The investment fund continued to grow and grants were made to more ministries. In 1987 a capital tithe campaign to the poor and Camp Mikell netted ECF about $400,000. Money went to the investment fund and to grants such as East Lake Housing Project community organizing and the Community Advocacy Ministry in Macon, which have produced lasting results.

More proactive grants were undertaken in 1994 and Bartlett left the foundation to devote full time to affordable housing programs. The Reverend Connie Dee Belmore became director with Linda Scott as assistant. The stock market's dizzying rise in the late 1990s was a double-edged sword for the ECF and the poor. The investment fund grew to $2.5 million, which provided more grants; however, the gap between the well-off and those in need grew even wider. More money and better programs addressing the needs of the poor are needed. Self-sufficiency ministries will need more attention. The new century has provided more challenges. ECF currently finds itself in a new cycle of the government's reduced commitment to the poor. ECF's response will depend on the toll on the poor welfare reforms take. Government cutbacks challenge the community to take up the call to action. Episcopal Charities Foundation is prepared to answer.

Text submitted by the Reverend Canon Debra Shew.

✠   ✠   ✠   ✠

CANTERBURY CLUB IN NORTHWEST GEORGIA, ROME

✠

Canterbury Club in Northwest Georgia invites all college students to come together in the spirit of Christian fellowship to explore and discuss matters of life and faith as a community of friends. The club continues to build on a rich history spanning more than two decades of bringing the Episcopal/Anglican experience to life on two Rome college campuses.

Early efforts on the Berry and Shorter College campuses in the 1980s resulted in the brief presence of a Canterbury Club at Shorter College and the development of an ongoing Episcopal Students Fellowship (ESF) at Berry College. The Reverend Janice Bracken Wright has served as the volunteer Episcopal chaplain to Berry College since mid-1983.

In the mid-1990s, the ESF changed its name to the more familiar Canterbury Club. The occasional participation of Shorter College students led to a more focused outreach on that campus in 2005. Currently over one hundred students, faculty, and staff from both colleges make up the Canterbury Club weekly mailing list.

The student-designed program of two or more meetings per week offers a creative mix of opportunities for worship, service, and fellowship throughout the academic year. Worship services include twice-monthly Tuesday evening Holy Eucharist services and weekly Sunday night Compline services. Annual Ash Wednesday and All Saints services, as well as an Instructed Eucharist, are offered for the entire Berry College community. Members also lead Morning Prayer chapel services at Shorter. St. Peter's, Rome, hosts an annual Canterbury Sunday with students filling all lay roles in the 11:00 a.m. Eucharist. A senior student, usually an officer, delivers the homily. Members also serve as choir members, lay readers, and chalice bearers at St. Peter's throughout the year.

Service opportunities include participation in Hunger Clean-up Day, Make a Difference Day, Saturday Community Soup Kitchens, and two seasonal parties at a local nursing home. Members participate in the Christmas Child and Angel Tree programs at the holidays and also host the Shrove Tuesday Pancake Supper as a gift to St. Peter's congregation.

Canterbury provides abundant fellowship opportunities. Students renew old, and make new friendships in a safe, welcoming environment. Spring and fall calendars include Tuesday night potlucks, as well as monthly Sunday lunches and weeknight dinners at local restaurants. Each semester, club members enjoy Sunday dinners at the homes of Berry and Shorter faculty advisors. Dinners at the chaplain's house close each semester, with Bishop Alexander attending the spring dinner each year since 2003. Other fellowship activities include ice cream socials, interactive games, and bowling.

Members often participate in inquirers classes at St. Peter's, leading to Confirmation or reception into the church. After graduation, members are well prepared to take leadership roles in their home churches. Many have pursued graduate degrees, two have taken positions as full-time lay youth ministers, and three have entered the priesthood in the Dioceses of Atlanta and Georgia.

The Canterbury Club was funded by the Diocese for over a decade, but is now formally sponsored by St. Peter's Church, where many of the students worship on weekdays and Sundays. The club is a community of faith in action, always growing, always open to new members and new ideas.

Text submitted by the Reverend Janice Bracken Wright. Photo by Mark Law.

Right: Members of the Canterbury Club of Northwest Georgia, in front of Old Ford Dining Hall at Berry College.

CHAPTER SIX

THE REFORMING CHURCH, 1983 TO THE PRESENT

NEWLY INSTALLED BISHOP CHARLES JUDSON CHILD WALKED AWAY FROM THE CATHEDRAL CHANCEL, SATURDAY, NOVEMBER 12, 1983, HIS VESTMENTS, COPE, MITER, AND STOLE flapping in all directions and ushered in an age of ecclesial flamboyance for the Diocese of Atlanta. Truly, the times were ripe for this unique former canon pastor and Suffragan Bishop to assume the helm. The Episcopal Church no longer bore its earlier character. A major theological and liturgical reformation was taking place and old denominational identities were falling to rising spiritualism, biblical literalism, megachurches, charismatic worship, and rebellion to some or all of these new forms of faith. In earlier days, Episcopalians quietly determined which parishes in an urban area were "High Church" or "Low Church." In the 1980s, the divisions fell along worship that could be termed "charismatic" and "traditional." The Diocese of Atlanta already reflected many of these tensions as Child began his episcopate.

Immediately upon assuming office, Bishop Child signed a covenant with the Roman Catholic Bishop, which provided for greater interchange among the congregations as well as shared retreats and spiritual events. In his first Diocesan newspaper article, the Bishop noted this covenant and encouraged the interchange some parishes were having with their local Lutheran congregations. This spirit of ecumenism remained a major aspect of Child's efforts.

On May 6, 1985, the Reverend Claiborne Jones became rector of the Church of the Epiphany, Atlanta. Reflective of the many women who had already taken their part in the priestly ministry throughout the Diocese of Atlanta; the Reverend Jones became the first woman to be called to the primary leadership of a parish. In 1985, there were 118 clergy in the Diocese and of these 108 were male and 10 female. Previously, all women served as assistants to male priests.

Bishop Child called for the election of a Coadjutor Bishop on September 3, 1986. This person would succeed him upon his retirement. The August *Diocese* published the photographs with the names and positions of fifteen nominated candidates. Five of these were currently serving parishes in the Diocese of Atlanta: the Reverends Frank K. Allan, St. Anne's, Atlanta; Robert H. Johnson, Holy Innocents, Atlanta; Harry H. Pritchett Jr., All Saints, Atlanta; E. Don Taylor, Holy Cross, Decatur; and James K. Yeary, St. Mark's, LaGrange. It took ten ballots with such a large slate, and the Reverend Frank K. Allan eventually won the Council's approval to be the first Bishop Coadjutor in Diocesan history. Only days later, the Reverend Don Taylor, rector of Holy Cross, Decatur, was nominated and elected Bishop of the Virgin Islands. Two years later, another earlier candidate, the Reverend Robert H. Johnson of Holy Innocents, was elected Bishop of Western North Carolina.

It had been some time since a Bishop approached the Diocese of Atlanta with immediate parish experience, as did Frank Allan who completed eleven years as rector of St. Anne's, Atlanta. He was forty-nine when elected and had also served St. Paul's, Macon, and St. Mark's, Dalton. When Judson Child resigned at the end of 1988, Bishop Allan appointed the first woman—the Reverend Nan Peete—to serve as canon to the ordinary. She also happened to be African American. Winds of change continued to whistle through the parishes of Atlanta, bringing relief to some and ruffling others. The American church ordained the first woman Bishop sending the Anglican primates into predictable contortions. The pro-life and pro-choice controversy over abortion filtered into the church and the sixty-ninth General Convention meeting in Detroit in early 1988 attempted to express the views of the church regarding this issue. "While we acknowledge that in this country it is the legal right of every woman to have a medically safe abortion, as Christians, we believe strongly that if this right is exercised, it should be used only in extreme situations."

Diocesan institutions also encountered changes during these years. Camp Mikell, already enjoyed by summer campers and annual visits of clergy, looked to encourage year-round conferences. The Appleton Home, having just celebrated 120 years of service, closed its dormitories to provide day therapeutic services to girls and young women in Middle Georgia. Emmaus House was founded in 1967 by the Reverend Austin Ford and continues to serve residents in the Peoplestown and Summerhill areas of Atlanta with a variety of programs for children, adults, and senior citizens. In 1997, the Cathedral Church of St. Philip celebrated its 150th anniversary. Cathedral communicant and Diocesan Chancellor Richard Perry produced a written history entitled *These Old Walls*. The Diocesan newspaper, for years, had held the title *Diocese*. Early in Allan's episcopate, he secured the services of journalist Cary Patrick, and the newspaper received an attractive new format and the name *DIOLOG*, which was circulated to homes throughout the Diocese and beyond.

The turn of the century marked Bishop Allan's retirement and an abortive attempt to elect a new bishop. After licking the wounds caused by withdrawing the election of the Reverend Robert G. Trache—due to irregularities determined by the Standing Committee—the Diocese enjoyed a brief interim under the Right Reverend Robert G. Tharp, and then nominated and elected a seminary professor, the Reverend Dr. John Neil Alexander, as the ninth Bishop of Atlanta. The scholar Bishop received his ordination on Saturday, July 7, 2001, at the Cathedral of St. Philip among a standing-room-only crowd of over two thousand. Bishop Alexander immediately appointed the Reverend Richard H. Callaway, rector of St. Julian's, Douglasville, to serve as his canon to the ordinary. The September–October 2001 *DIOLOG*, noted that Bishop Alexander assumed responsibility for a Diocese with more than fifty-four thousand members in North and Middle Georgia—the tenth largest in the Episcopal Church. Like earlier Bishops, Alexander's entry into this unique leadership ministry found him confronting both already established controversies as well as a new one brought about by the election of an openly gay bishop in the Diocese of New Hampshire. Indeed, the Episcopal Church and the Diocese of Atlanta remain a reforming community; and the Bishop holds high the Gospel of Jesus Christ, which unites and heals the divisions of God's people.

Text submitted by the Reverend William P. McLemore.

✠   ✠   ✠   ✠

St. Clare's Episcopal Church, Blairsville

✛

St. Clare's exists today because in the early 1980s a few Episcopalians in the Blairsville area stepped out to declare: "We need a church here." As more people moved into the area and caught the fever, "we met, achieved recognition, and we grew."

As the worshipping community began to grow they were among the first groups to "Adopt A Mile" of highway as their own to clean up. Many friendships grew as members proudly picked up litter. Bake sales and yard sales were held. As individuals, members participated in various community organizations and encouraged everyone to put Episcopal Church decals on their vehicles and St. Clare's continued to grow.

After meeting in a vacant Methodist Church in the downtown area and later in another older unused church out of town, they were delighted to have the opportunity to hold services in a chapel on the campus of Young Harris College. With greater seating, they presented folk masses frequently and extended coffee hours after services. As several interim priests traveled over the mountains to lead the services, the congregation grew. Now a mission of Grace Calvary, Clarkesville, they moved on to searching for property where they could build a "real Episcopal Church." The members chose and were approved as St. Clare's and the mission statement reflected her philosophy of serving and caring for others.

A parishioner deeded a house to the congregation and the sale of that property, and a loan from another member provided "seed money" for the purchase of ten acres at the present location. The church subsequently gave two acres to their very first outreach project, Mountain Learning and Child Care Center, which was completed shortly before St. Clare's was finished. The first vicar, the Reverend Carter Maddox, began holding services and ground was broken—the congregation was up and still growing. Luckily there were experienced construction workers in the congregation and everyone participated wherever able. Bishop Allen consecrated the debt-free church in May 1995. There was great rejoicing, while they grew.

Following the retirement of the Reverend Maddox, the Reverend Susan Johnson accepted the call to be the first full-time rector. The Memorial Garden has been completed, the paving and scenic landscaping of the parking lot is finished, they have a new mission statement, and an active Daughters of the King and Education for Ministry (EFM) is on-going. St. Clare's Parish is ready to grow still more.

Text and photo submitted by Ms. Pat Seymour.

Opposite page: St. Clare's Episcopal Church, Blairsville.

✛   ✛   ✛   ✛

ST. JOSEPH'S EPISCOPAL CHURCH, McDONOUGH

✠

Henry County's first efforts to establish an Episcopal parish began in 1955 when several local families began a mission under the sponsorship of St. George's Episcopal Church, Griffin. Meeting in the local Woman's Club annex, the group worked enthusiastically and grew with several additional families. Then rural Henry County (about three thousand people) simply did not provide the members hoped for and in 1957 Bishop Claiborne closed St. John's mission.

After almost thirty years a new effort began, with a much larger population in a now suburban county. In 1986 an effort was initiated by resident Episcopalians along with a number of families from St. Simon's Church, Conyers. Bishop Child was petitioned and after initial skepticism, consented to forming a worshipping community. The first service was Holy Eucharist on Christmas Eve, 1986. Almost all the previous members of St. John's were involved in the effort. The potential for growth was there and by March of 1987 Bishop Allan had laid out the necessary goals for incorporation and appointed the Reverend H. Donald Harrison as priest-in-charge.

The church grew rapidly and moved its services in September 1987 to the chapel of the Rainer-Carmichael Funeral Home. In early 1987, Alex and Claire Crumbley donated half of the seven acres adjoining their home and the other half was purchased and donated by Harold and Willathea Jackson. The startup was so successful that in January 1988, at Diocesan Council, St. Joseph's was admitted as a self-supporting parish with seventy members. The Reverend H. Donald Harrison became its first rector and served with energy and distinction for the next ten years

The membership became active and engaged in ministry and service from the beginning. Youth groups and choirs were formed, Sunday school was taught and Christian education became an expected feature of parish life. Valerie McDonald has been tireless in her leadership of the Sunday school at St. Joseph's. Neighborhood home groups formed and the church began to reach out to the community. "In His Name

Exterior of St. Joseph's Episcopal Church, McDonough.

Food Pantry"—the county's first—was spearheaded by Episcopalians working with other likeminded Christians in the community. Carlotta Monningh of St. Joseph's served as the first executive director. Three other members of St. Joseph's served as executive director in the following years. An Education for Ministry curriculum has operated since 1987.

A Palm Sunday 1989 groundbreaking ceremony was held on the seven acres and the church moved into its new facility on May 27, 1990. Harold Jackson hand-crafted the beautiful sanctuary appointments including the cross, altar, altar rail, clergy chairs, acolyte benches, and baptismal font. The new facility offered new opportunities for service. It did not take long for the building to open to a much-needed Alcoholics Anonymous chapter—now grown to six. Other community groups including a local mothers' group, the Girl Scouts, and a TOPS group use the building. In 1997, with the growing congregation began a capital campaign to construct a new Parish Hall and Sunday school wing completed in 1999.

The Reverend Loree Reed was called as associate priest in July 1997, and spear-headed expansion of the Christian education program. Father Harrison resigned in August 1998 and the Reverend Dr. Gene Robinson was called as interim in December 1998. After a lengthy search, the Reverend John G. Bancroft became St. Joseph's second rector in June of 2000.

St. Joseph's has worked at becoming an effective program parish of almost four hundred members. It continues to actively serve in the community and to pay off existing debt and make necessary improvements to the facility. Its members remain very active in the community, serving in adult literacy, the hospital auxiliary, and various other community efforts. Most would agree that while its accomplishments to date have been very significant, its best years are truly yet to come.

Text and photos submitted by the Reverend John Bancroft.

Right: Interior of St. Joseph's Episcopal Church, McDonough.

THE EPISCOPAL CHURCH OF THE ANNUNCIATION, ROSWELL

✛

The name Annunciation is based on Luke 1: 26–36. The Angel Gabriel comes to Mary and announces to her that she will bear the Messiah. The lily, the symbol of the Virgin Mary, recipient of the Annunciation, has come to symbolize purity and virginity.

Annunciation's mission is "to know God, to make Christ known, and through the power of the Holy Spirit, to accept and serve others as Christ accepts and serves us." Although small in size, the church is large in spirit. They are a friendly church made up of longtime Episcopalians and those who have joined the congregation from other religious backgrounds. They are united by their liturgy and worship, while having the freedom to think, question, and grow.

In September 1985 a letter to Bishop Child from the clergy of the Marietta Convocation indicated a need for a congregation in northeast Cobb and south Cherokee Counties. At the 1986 Annual Council, the Marietta Convocation resolved to sponsor a new mission. Eighty-nine letters were sent to area Episcopalians, inviting them to meet at Mountain View United Methodist Church on February 12, 1987, and forty-five people attended. The Reverend Bill Swift was named vicar for the new mission.

A worship service and second organizational meeting on March 12, 1987, was held at Mountain View. On April 5, 1987, the first Sunday service was celebrated at Modesto House on Arnold Mill Road. A Steering Committee formed and voted to name the new mission "The Episcopal Church of the Annunciation." Bishop Allan received the first confirmation class on August 27, 1987. In September the con-gregation moved to the Academy of Ballet Arts in Roswell due to increasing numbers; soon after, Foyer groups started; and the first issue of *Annuncations* newsletter was distributed.

A contract was signed for property on Jamerson Road on October 19, 1987. On November 1 the first Vestry was elected. The Feast of the Annunciation and the first anniversary were celebrated March 25, 1988. An Altar Guild was started by Anne Whittle. The Academy of Ballet Arts was outgrown and the congregation moved to Davis Elementary School on Jamerson Road where acolytes served for the first time. The new church property on Jamerson Road was blessed on January 17, 1989.

Church of the Annunciation, Roswell.

Ground was broken on September 3, 1989, and an adult education program began with two classes between services. The last service at Davis Elementary was February 18, 1990. The Right Reverend Frank K. Allan dedicated and consecrated the building the next week. The new building was made possible by generous donations of time, talent, and funds by the parishioners. The ordination of Alan Sandlin, Annunciation's former choir director, occurred at Annunciation on June 8, 1991.

Father Swift officiated at his last service on February 14, 1993, with Father Al Daviou, the second vicar, celebrating his first service on February 6, 1994. The Reverend Thomas H. Conley, the third vicar, celebrated his first Sunday service on August 25, 1996, and in August 1999 left to become canon of pastoral care at the Cathedral of St. Philip. The Reverend Hendree Harrison was appointed priest-in-charge on April 1, 2000.

Since 2000, Annunciation has continued to thrive and no longer receives aid from the Diocese and pays its full share to the Diocese annually. About seventy households of active members with Sunday attendance of eighty to one hundred people support the mission. The Christian education program was revitalized in the fall of 2000. Memorial funds provided improvements in the nave, beautiful additions to the altar, as well as kneelers, prayer books, and hymnals.

Current outreach projects include MUST Ministries in Cherokee County and a print-cartridge recycling program produces money to support missionaries in Northern Iraq. Fundraising goes exclusively to outreach. The youth and children's Sunday school classes sponsor Christmas stockings for Emmaus House and Christmas shoeboxes for Operation Christmas Child. Parishioners' ties to active duty military result in regular care packages sent abroad. An Episcopal Church Women (ECW) Guild makes afghans for shut-ins.

Members celebrate their church family in many ways: "Hendree's Barbecue"; a parish picnic at Allatoona; an Easter Feast; covered-dish lunches after church; covered-dish suppers in parishioners' and the priest's homes; workday hot dog lunches; Lenten soup suppers; and receptions after baptisms. A remodeled Activities Building to better accommodate their fellowship and a new playground built in 2001 are welcomed additions.

Text submitted by Linda Werner. Photos by Geoffrey Myers.
Left: Church of the Annunciation, Roswell.

CHURCH OF THE HOLY FAMILY, JASPER

✠

In the fall of 1986 a small group of Episcopalians met to make plans for realizing their shared visions: an Episcopal Church in Jasper. They had been driving to Episcopal Churches in Canton and Cartersville, or attending local churches of other denominations; two had been part of an earlier unsuccessful attempt to start a church. Under the focused leadership of Beverly McCormick a place to worship was found in the friendly New Lebanon Presbyterian Church, and the Reverend Paul Ross—a quintessential circuit-riding priest—agreed to add an early morning service to his Sunday schedule of services in Canton and Calhoun. On the first Sunday of Advent 1986 the first service of what was to become Church of the Holy Family was held at 7:45 a.m. at the Presbyterian Church with the Reverend Ross celebrating. Eucharistic minister was Jim Wilbur who has served continually for almost twenty years and is now head verger.

Of the nineteen persons who signed the guest book that day, five were out-of-town guests, two were Altar Guild ladies from St. Clement's, and twelve became the nucleus of the new congregation. It was several weeks before attendance again reached double digits. The church soon had its own Altar Guild person and three Eucharistic ministers. The Nineteenth Hole at Bent Tree became a substitute Parish Hall and after the service everyone went "up the mountain" for breakfast.

The name chosen was St. Francis of the Mountains, but on his first visit the Right Reverend Judson Child requested that the name be changed to Church of the Holy Family. He said he had always wanted to have a Holy Family Parish in his Diocese. If there was any reluctance it soon disappeared as the small congregation began to grow into its name, becoming indeed a holy family. In those early days there was already an emphasis on outreach. Families were adopted at Christmas, and members were volunteers for Meals on Wheels, Hospice, DFACS, and for driving patients to appointments.

When the Reverend Ross retired the Reverend John Bolton became vicar

Exterior view of Church of the Holy Family, Jasper.

A service at Church of the Holy Family, Jasper, with Bishop Alexander.

The first rector of Holy Family, the Venerable Dr. Jerry Zeller, came in 1996, providing dynamic leadership throughout the planning and building of the new church. During his tenure Holy Family was blessed to have in the congregation priests who often served as celebrants or preachers, notably: the Very Reverend John Sanders (retired dean of the Cathedral of St. Philip); the Reverend Joe Holt (retired Lutheran pastor); and the Reverend Ted Hackett (professor at the Candler School of Theology). The Reverend Frank Wilson served first as associate rector and then interim rector after Dr. Zeller's retirement. The Reverend William Harkins served the parish as postulant, deacon, and priest. The Right Reverend J. Neil Alexander, ninth Bishop of Atlanta, celebrated the new ministry of the Reverend Mary Johnson as rector of the Church of the Holy Family on February 27, 2005.

Outreach has always had the highest priority at Holy Family. Both the Community Food Pantry and the Good Samaritan Health and Wellness Center were initiated by members of Holy Family but have become community-wide programs with leadership, funding, and volunteers from many other groups as well. The Food Pantry provides families with food and counseling during crises. Good Samaritan is a nonprofit, volunteer-operated free clinic providing health services to the medically underserved in Pickens County. Within the church the outreach ministry and the pastoral care ministry, which works closely with the Casserole Patrol, provide ongoing care to members and to the community as a whole. Grace happens!

Text and photos submitted by Mrs. Louise Wilbur.

for the churches in Calhoun and Jasper. The next vicar, the Reverend Sam Buice, also served both churches. The Reverend Scott Trotter was Holy Family's first full-time vicar. Holy Family became a parish in 1991.

After leaving the Presbyterian Church, Holy Family met in a church building leased from the Chapel Assembly of God and then at the Chapman Funeral Home before moving into modular units made possible by the Diocese of Atlanta. At this time Holy Family had purchased twelve acres of land and the modular church was installed in 1995 on the original plot of the now forty-acre campus. This served Holy Family well until the move, in May 2002, into the beautiful new church designed by architect Garland Reynolds. It has been described as "North Georgia mountain gothic." The church was dedicated and consecrated by the Right Reverend J. Neil Alexander on September 8, 2002.

St. Elizabeth of Hungary Episcopal Church, Dahlonega

✠

In 1987 the first Episcopal Bishop to visit Dahlonega in an official capacity was the Right Reverend Frank K. Allan. Clergy representing almost every denomination in town, the mayor, and the curious all came to pay their respects to Bishop Allan.

While Bishop Allan was putting away his regalia after the service, the worship space was magically transformed into a banquet hall in under five minutes! Then men marched into the room carrying tables already laden with a feast, beautifully presented in silver and crystal dishes on lace tablecloths with silver candelabra. The bishop was stunned!

This is just one example of the teamwork of that close-knit group of about thirty friends. They were holding services in Dahlonega's historic Women's Club. Sunday school was taught in the kitchen, and hymns were played on an ancient upright piano that was missing several notes.

The story of St. Elizabeth's begins with Louise Boyd, a "Cathedral-trained" Daughter of the King, who became a guiding light. She and several others decided that attending Grace Church in Gainesville was too far to drive every Sunday. So in 1981, this pioneering group received permission from Grace Church's rector, Father Nat Parker, to organize Grace Chapel in Dahlonega.

A temporary worship space was found at the chapel at Lumpkin County Hospital; later moved to the Lumpkin County/Dahlonega Senior Center, and then to the

St. Elizabeth of Hungary, Dahlonega.

parishioner. The cross was originally part of the rood screen at St. Michael's and All Angels' Episcopal Church in Baltimore, Maryland. When the chancel burned in 1961, Milton (Bunky) Schul, later a Nativity parishioner, salvaged the charred remnant from a dump truck.

In November 2000, the congregation dedicated "The Memorial Garden of the Resurrection" as a permanent reminder of that community's legacy. After September 2001, a conversation initiated by Nativity grew into what is now the Fayette Interfaith Community Network, comprised of area Christians, Jews, and Muslims. In November 2003, Nativity became a full parish and with renewed emphasis on stewardship.

Throughout this congregation's life, it looked to the greater community. In Fayetteville, Nativity has worked with and through the Fayette Samaritans (a local clearinghouse for food, clothing, and financial aid); Azalea Estates Assisted Living; Holy Comforter Episcopal Church; LaFayette Nursing Home; Southern Crescent Habitat for Humanity; Bethlehem Ministries; Compassion International; Episcopal Relief and Development; Food for the Poor; United Thank Offering; and provided meeting space for home schooling.In November 2004, Bishop Alexander dedicated a second building, providing classrooms for Sunday school for all ages. Today, the congregation is a fast-growing and diverse Episcopal family, emphasizing spirituality, community, and celebrating Christ's love above all.

Text and photos submitted by Martha Clatterbuck.

✢   ✢   ✢   ✢

Allan announced the Reverend Patricia Merchant as ver the next eight years, the congregation worshipped ng Sunday school, Bible study, and outreach programs. ant left and the Reverend Katherine Roberts was appended Bob Hudak became full-time vicar on April 1 of

ent home at 130 Antioch Road. The first service was a Palm Sunday "Liturgy of the Palms" shared with St. t door. Bishop Allan dedicated the building in June. rated a cross that had been restored by Robert Haynie, tte County Episcopal Mission and former Resurrection

---

Women's Club. A priest from Grace Church came to Dahlonega to celebrate twice a month. On other Sundays, registered lay readers from Grace Church rotated with several of the members to lead us in Morning Prayer.

Things started really popping on June 5, 1988, when they moved their services to the Dahlonega Presbyterian Church. Encouraged by Bishop Allan, they broke away from the patronage of Grace Church and became St. Elizabeth's, an official parish of the Diocese.

Outreach had been the congregation's mission from the outset, so they chose St. Elizabeth of Hungary—a queen who spent her fortune building hospitals and helping the sick, the poor, and the elderly—for their patron saint.

Chancel of St. Elizabeth of Hungary, Dahlonega, with the Reverend Paul. B. Roberts.

Projects supported by the church over the years include Rainbow Children's Home, CASA, Emmaus House, Peruvian Amazon Conservation, Jars of Clay, NOA, Family Connection, Habitat for Humanity, Project Hope, White Christmas, and the Community Helping Place. Members have paid electric bills, taken children to school, helped students with special needs, provided transportation to medical facilities, and provided Meals-on-Wheels—the list goes on. St. Elizabeth's has provided prominent leadership in establishing several of Dahlonega's philanthropic organizations. Church members were among the founders of NOA, a local shelter for abused women and children.

Hurricane Hugo in 1989 caused the establishment of a local chapter of Habitat for Humanity. At one time, at least half of the congregation was actively involved in repairing and renovating existing dwellings, locating suitable land, building new homes, and comprised half of Habitat's Board of Directors.

The Community Helping Place (CHP) is a local ecumenical ministries organization. St. Elizabeth's is the only church that includes CHP in their outreach budget, and also offers generous support with leadership, labor, and goods.

On June 5, 2000, St. Elizabeth's opened the doors of its own church on the outskirts of Dahlonega. The church's beautiful antique altar was given to them in 1985 by St. Catherine's in Marietta, which had received it from St. James' in Marietta, where it was first installed in 1876. Almost everything in the church has been designed, created, and donated by members.

The overwhelming generosity and talent of every individual in this congregation is the foundation of this thriving parish. They embrace growth and change, and try to make all who walk through their doors feel like they have just come home.

Text and photos submitted by Roberta Niles.

✢   ✢   ✢   ✢

Church of the Nativity, Fayetteville

✣

The Fayette County Episcopal Mission in Fayetteville celebrated its first Eucharist on November 4, 1990, although the congregation was already thirty-six years old. In November 1964, parishioners from St. John's in College Park met to consider forming a new parish in East Point. The Reverend Edwin Coleman led Evening Prayer at Continental Colony School on December 4, 1964, sponsored by St. John's, Incarnation, and St. Mary's. The Reverend Dr. Henry Stokes Jr., curate of St. John's, assumed the additional duty of vicar of the new mission. Father Stokes became full-time vicar in January 1966, and the parish incorporated as "The Episcopal Church of the Resurrection."

In June 1969, Bishop Randolph Claiborne Jr. dedicated a new building at 2670 Hogan Road in East Point, with a parish of over 450 members. The Navy Department placed a one-thousand-pound brass Coast Guard buoy bell on permanent loan. The church had acolytes, *Butterfly* (the newsletter), choir, church school, lay readers, Men's Club, Parish Life, ushers, youth, and Episcopal Church Women (ECW), who ran the Old Curiosity Shop, a successful business.

In November 1979, the Reverend Gene Britton was called. He indicated that the church "was founded . . . in an all-white suburban neighborhood and enjoyed instant success . . . [but] soon after [going] into debt for the lovely new facility, [it] became a white island in a sea that was turning increasingly black." The church explored options to expand their now shrinking financial base: community outreach, merger with Incarnation or St. Mary's, or sale of assets.

In July 1987, unable to support a full-time priest, Resurrection called the Reverend Delmas Hare. In March 1989, the Bishop Frank K. Allan celebrated Good Friday Liturgy and secularization of the building. The parish's liturgical appointments were divided between the then-new student centers at Atlanta and Emory Universities.

Church of the Nativity, Fayetteville.

The Episcopal Church of St. Mary and St. Martha of Bethany, Buford

✣

The Church of St. Mary and St. Martha was formed in 1992 when a small group of dedicated Christians planned an Episcopal Mission in northeast Gwinnett County. After worshipping in private homes, the Reverend John Dukes celebrated the first Eucharist at a picnic at Lake Lanier on August 2. That morning was quite foggy, so visibility was limited. The invited bagpiper drove around for an hour, but was hopelessly lost. He parked his car, walked to the banks of the lake and started playing "Amazing Grace." It was so spiritually moving for the small gathering of worshipers hearing the beautiful bagpipe sounds lofting across the waters, as the fog began to lift. What an inspirational way to begin our history.

Regular services were held in Tapp Funeral Home's Chapel, whose owners did not charge rent because they wanted their gift of space to spread Christianity to the community. That kindness allowed the small mission to save money toward the purchase of land in 1994. The Reverend John Dukes resigned in January 1995 and the Reverend Charles M. Girardeau became the second vicar on August 15, 1995.

The present building was completed in the spring of 1998. On May 17, the Sunday morning service began in the Chapel at Tapp. While singing "Lift High the Cross," parishioners walked out of the Chapel, got into their cars, and began a procession following Father Chuck in his 1994 purple pick-up truck to the church's new location. An acolyte sat in the bed of the truck, holding high the cross, robes billowing in the wind as members drove behind with headlights beaming, and onlookers wondering what this was all about. The congregation gathered again on the front porch of the new building, sang the final verses as they filed inside together. Immediately there was a Baptism, then a Eucharist, and members finally felt at home. Full Parish status was achieved in June 2000 and Father Chuck became the first rector shortly thereafter.

From the beginning, St. Mary and St. Martha has had a strong sense of community, friendship, and mutual support. The name was the result of a vote taken by parishioners, and approved by Bishop Frank Allan. It is a very fitting name for this congregation, which devotes equal emphasis to worship and service.

The decision to confirm the election of the Reverend Gene Robinson as Bishop in the Diocese of New Hampshire had a significant impact on this parish. It suffered the loss of one-third of its worshiping congregation and one-third of its financial support.

Since that time, however, the parish has eme[...] Today, St. Mary and St. Martha serves a strong an[...] mately 420 baptized members and the surrounding[...] port of food donations to the North Gwinnett C[...] volume of food contributed, despite the fact that [...] tions to support them. The Parish has supported [...] Wheels program for many years; it was awarded the [...] A unique horse ministry program is offered to the [...] a shelter for victims of domestic violence. These ar[...] commitment to service to the community.

"We are *united* in our *passionate* worship of God, [...] and *loving service* to our Lord, the community and one[...] the Holy Spirit." Amen.

Text and photos submitted by the church.

Opposite page: St. Mary and St. Martha of Bethany, Bufor[...]

Youth activity, St. Mary and St. Martha of Bethany, Buford.

CHURCH OF THE RESURRECTION, WHITE COUNTY

✠

The Episcopal Church of the Resurrection is situated on thirty-four beautiful acres in the rolling hills of White County flanked by Yonah and Sal Mountains. Entrance to the church property is over a wooden bridge that crosses Brasstown Creek. The Reverend Barbara Brown-Taylor with the support of twelve White County families started Resurrection as an aided parish of Grace-Calvary in 1993. The first Eucharist attended by sixty-five worshipers was January 27, 1993, in the hallway of the Historical White County Courthouse in Cleveland. Also at this first Eucharist the name was approved unanimously. Due to Courthouse renovations at that time, members came on Saturdays with buckets, brooms, and mops to clean up the building for Sunday worship. In May 1993, the Reverend Barbara Brown Taylor selected the Reverend Steve Lipscomb as associate priest at Grace-Calvary and the vicar at Resurrection. Father Lipscomb became the priest at Resurrection when parish status was granted by the Diocese on November 13, 1993.

Worship services moved to the White County Bank annex in early 1994 when restoration of the Courthouse was completed and the search for a permanent location began. The current site on Duncan Bridge Road became available when the Palm Sunday tornado in 1994 destroyed the new home of a parishioner. The property was purchased by Resurrection and the first phase of their building program was dedicated on Pentecost Sunday 1996.

The narthex is decorated with butterflies, which is one of the symbols recognizing the birth of Church of the Resurrection. Entering the nave, many have said there is a feeling of peace and you can feel God in your presence. The baptismal font was sculpted from the limb of a hundred-year-old cedar tree and a pan used to pan for gold on the Chattahoochee in the 1850s add a note of history to the modern church design. All furniture and fixtures are made from natural red oak.

Phase II of the building program began in 1999 with additional education space and a pre-K school to benefit both the church and the community. Construction was completed and the pre-K school opened in September 2000. Four-hour classes are held for three- and four-year-old children to master the skills necessary for entry into K-12 schools. The school is highly respected in the area by both teachers and parents for the excellent preparatory work.

Resurrection has nine major ministries: worship, Christian formation, pastoral care, parish life, membership and assimilation, community and public relations, building and grounds, and finance and stewardship. Of the ministries, outreach is recognized most highly by the community through supplying food and other supplies to area families in need. Events sponsored by Resurrection serving the community in general include the Fall Festival and Yard Sale. All proceeds go to community outreach. The monthly newsletter, *Resurrection Light*, is distributed to all congregation members to keep them informed about ongoing church activities. Church facilities are made available for other community events and programs including the Divertimento Concert series, AA, and local homeowners groups.

In its twelve years Resurrection has grown from the originating 12 families to over 175 families with an average Sunday attendance of 120 parishioners and guests. The church has a wide diversity of ages from the very young to the elderly. This requires that we have programs to support their varying interests including Daughters of the King, a weekly luncheon for women, a weekly breakfast for men, Cursillo, Foyers, Sunday School for all ages, a youth fellowship group, a monthly fellowship dinner, and others.

Text submitted by Jaymi and Chuck Hampton. Photos by Chuck Hampton and James Owens.
Opposite page: The Church of the Resurrection, White County.

Members of Church of the Resurrection with their unique baptismal font.

✠   ✠   ✠   ✠

St. Aidan's Episcopal Church, Alpharetta

✠

In 1993 at St. David's in Roswell, the Right Reverend Frank Allan announced that the Diocese would open a mission church in the Alpharetta area. In early 1994 St. Aidan's was started on Easter Sunday, April 3, at sunrise in Windward Park. About seventy-five people gathered as the priest-in-charge, the Reverend Noel Burtenshaw, led the service.

Before a year passed, St. Aidan's moved from being an aided parish to being recognized as a full parish. The name St. Aidan's was chosen because St. Aidan of Ferns (not Lindesfarne) was a missionary monk sent to preach the gospel by St. David in seventh-century Ireland, and the relationship between St. David's and St. Aidan's has remained strong through the years.

Father Noel led the parish for ten years and became the inspiration and driving force for the new church. Father Noel worked many long hours and nurtured the community spirit for the new church, which adopted as its mission statement: "To Know Jesus Christ and Make Him Known."

The new St. Aidan's congregation met for regular worship first on June 26, 1994, in a leased space of the AT&T Building in Alpharetta, and during the first year everyone pitched in because of the limited space for worship and mid-week storage. Prayer books, vestments, the altar items, and a large, standing cross had to be brought in every Sunday, and many of the children's Sunday school classes were held in corners of the hallway.

St. Aidan's Episcopal Church, Alpharetta.

The next temporary space of meeting was the Alpharetta Senior Center, which was large enough to accommodate the growing membership of St. Aidan's, but soon the congregation purchased the present nineteen-acre site at 13560 Cogburn Road, built a church to seat four hundred, and held its first Holy Eucharist on Palm Sunday 1997.

Some of the ministries at St. Aidan's include the Towel Train—a group that collects discarded but usable towels and other linens from hotels and takes them to shelters and people in need; yearly Habitat for Humanity builds; Heifer International; regular support and involvement with North Fulton Community Charities; mission trips both domestic and international; a wonderful prayer chain; exuberant and active Christian Education; and a large and active Daughters of the King chapter.

Father Noel retired in June 2003, but that didn't keep parishioners from beginning the next phase of growth—a Parish Hall for education and fellowship, which was completed in September 2004. The Reverend Robert Wood was called as St. Aidan's next rector the very next month, so one of the first events in the new Parish Hall was a grand reception, following his institution by the Right Reverend Neil Alexander on January 19, 2005.

In their first year in the new building, the people of St. Aidan's have also welcomed over 120 each Sunday for a full breakfast cooked by the men of the parish, doubled the size and scope of Vacation Bible School, and hosted other parish-wide fellowship events, including a gala reception on the Feast of Pentecost 2005 to honor Father Noel by naming the Parish Hall as Burtenshaw Hall.

Text and photos submitted by members of St. Aidan's Church.

St. Aidan's, Alpharetta, Dedication of Bartenshaw Hall.

ST. TERESA'S EPISCOPAL CHURCH, ACWORTH

✝

The history of St. Teresa's began at Annual Council in November of 1994. It was during his address that Bishop Allan laid out his vision for a new parish in the West Cobb area, and he called for a missioner to make it a reality. Working as assistant at St. Catherine's in Marietta, Michael Billingsley was moved by that call and scheduled a meeting with Bishop Allan to discern his vision for new ministry in that area. Over the next several months, Michael Billingsley met with the rectors of four Episcopal parishes in the North Cobb area to discuss mission plans.

In October of 1995, Michael Billingsley was named missioner and vicar, and launched a feasibility study for the West Cobb Mission. In January of 1996, volunteers from the four surrounding parishes were solicited and asked to make a two-year com-

mitment and become lay missioners that would gather together as the "Mission Development Committee" to brainstorm plans for establishing and supporting an Episcopal Church in West Cobb.

Letters addressed to 640 Episcopalians in five surrounding zip codes were mailed out, and in March of 1996, forty people responded and gathered for their first organizational meeting at the home of Gary and Carlotta Roberts from Christ Church in Kennesaw. Those present signed a petition to form a "Worshipping Community" in West Cobb. On April 3, 1996, Bishop Allan accepted the petition and gave permission to form a community. That same month, a Bishop's Committee was formed and they began work on choosing the name.

St. Teresa's Episcopal Church, Acworth.

Permission was granted for the community to begin Evening Prayer in May of 1996. The new worshipping community had its first service of Evening Prayer that same month in the home of Peter and Ethel MacKenzie of Powder Springs. Sunday worship space was found and a contract was negotiated with Ford Elementary School on Mars Hill Road to use their gym. A "Commissioning Service" was held for the newly formed community at St. Catherine's on Sunday July 7, 1996. A processional cross and other gifts were given and a picnic was held to celebrate the event.

The Right Reverend C. Judson Child was the celebrant at the first public service of the Holy Eucharist on Sunday July 14, 1996. Bishop Child consecrated communion vessels and the processional cross in the service that was attended by 164 faithful worshippers. Since the community was meeting in a public school, all items and books used for worship were portable and packed each week into a van.

At Annual Council in November of 1996, St. Teresa's was admitted into the Diocese of Atlanta as a parish, and the Bishop's Committee became the Vestry. With the consent of Bishop Allan, the new Vestry called the Reverend Michael Billingsley as the first rector. The first Parish Meeting was held in January of 1997 and the first Vestry members were elected.

The search for land began shortly after that first Parish Meeting, and 14.25 acres were purchased on the corner of Ford and Mars Hill Roads for $475,000. In the late fall of 1998, conversations with architects resulted in plans and conceptual drawings of a large, ten-thousand-square-foot multipurpose building. The Diocesan Architectural Committee approved the design in early 1999 and the date was set for groundbreaking. In July 1999, Bishop Child celebrated at the groundbreaking service on the property and turned the first shovel of earth at the location where the altar would be placed.

Construction on the first building of St. Teresa's began September 4, 2001, and the first service in the building was Ash Wednesday, February 13, 2002.

St. Teresa's founding rector, the Reverend Michael Billingsley, resigned his position in May 2005 and moved to the Boston area. The parish continues in ministry and is currently searching for a new rector.

Text and photos submitted by the Reverend Scott Kidd.

✢   ✢   ✢   ✢

St. Teresa's Episcopal Church, Acworth.

St. Gabriel's Episcopal Church, Oakwood

✠

In early 1996 Bishop Frank Allan and the clergy and Vestry of Grace Episcopal Church began to discuss the need for an additional Episcopal Church to serve the southern end of Hall County. The Reverend Jim Shumard, assistant rector at Grace was given the responsibility of forming a task force to work toward the establishment of a congregation somewhere in the Oakwood/Flowery Branch area.

In the summer of 1997 the Reverend Sollace M. Freeman ("Mike"), associate rector of Grace Church was asked by the rector, the Reverend Fred Jones, and Bishop Allan to take on the responsibility of vicar for the new church and to proceed with the securing of appropriate property. With the help of the task force, property owned by the Oakwood Assembly of God (OAG) was selected, and efforts were begun to raise the $535,000 needed for the purchase and renovations. Over the next several months individual loans from fourteen families—St. Gabriel's and Grace Church members—totaling $535,000 were secured for five years on an "interest only" basis. The names of these early supporters have been kept in the archives of St. Gabriel's Church.

On Monday night, December 15, 1997, fourteen people met together for the first service of the new church at the OAG. They continued to meet each Monday night for Holy Communion until May 4, 1998, by which time the weekly attendance was fifty-plus.

In March of 1998 the property was purchased from the OAG. The OAG congregation then began to rent the facility from the Episcopal congregation until renovations

St. Gabriel's Episcopal Church, Oakwood, dedicated May 10, 1998.

Chancel of St. Gabriel's Church, Oakwood

years. Following the death of Lou Fockele in 2002 and with the permission of his wife, Jean, the source of this contribution was made public in 2003.

St. Gabriel's was accepted into parish status at the Diocesan Council in November of 1998. Father Mike Freeman was elected by the Vestry as the first rector of St. Gabriel's as of January 1, 1999.

By January of 2003 Sunday attendance was averaging 165, a four-classroom addition had been completed and a half-time director of religious education had been hired. However, following the approval of the election of Bishop Robinson about 25 percent of the membership, six of nine Vestry members, including both wardens, left the Episcopal Church. The "road to recovery" has been difficult but the faith and perseverance of the remaining members has sustained the congregation and St. Gabriel's continues as a viable and vital part of the Diocese. On October 31, 2005, Father Freeman announced his decision to retire on January 8, 2006. As of this a new rector has not been called.

Text and photos submitted by the Reverend Mike Freeman.

✠   ✠   ✠   ✠

on their new site could be completed. They continued to hold Sunday services and other weekday gatherings until May 1998. During this period, the members of the new congregation, which included about forty "one-year loaners" from Grace Church, began the renovation of the worship space and Parish Hall.

St. Gabriel's was officially registered with the Georgia secretary of state as "The Episcopal Mission of South Hall" on March 9, 1998. On March 30, 1998, the name St. Gabriel's was adopted with Bishop Allan's approval.

Two hundred and fifty people from Grace Church, St. Gabriel's, and the community joined together with Bishop Allan, at 3:00 p.m. on May 10, 1998, for the dedication of the building and property. Offering of $10,168 was contributed at that service toward the budget of the congregation. In addition an anonymous gift of $100,000 was given to the congregation by a Grace Church family to be used by the church during its early

St. Thomas of Canterbury Episcopal Church, Thomaston

✠

Like many great ideas, St. Thomas of Canterbury Episcopal Church in Thomaston began as a vision. In the 1930s, a family in the small town of Thomaston opened a fund with $10,000 for the sole purpose of establishing a parish called St. Thomas in Thomaston. About sixty years later, with no knowledge of the family or the growing fund, Joanne Britt began to pursue this dream. She published a small invitation in the local newspaper for others to join in discussion on establishing an Episcopal parish. Deborah Green and Tracy Chandler responded and the trio met with the Reverend Don Harrison and soon the idea became reality.

On May 19, 1997, a meeting of inquirers was held with the Reverend Richard Callaway. Eight people attended and enjoyed banana pudding. To this day, it seems that banana pudding is served at every parish covered dish gathering. A month later, a second meeting with fifteen potential parishioners met with Bishop Frank K. Allan. On June 29, he led the group's first Eucharist at Bill and Kathy Anderson's home. Twenty-four parishioners celebrated communion. Meetings continued about once a month and on August 17 an instructed Eucharist was held at Silvertown Methodist Church, and Eucharist continued to be celebrated there as often as possible for several months.

During 1998 parishioners began meeting regularly on Sundays at Silvertown Methodist and on February 15, the Reverend Ellen Neufeld became the first priest-in-charge. In

Entrance to St. Thomas of Canterbury, Thomaston.

Interior of St. Thomas of Canterbury, Thomaston.

with her guidance the church enjoyed progress and growth; however she resigned in June 2003 due to family illness.

For the next several months, the true spirit of St. Thomas really shone as the parish had to find a way to operate without a priest. St. Thomas had always been a family, first and foremost and the combination of strong lay leadership, the culture of abundant and varied talent, and old-fashioned diligence sustained the parish during the period of uncertainty. On July 1, 2004, the Reverend Brian K. Davy, one of several regular supply priests, became vicar of St. Thomas of Canterbury. His father-like demeanor and his wonderful sermons were the medicine needed to revitalize the parish and he continues to lead the parish.

The parish continues to grow—physically and spiritually. Outreach endeavors to the community, throughout the Diocese and beyond, change as the spiritual needs change, but never the effort put into them. Though visitors and members come and go, the family culture never changes. St. Thomas is a small community, as were the earliest Christian communities. All who are seeking God are welcome, and the church welcomes all to become part of their loving and supportive family.

Text and photos submitted by Matthew T. McGaha.

✠ ✠ ✠ ✠

July the parish rented a former Catholic Church building at 400 Georgia Avenue in Thomaston. Much work by all was needed to make it suitable for service. A keyboard was the first major purchase. Beautiful music has been heard from the instrument and the congregation every Sunday morning since. The first Eucharist in the new space was held on August 9, and the first Christmas service was held there.

In September 1999, the Reverend Neufeld left and the parish went through a few months led by their own, the Reverend George Welch, a retired priest, enjoying his delightful sermons and the variety provided by other supply priests supplied by the Diocese. In February of 2000, the Reverend Donna Gafford became priest-in-charge and

St. Nicholas Episcopal Church, Hamilton

✛

St. Nicholas started seven years ago. They came together to develop a common vision. From these sessions came their mission, "For the Glory of God and Service to the Community," and a common dream of creating a place for worship, spiritual outreach, service, memorials, education, and childhood enrichment.

They reach out to visitors to Callaway Gardens and to young families. They work to build a Christian community and a place for worship and spiritual renewal. From this foundation they believe will spring strong commitment to loving enrichment of the lives of children and to caring service to the wider community.

In August 1998, under the leadership of the Reverend Tom Jones of Trinity Church in Columbus, fifty people from Harris County and environs gathered at Callaway Gardens to explore establishing an Episcopal Church in the Hamilton area. For the next year, the group met monthly for Evening Prayer in borrowed facilities, in the Hamilton Baptist Church. In December 1998, Trinity asked the Reverend Beverley McEachern to be their priest-in-charge. Under her leadership, they began weekly Sunday morning services in August 1999 at the Pine Mountain Valley Seventh-Day Adventist Church.

That same month, the Pine Mountain Benevolent Foundation gave St. Nicholas five acres of land east of Hamilton; the church purchased another three acres at 69 Mobley Road near the new high school. On February 20, 2000, Bishop Frank K. Allan launched St. Nicholas as a worshiping community. On October 6, 2001, his successor Bishop Neil Alexander visited St. Nicholas to consecrate the land.

Bishop Allan confirmed their first three new members in February 2000. Since then, another thirty have been confirmed. From about ten families they now have over fifty families and almost one hundred people who are members or active affiliates.

St. Nicholas Episcopal Church, Hamilton.

Members at St. Nicholas, Hamilton, celebrate a twenty-fifth anniversary.

board-and-batten, composite siding on a stone veneer foundation. A cathedral ceiling enhances the interior worship area, designed to seat one hundred people. The building has a sacristy; three large classrooms that serve as extra seating for meals, weddings, or funerals; a small kitchen; and administrative offices.

The congregation anticipates creating memorial gardens within the next year. They hope to gather and preserve the records of old cemeteries in the county. Longer range, their vision includes a quality primary school, beginning with a preschool that offers scholarships in the community, based on need.

On Sunday afternoon March 9, 2003, Bishop Neil Alexander consecrated St. Nicholas' new worship hall. More than 150 members and friends attended the service, which officially established the county's first Episcopal Church in modern times. In his sermon, Bishop Alexander congratulated St. Nicholas for "this marvelous building." He observed that the opening of a new church is "a sign of God still mightily at work in the lives of his people. . . . It is an offering to God in prayer, in praise, and in thanksgiving . . . an incredible act of faith, commitment, and determination."

Text submitted by Connie Blackmon. Photos by Dr. Larry Correnti.

The church's first Vestry, elected in 2000, has worked to establish a strong financial base. Their priest works for them four days per week; they have had a regular organist since Pat Newton joined the church in 2000. They have an active Altar Guild, Lay Episcopal Ministers, a Flower Guild, adult acolytes, and an acolyte-training program.

Their primary outreach ministry is through FOCUS, an interdenominational charity composed of a coalition of Harris County churches. They also participate in the Harris County Cancer Society's Relay for Life and sponsor needy children at Christmas.

On Sunday, January 12, 2003, they held opening service in the new Parish Hall: a thirty-eight-hundred-square-foot structure of Carpenter Gothic architecture with-

St. Columba's Episcopal Church, Suwannee

✛

St. Columba's is the Diocese's ninety-third parish and one of the country's fastest growing new parishes. On the Feast of St. Joseph, March 19, 2005, they celebrated another milestone when more than two hundred members celebrated the groundbreaking for their new church just eighteen months after their first service. Completed in the spring of 2006, St. Columba's Church, is located on James Burgess Road in south Forsyth County, in close to Johns Creek where Forsyth, Gwinnett, and Fulton Counties meet.

Since their first Mass in September 2003, St. Columba's has grown to more than seven hundred communicants. St. Columba's was initiated in July 2002 when Father Tripp Norris became the founding priest. On December 15, 2002, St. Columba's held its first meeting in a local hotel, not a particularly sacred space. But like every place they have gathered, the Holy Spirit transformed them into places of beauty. They met for over two years in the South Forsyth Middle School Cafeteria, where it was all too common to genuflect in dried spaghetti sauce or mustard!

Under those circumstances, one might wonder how they managed to thrive as a congregation. It's simply that in a time where many churches focus on Power Point and video, they have offered traditional worship steeped in the richness of Anglican tradition and grounded in the things that matter most—faith, family, and fellowship. Their continued growth in number and witness is also due to their reputation of "Radical Hospitality." From the first meeting when four invitations were handed to each family to share with others, Radical Hospitality has been their motto. Inviting friends to church works, and at each gathering their numbers have grown.

St. Columba's, Suwanee, proposed elevation rendering.

Radical Hospitality goes beyond an invitation; it is a call to regularly tell others about God's presence in their lives. Sharing the Good News is the blessing that has enabled them to grow at an average of two families each week. Radical Hospitality is a feeling, a personality, and the greeting one receives when entering their doors. It spills into all of their ministries—from the dedicated group of "Glad Tidiers" that met each and every Saturday morning to convert a middle school cafeteria into a church; to all the greeters, ushers, lectors, Flower and Alter Guild volunteers, choir members, and Sunday school teachers that make the church function. It extends to the community as well. Through outreach programs, they have provided more than one hundred needy children and their families with Christmas gifts, lunch to more than five hundred foster children and their foster parents, participated in the annual AIDS and Hunger Walks, and delivered Meals on Wheels.

Like true Episcopalians, they work hard and play hard too! St. Columba's offers fellowship for everyone: EYC for our teenagers, ECW, Knights of 'Columba'—the parish men's group, monthly dinner groups, an after church "lunch bunch," and a weekly coffee shop book study group. "It has been an exciting journey thus far. Blessed with an active, Spirit-filled, growing congregation, together, we've experienced many "firsts—many new friendships, new ministries, new outreach programs, and a new building. God has indeed called us here, and we can't imagine a better beginning!"

Text submitted by Pamela Bartz. Photos from the church archives.
Left: St. Columba's Easter Altar.

✠   ✠   ✠   ✠

THE YOUTH DEPARTMENT OF THE EPISCOPAL DIOCESE OF ATLANTA

✠

The Diocese of Atlanta provides a variety of events and opportunities to the youth and youth leaders of the Diocese. Youth in grades ten through twelve are able to apply to be on the Diocesan Youth Committee (DYC). The committee plans all the activities during actual retreats including theme, small group interactions, and afternoon activities. The committee meets for a training weekend several months prior to the retreats. The DYC is also responsible for planning the "Episcopalooza," a lock-in hosted by the Diocese and a local parish. The night is filled with music, singing, art, and drama produced by the high school youth of the Diocese.

The junior- and senior-high DYC retreats are held the first weekends of December and January at Camp Mikell for youth in grades six through twelve. The weekend consists of discussing theme-related issues, small focus groups, praying and worshiping together and dancing. "Happening" is a renewal weekend for youth in grades ten through twelve held at Camp Mikell twice a year. It's a powerful encounter in which young people minister and bring Jesus Christ alive within a community of disciples. The weekend includes talks, small focus group interactions, singing, and praying.

The "New Beginnings" retreat is designed to respond to issues, concerns, and needs of teenagers in grades six through nine. It is a spiritual growth and renewal weekend held in the fall at Indian Springs and in the spring at Camp Mikell. The weekend is filled with talks, skits, sharing, praying, and singing. After having attended these retreats, a young person can be on the "New Beginnings" or "Happening" team, and plan retreats for upcoming youth.

Every March the Hunger Walk takes place at Turner Field. Youth and other groups raise money to support the Episcopal Charities Foundation. "Vocare" is the newest weekend retreat added to the Diocesan calendar, and is a renewal weekend for young adults aged eighteen through twenty-nine held at Camp Mikell. The focus is on Christ in everyday life and provides opportunities for reflection on life's callings.

Each summer the Diocesan Mission Trip engages youth in grades ten through twelve. It is an opportunity for youth to experience a wider vision of the world and to deepen their relationship with God through services either in the United States or in another country.

Bishop Alexander with the 2005 Diocesan Episcopal Youth Event group.

2005 Diocesan Ecuador Mission Trip group.

is hosted at a Diocesan camp within the province. The national church sponsors the Episcopal Youth Event (EYE), another triennial event for senior high youth. This weeklong EYE event is held in a university setting in the United States. Province IV Network Meeting, an annual meeting of the province, targets Diocesan coordinators and two youth representatives. This networking meeting focuses on sharing ideas, suggestions, and concerns in developing ministry opportunities for the province.

Youth leader opportunities are offered within the Diocese to adults who work with young people. Each month (except summer) there is a meeting designed for youth workers to network, pray, share ideas, and discuss topics and upcoming events. Every March the Diocese sponsors a Diocesan-wide Ministry Fair and offers workshops for youth leaders.

An internship position to the Diocesan Youth Coordinator is open during the summer or the school year for a youth interested in learning how to coordinate youth events. One youth and one alternate from each of the ten convocations are elected to be Annual Council representatives every year. Each delegate has voice, vote, and a seat. Two youth representatives have seats with voice and vote on the Mikell Board of Governors.

The Diocese is active in provincial and national events, which give opportunities to interact with other youth from all over the country. Province IV sponsors the Provincial Youth Event, a triennial event for senior high youth and adults who work with them,

The Youth Workers' Conference is a yearly training conference that provides support to youth leaders/volunteers and their ministry. It is a time for learning, community building, networking, and spiritual reflection. Youth leaders are invited to participate in DYC, New Beginnings, and Happening Retreats.

The Diocese is proud of its youth and the events that it sponsors and supports. The youth of the Diocese benefit greatly from their experiences and the relationships that they make.

Text and photos submitted by Kim Smith, Diocesan Youth Coordinator.

SELECTED BIBLIOGRAPHY

✝

Bonner, James C. *The Georgia Story*. Oklahoma City: Harlow Publishers, 1961.

_____. *Milledgeville: Georgia's Antebellum Capital*. Macon [GA]: Mercer University Press Reprint, 1985.

Brisbane, Dr. Robert, et al. *History of St. Paul's Episcopal Church, Atlanta, n.d., edited and updated by Mrs. Harriett Witsell Bowens*. Atlanta: St. Paul's Episcopal Church, 2005.

Christ Episcopal Church, Macon, Georgia, Archives. Macon [GA], various documents from years through 2005.

Christ Episcopal Church, Norcross, Georgia. *Christ Church Episcopal Profile*. The Search Committee. Norcross [GA]: 2004.

_____. *Our Story—The First 25 Years, Christ Church Episcopal, Norcross*. Norcross [GA]: 2003.

Coleman, Kenneth, ed. *A History of Georgia*. Athens [GA]: The University of Georgia Press, 1977.

Collier, Caroline. *Parish Profile of St. Stephen's Episcopal Church*. Milledgeville [GA]: St. Stephen's Episcopal Church, 2005.

Collins, Doris. *The Episcopal Church in Georgia from the Revolutionary War to 1860*. Unpublished master's thesis. Atlanta: Emory University, 1957 (1961).

Emmanuel Episcopal Church Archives. Selected historical documents. Athens [GA]: through 2005.

Fleming, The Reverend Samuel C. W. "A Short History of The Church of Our Saviour." Atlanta: 1944.

Hart, Oliver. J, Rector comp. *The History of Christ Church Parish, Macon, Georgia. March 5, 1825–March 5, 1925*. Macon [GA]: Lyon, Harris & Brooks, Printers and Binders, 1925.

Hinton, Virginia C. *A Living Heritage: St. Stephen's Episcopal Church, Milledgeville, Ga., 1841–1907, with research by Janice A. Hardy and editing by Claire H. Shepard, edited with notes by the Rev. Dr. C. K. Robertson*. United States of America: Xlibris Corporation, 2003.

Hopewell, James F. *Congregation: Stories and Structures*. Philadelphia: Fortress Press, 1987.

Kell, Mrs. John McIntosh. "Memoirs of a Parishioner [of St. George's Church—Griffin], March 23, 1913." Griffin [GA]: St. George's Episcopal Church, 1913.

Kollock, John. "Grace-Calvary Church, Episcopal, Clarkesville, Georgia." Clarkesville [GA]: Grace-Calvary Church, circa 2000.

Langford, Margaret Ellis. *All Saints Episcopal Church: To Celebrate, To Seek, To Serve. 1903–2003*. Korea: All Saints Episcopal Church, Atlanta, Georgia, 2003.

Lee, Susan Elizabeth. *Alive In Atlanta, A History of St. Luke's 1864–1974*. Atlanta: St. Luke's Episcopal Church, circa 1974.

Linley, John. *Architecture of Middle Georgia: The Oconee Area*. Athens [GA]: University of Georgia Press, 1972.

_____. The Georgia Catalog: Historic American Building Survey, Athens [GA]: University of Georgia Press, 1982.

Malone, Henry Thompson. *The Episcopal Church in Georgia 1733–1957*. Atlanta: The Protestant Episcopal Church in the Diocese of Atlanta, Foote & Davies, 1960.

Marshall, James P., Jr. *The History of All Angels Episcopal Church, Eatonton, Georgia*. Eatonton [GA]: manuscript 2000.

Mitchell, The Reverend Donald G., Jr. *One Hundred Years of St. Paul's Episcopal Church in Macon, Georgia*. Macon [GA]: Southern Press, 1970.

Payne, Calder. W., comp. *The History of Christ Church Parish, Macon, Georgia*. Sesquicentennial Edition. Macon [GA]: Omnipress, Inc., 1974.

Perry, Richard P. *These Old Walls: A History of the Episcopal Cathedral of St. Philip, Atlanta, Georgia, 1947–1997*. Atlanta: Eagle-Empire Printing, circa 1996.

Pettway, The Reverend Roy. *History of the Church of Our Saviour*. Atlanta: The Church of Our Saviour, 1964.

St. Bede's Episcopal Church. *1984 Parish Profile of St. Bede's Episcopal Church*. Atlanta: 1984.

_____. *2002 Parish Profile of St. Bede's Episcopal Church*. Atlanta: St. Bede's Episcopal Church, 2002.

St. David's Episcopal Church. "Strategic Plan for St. David's Episcopal Church." Roswell [GA]: n.d.

St. Gregory the Great Episcopal Church. *1995 St. Gregory the Great Episcopal Church Profile*. Athens [GA]: 1995.

_____. *2005 St. Gregory the Great Episcopal Church Profile.* Athens [GA]: 2005.

St. Gregory the Great Episcopal Church Archives. "Letter to the St. Gregory the Great Congregation from Rebecca Baggett, Senior Warden, February 25, 2003." Athens [GA]: 2003.

_____. "Oral Interviews, Peter Rice, first senior warden and other founding members of St. Gregory the Great Episcopal Church in 2000." Athens [GA]: 2000.

St. Matthias' Episcopal Church Archives. "Oral interviews with Mildred Dillon and Bertha Guimond, by Bonnie Finne Churchill." Toccoa [GA]: 2005.

_____. Selected historical documents. Toccoa [GA]: St. Matthias' Episcopal Church, various dates.

St. Michael & All Angels Episcopal Church. The parish web site: www.stmichael.cc. Stone Mountain [GA]: 2005.

St. Michael & All Angels Episcopal Church Archives. "A Brief History of the First Fifty Years." Stone Mountain [GA]: n.d.

St. Stephen's Episcopal Church Archives. Selected documents and journals. Milledgeville [GA]: various years through 2003.

St. Timothy's Episcopal Church. *St. Timothy's Episcopal Church Centennial.* Decatur [GA]: St. Timothy's Episcopal Church, 1998.

St. Timothy's Episcopal Church Archives. "Profile of St. Timothy's Episcopal Church." Decatur [GA]: St. Timothy's Episcopal Church, n.d.

Stancil, Dorsey, ed. *History of the Episcopal Church of St. Edward the Confessor: A Celebration of Thirty Years.* Lawrenceville [GA]: 1999.

The Diocese of Atlanta Archives. "The Jesse T. Collins Photograph Collection." Atlanta: 1998.

_____. "Diocese." Atlanta: The Diocese of Atlanta, selected volumes and dates, 1963 to 1986.

_____. "Journals of the Councils of the Diocese of Atlanta." Atlanta: The Diocese of Atlanta, various volumes and dates, 1907–2004.

_____. "DioLog." Atlanta: The Diocese of Atlanta, selected volumes and dates, 1987–2005.

_____. "The Diocesan Record." Atlanta: The Diocese of Atlanta, selected volumes and dates 1925–1961.

The Episcopal Church of the Epiphany. "Parish Profile 2005." Atlanta: The Episcopal Church of the Epiphany, 2005.

The Episcopal Church of the Nativity. "Vision, History and Proposal." Fayetteville [GA]: The Episcopal Church of the Nativity, circa 1995.

The Episcopal Church of the Nativity Archives. "Mission News." Fayetteville: The Episcopal Church of the Nativity, various dates.

_____. "Oral interviews by Martha Clatterbuck: Bette and Robert Haynie, the Reverend Bob Hudak, Judi McNeirney, Louise Stroberg, and Dick Tally." Fayetteville [GA]: 2005.

_____. Records of the Church of the Resurrection. Fayetteville [GA]: Church of the Nativity. Selected documents with various dates.

_____. "Mission News." Fayetteville [GA]: The Episcopal Church of the Nativity, selected issues, 1991.

_____. Selected clergy and lay letters, 1989–2001. Fayetteville [GA]: The Episcopal Church of the Nativity, various dates.

_____. "Stable Cable." Fayetteville [GA]: The Episcopal Church of the Nativity, selected issues, 1997.

The Episcopal Church of the Resurrection. "Dedication Service Booklet, June 15, 1969." East Point [GA]: The Episcopal Church of the Resurrection, 1969.

Trinity Episcopal Church Archives. Columbus [GA]: selected documents, various years through 2005.

Van Keuren, Robert E., Jr., ed. *St. Bartholomew's Episcopal Church 1954–2004: A Jubilee History.* St. Bartholomew's Episcopal Church. Atlanta: 2004.

Walters, Katherine Bowman. *OCONEE RIVER: Tales To Tell.* The Eatonton-Putnam County Historical Society, Inc. Spartanburg: The Reprint Company, Publishers, 1995.

Willoughby, Lynn. *A Power for Good: The History of Trinity Parish, Columbus, Georgia.* Macon [GA]: Trinity Episcopal Church in association with Smyth & Helwys Publishing Company, 1999.

Wolfe, Gerald R. *The House of Appleton.* Methuen [NJ] and London: The Scarecrow Press, 1981.

Wyatt, Dr. C.L. *"Upon This Rock" History of St. Peter's Rome.* Rome [GA]: St. Peter's Episcopal Church in association with Wallace Printing, Rome [GA], 1994.

INDEX

✠

THE CENTENNIAL PRAYER - THANKS

Almighty God, giver of all good things:
We thank you for the gathering of Episcopalians in St. Paul's, Augusta, February 24, 1823, which gave birth to the work of our church in Georgia as a Diocese.
We thank you, Good Lord.

We thank you for the election of the Reverend Dr. Stephen Elliott as the first Bishop of this Diocese in Grace Church, Clarkesville, May 5, 1840. We are indebted to his pioneer spirit and the leadership he provided.
We thank you, Good Lord.

The Civil War found the destruction of many of our churches in Georgia and brought great grief to the people, clergy, and Bishop. Yet, today, we are thankful for the tenacious spirit of the Episcopalians who worked for the recovery of our parishes.
We thank you, Good Lord.

In 1866, Bishop Elliott died and a year later the Reverend John Watrus Beckwith was elected Bishop. We offer our thanks for the good ministry of both of these Bishops.
We thank you, Good Lord.

November 23, 1890, Bishop Beckwith died after twenty-four years of service as chief pastor of the Episcopal community in Georgia. Two years later, the Reverend Cleland Kinloch Nelson was chosen to succeed him. We thank you for the life and ministry of both of these dedicated men.
We thank you, Good Lord.

Lord, you blessed the churches of Georgia so much that the growth in people, clergy, and parishes, led to the formation of the Diocese of Atlanta in 1907, which comprised the northwestern corner of the state. The Episcopal Church in Georgia now consisted of two Dioceses to provide pastoral leadership. Bishop Nelson chose to remain with the Diocese of Atlanta. We thank you for the vision and effort of your people and clergy that preceded this important division.
We thank you, Good Lord.

Bishop Nelson's earthly ministry ended in February 1917 and the Diocese elected the Reverend Henry Judah Mikell as Bishop. He was consecrated on All Saints Day, 1917, in St. Philip's Cathedral, Atlanta. We offer our thanks for the leadership of Bishop Nelson through the division of the Diocese and the spirit that Bishop Mikell brought in his new Episcopate.
We thank you, Good Lord.